# SELLING THE
# HOLOCAUST

# SELLING THE
# HOLOCAUST

FROM AUSCHWITZ
TO SCHINDLER
HOW HISTORY IS BOUGHT,
PACKAGED, AND SOLD

TIM COLE

Routledge
Taylor & Francis Group

NEW YORK AND LONDON

First published in 1999 by
Gerald Duckworth & Co. Ltd.

Published in 2000 in the United States of America by

Routledge
711 Third Avenue,
New York, NY 10017, USA

2 Park Square, Milton Park,
Abingdon, Oxon OX14 4RN

*Routledge is an imprint of the Taylor & Francis Group, an informa business*

ISBN 0-415-92581-9 hb / 0-415-92813-3 pb

A catalogue record for this book is available from the Library of Congress.

*Typeset by Derek Doyle & Associates, Mold, Flintshire*

# CONTENTS

*For Julie*

# Acknowledgments

I first began thinking about how the Holocaust has been represented after what proved to be the jarring experience of visiting Auschwitz in the Spring of 1994. I had gone there on a pilgrimage of sorts, while researching for my PhD thesis on the Hungarian Holocaust. However, what struck me about this place, which I had read about but never visited, was that there were two quite different Auschwitzs for the tourist to visit. That night in my hotel room in Kraków, I read Jonathan Webber's Frank Green Lecture 'The Future of Auschwitz: Some Personal Reflections'. This started me thinking not just about the Holocaust as a historical event, but also how that historical event has been represented in the last fifty or so years. From asking the question 'how', I have increasingly been drawn to ask the question 'why', and in many ways it is those two questions which are central in this book.

This is a book which was in large part taught before it was written. My ideas owe much to the University of Bristol graduate and undergraduate students with whom I have enjoyed discussing how and why the Holocaust has been remembered and represented. The process of putting those ideas into print has been helped along by a large number of individuals. I am thankful to John Vincent for first introducing me to Robin Baird-Smith at Duckworth. It was Robin's initial enthusiasm which prompted me to start writing, and his patient advice and encouragement which have helped bring this book to completion. Also critical in that process has been my editor, Martin Rynja.

Over the last year and a half, I have been struck again and again by how much writing is a cumulative process. I owe a particular debt of gratitude to the many historians and journalists who have reflected on the memorialisation of the Holocaust over the course of the last twenty or so years. In particular, the writings of Omer Bartov, Saul Friedlander, Geoffrey Hartman, Lawrence Langer, Edward Linenthal, Judith Miller, Jacob Neusner, Alvin Rosenfeld,

Tom Segev, Jonathan Webber, Isabel Wollaston and James Young have both guided and stimulated my own thinking to a considerable degree. Their influence is to be felt in the following pages, in a book which makes no claims to being either the first or the last word on Holocaust memorialisation. Rather, it builds on what has gone before, and hopefully provokes questions which others will take further.

The collaborative nature of scholarship has also been brought home to me through the support and encouragement of many of my colleagues at the Department of Historical Studies at the University of Bristol. I am particularly thankful for the bibliographical references given to me by Bernard Alford, Tony Antonovics, Robert Bickers, Peter Coates, Kirsty Reid, Hugh Tulloch and John Vincent, and the useful feedback given to me by colleagues when I used some of the material from the chapter on Auschwitz to speak to the half-day conference organised by the department's 'Reputations' research cluster. Reflecting more generally on the theme of 'Reputations' – as this research cluster does – has stimulated me to think more fully about how and why the 'Holocaust' has gained the kind of reputation it has at the end of the twentieth century. Further afield, our Erasmus link department in Hannover gave some very useful feedback to a seminar paper on Anne Frank, as well as introducing me to Thomas Rahe at Bergen-Belsen, who gave me an insight into some of the questions being asked by someone at the cutting face of 'Holocaust' memorialisation. The University of Bristol has provided me with not only a stimulating environment for both teaching and research, but also with financial support from the Arts Faculty Research Fund and library resources. I am particularly grateful for the efficient help of the staff at the Inter-Library Loans department of the University of Bristol Library whom I have called upon many times since arriving in Bristol.

One of the greatest pleasures in researching this book was enjoying the kind hospitality of friends who provided a bed, meals and conversation as I travelled. I am particularly thankful to Mark, Connie, Annie and Nathan Dever in Washington, DC; Harry and Gladys Evertsen in Houston; David and Alison Boubel in Dallas; and Jon Doye and Sue Bird in Amsterdam. I am also thankful to Jon Doye and Sue Bird for reading and commenting so thoroughly on a final draft of this book. Thanks also to Bob and Pat Evertsen, who spent hours searching for obscure books in San Antonio bookstores, and to Matthew Sleeman and Jeremy Lindsell, who drove down to Bristol to restore my sanity as I came towards the end of writing this book. Their friendship is something which I value.

Above all others, three people deserve special thanks. My parents – Roger and Christine Cole – first taught me to take an interest in the past and to question everything in both the past and the present. My wife – Julie – has not only been dragged around more Holocaust museums in the last year than most people visit in their lifetime, but has listened and responded to my initial reactions to those museums. Her comments during the process of writing this book have been insightful, and her critical reading of the final draft extremely useful. She has been a wonderful companion during the last year and a half of writing, and it is therefore to her that this book is dedicated. I hope that she will now allow me to write the next one!

Tim Cole
Bristol
December 1998

# Introduction to the Paperback Edition

This morning on the radio, I heard something I've been expecting to hear for a long time: a Republican congressman from California stated that if Europe had not taken guns away from its citizens, the Jews would not have been defenseless when the Nazis came for them. Invoking the Holocaust to teach a lesson of the dangers of gun control did not exactly surprise me. After all, the Holocaust has been used to lend weight to a remarkable variety of positions. But when I listened to the congressman further, I was struck that he made direct reference to *Schindler's List* rather than to the Holocaust. His realization came, he recounted, while watching the movie. In a scene where a group of 'Nazis' round up a group of Jews, he noticed that the Nazis were the only ones with guns; hence he realized the importance of the freedom to bear arms.

By referencing *Schindler's List*, the congressman was invoking what I call the 'myth of the Holocaust' rather than the historical event that has become known as the Holocaust. This 'mythical' celluloid rendition of the event is one that among other things, stresses – as I discuss in Chapter 3 – Jewish passivity. Spielberg did not make a movie about the Warsaw ghetto uprising – where a number of Jews *were* armed, although that ultimately did little to change the fate of Warsaw's Jews – but about a group of Polish Jews who are saved through the actions of one (Ger)man. Thus the congressman's lesson comes not from an engagement with the complexity of the Holocaust but from the streamlined simplicity of a Hollywood movie.

In researching and writing *Selling the Holocaust*, I became more and more skeptical not only of the myriad representations of the Holocaust in contemporary culture of which *Schindler's List* is the most dominant but also of the frequent attempts to draw simple lessons from this complicated past. As a scholar of Holocaust history, I fear that all too often the 'Holocaust' that is being bought, packaged and sold in the present bears little relation to the actual events in the past. And thus the lessons drawn appear banal at best.

Yet, tellingly, that packaging of the past has assumed an importance all its own. As I mention in the pages that follow, tourists in Krakow, Poland, do not visit the ghetto area because that is where the Holocaust ghetto was located. Rather, they visit the ghetto area because that is where Spielberg filmed his movie. Such is the dominance of *Schindler's List*.

The discourse of *Schindler's List* has not simply been adopted by Republican congressmen for political bromides; it has also been used in a controversial television commercial in an election campaign in Virginia. By showing the scene from *Schindler's List* where an inmate is shot in the back of the head for no apparent reason, the sponsor sought to portray his opponent as 'Nazi-like' in his policies.[1] Subsequently, the commercial was criticized, not because it incorporated a scene from *Schindler's List*, but because it sought to equate the opponent's policies with the Holocaust. What was not questioned was that *Schindler's List* was considered to be synonymous with the Holocaust.

This equating of *Schindler's List* with the Holocaust has led – as Jeffrey Shandler suggests in his fascinating book on American television and the Holocaust – to Steven Spielberg's emergence as 'the most prominent public figure in America associated with Holocaust memory.'[2] Shandler points to the decision to have Spielberg introduce the 1993 TV screening of *The Nuremberg Trial* as signaling that after the release of *Schindler's List*, Spielberg's familiarity can be seen as 'rivaling and perhaps even eclipsing that of Elie Wiesel.' 'This,' he argues, 'is a telling development, evincing a larger shift in Holocaust remembrance from its focus on survivors to a newer center of attention: the creators of Holocaust mediations.'[3]

If, as the historian Peter Novick suggests, in the 1960s Elie Wiesel – the survivor – replaced Anne Frank – the victim – as the symbol of the Holocaust in the United States,[4] then Shandler suggests that in the 1990s Steven Spielberg – the creator of Holocaust representation – has replaced Elie Wiesel – the survivor – as the symbol of the Holocaust in the United States. This signals a new phase. In the 1960s and 1970s there was considerable interest in the events of the Holocaust – hence Wiesel's rise to prominence. In the 1990s, it is not the events but the *representation* of those events that has triggered interest – hence Spielberg's dominance. A movie like *Schindler's List* has assumed a life of its own apart from the Holocaust.

It is not simply that Spielberg has emerged as the Holocaust spokesman and that *Schindler's List* has emerged as the Holocaust movie. The very act of watching *Schindler's List* has entered into contemporary popular culture as a shared generational experience. This can be seen in the plotline of an episode of the popular television show *Seinfeld*. In it, Jerry, who is Jewish, is caught making out with his girlfriend at the movie theater while *Schindler's List* is playing. In subsequent scenes, Jerry tries, but fails, to stop people from finding out that he broke this cultural taboo.[5] The humor works because we know that *Schindler's List* is not simply an ordinary movie. It is a movie that has become shorthand for the Holocaust. But it also works because the very act of watching this movie in particular is a shared experience upon which a comedian such as Seinfeld can draw.

For a whole generation, the act of watching *Schindler's List* is more or less a given. Thus, in Alex Garland's 1996 novel *The Beach*, knowledge of *Schindler's List* is assumed. In a scene where Richard and Jed are watching TV at a café in a Thai beach resort, the passing of time in the movie becomes a measure of the passing of time in the café.

> While we waited for our food we watched TV. There was a video at the far end of the café and it was playing *Schindler's List*. Schindler was on a horse watching the ghettos being emptied, and he'd noticed a little girl in a red coat.
> 'How about that coat?' Jed asked, sipping his coke.
> I sipped my Sprite. 'What about it?'
> 'Do you reckon they painted it on the film with a brush?'
> 'On each frame? Like animation?'
> 'Yeah.'
> 'No way. They would have done it with a computer, like *Jurassic Park*.'
> 'Oh.' Jed drained the bottle and smacked his lips. 'It's the real thing.'
> I frowned. '*Schindler's List*?'
> 'No, you twerp, Coke.'
> The food must have taken ages because by the time it arrived, Schindler was looking at the red coat again. If you've seen the film you'll know that's an hour after he first sees it, if not more.[6]

In Garland's novel, it is irrelevant that *Schindler's List* is a movie about the Holocaust. Rather, what is relevant is that this is a movie that for an author born in Britain in 1970 – Garland is like myself in that respect – is one that has been watched once if not several times. It is one of our generation's shared cultural experiences. We are, after all, part of the *Schindler's List* generation.

In many ways, writing *Selling the Holocaust* was inspired by being a member of that generation. My own personal history – and even more so the histories of my students – coincides with the period that I term 'the rise of the myth of the Holocaust.' The earlier period in which knowledge of the Nazis' mass murder of Europe's Jews was hazy at best is outside of my own personal experience and the experience of my students.

The history of the rise to prominence of the Holocaust that I trace in the pages that follow is one also outlined by Peter Novick in *The Holocaust in American Life*. There is a burgeoning amount of scholarship being produced on the issues discussed here, and while there are many similarities between Novick's and my approach, there are also important differences. In Novick's important study – which was published after I completed *Selling the Holocaust* – he points out the relative silence about the Holocaust within America in general and the American Jewish community in particular in the late 1940s and 1950s. He contrasts this with the emergence of a 'distinct thing called "the Holocaust" ' in 1960s America,[7] and contemporary 'Holocaust-fixation.'[8] This chronology of the rise of the Holocaust is one that broadly parallels my own, although Novick does lay greater stress upon 1973 as the turning point – if there was a turning point – in Holocaust consciousness, whereas I would tend to see 1967 as more significant.

However, where I think we differ is in explaining why this history of silence was followed by intense interest in the Holocaust. For Novick, the answer lies with the American Jewish community leadership, which forms the focus of his study. While acknowledging a combination of 'the spontaneous and the contrived' in explaining the emergence of Holocaust consciousness,[9] Novick clearly leans toward the latter. In particular, he suggests that the American Jewish community leadership suppressed talk of the Holocaust in the immediate post-war years. From the 1970s onwards, however, all this changed, with Novick claiming 'massive investments by Jewish communal organizations in promoting "Holocaust consciousness" '.[10] Thus his approach is very much 'top-down,' with the decisions made by American Jewish community elites impacting the Jewish community (both problematic concepts), and in turn impacting non-Jewish America.

In what is perhaps the most problematic element of his argument, Novick suggests that once America's Jews gained Holocaust consciousness, then it was more or less inevitable that America at large would know about this event. This dissemination is seen to be more or less inevitable, given – Novick claims – 'that Jews play an important and influential role in Hollywood, the television industry, and the newspaper, magazine, and book publishing worlds.'[11] Rejecting notions of a 'Jewish conspiracy,' however, Novick argues that 'in large part the movement of the Holocaust from the Jewish to the general American arena resulted from private and spontaneous decisions of Jews who happened to occupy strategic positions in the mass media.'[12]

Although it is clear that Novick does see the second phase of dissemination – from Jewish America to America at large – to be largely spontaneous, he sees the earlier first phase of dissemination – from Jewish American elites to Jewish America – as far more intentional. However, unlike Norman Finkelstein – whose 1997 article I critique in *Selling the Holocaust* and whose book-length *The Holocaust Industry* will be published in mid 2000 – that decision to promote Holocaust consciousness is not explained solely in terms of support for the State of Israel.

For Finkelstein, Holocaust consciousness was manipulated by the pro-Israel lobby in the United States after the 1967 war. However, for Novick, there is a need to look to domestic factors as well as matters of foreign affairs. Thus he sets decisions by American Jewish elites to highlight the Holocaust – from the 1970s onwards – not only in the broader context of Israeli geopolitics but also in the specific context of the stressing of ethnic exceptionalism and the growing importance of the story of victimization. For Novick, the Holocaust has emerged not simply as the Zionist narrative that Finkelstein suggests, but also – and more importantly – as an (if not the) ethnic narrative for America's Jews. He argues that 'the Holocaust, as virtually the only common denominator of American Jewish identity in the late twentieth century, has filled a need for a consensual symbol.'[13]

While I would certainly see evidence of the 'Holocaust' being used both as an ethnic marker for American Jews and as a means of garnering support for Israel, the emergence of the Holocaust within the United States – let alone elsewhere – cannot be explained solely (or even primarily) in terms of these two factors. As I suggest in *Selling the Holocaust*, the United States Holocaust Memorial Museum is perhaps best seen as 'selling' not an ethnic narrative – let alone a Zionist narrative – but a nationalist one. I discuss this further in Chapter 6, where I suggest that the US Holocaust Memorial Museum is first and foremost an *American* museum. Moreover, there is clear evidence of the contestation of both ethnic and Zionist narratives within the American Jewish community and Israel. This suggests that, far from monolithic acceptance within a monolithic 'Jewish community,' Holocaust consciousness has been – and is being – questioned.

By focusing on the American Jewish elite in particular – and the American Jewish community in general – Novick's answers reflect, in part, where he asked his questions. I think there is a need to explore the appeal of the Holocaust to both non-Jewish America and the much wider world. While American Jews have been crucial players as both producers and consumers of the 'Holocaust,' there has been a far wider resonance both within and outside of America. The 'Holocaust' has entered more than simply 'American life.'

In an article that reflects upon my own work alongside that of Novick and Finkelstein, the British historian David Cesarani argues that behind the 'impatience with Holocaust memorialization' lies a 'continuing, stubborn resentment of Jewish difference.' In particular, he claims that 'behind Peter Novick's criticism of "particularism" is an assimilationist agenda' and that 'in Finkelstein's anti-Zionism this is quite explicit.'[14] While Cesarani may be right to see Novick writing as an assimilationist, I think Novick also writes as a historian, as I do myself, and in doing so, offers a powerful critique of – not simply 'impatience with' – contemporary Holocaust memorialization. In a memorable passage where he dismisses the drawing of 'bumper sticker' lessons from the Holocaust, Novick notes that

> along with most historians, I'm skeptical about the so-called lessons of history. I'm especially skeptical about the sort of pithy lessons that fit on a bumper sticker. If there is . . . any wisdom to be acquired from contemplating an historical event, I would think it would derive from confronting it in all its complexity and its contradictions.[15]

*Selling the Holocaust* is written in that same spirit of critical – and skeptical – historical inquiry. And a year or so on from writing, I admit to remaining skeptical of many of the more recent offerings of the 'Holocaust' by popular culture.

The spate of Holocaust movies in the late 1990s, foremost amongst them Alberto Benigni's *Life Is Beautiful*, continued in the tradition of Spielberg's treatment of the Holocaust to opt for 'happy endings.' Awarded three Oscars, *Life Is Beautiful*, like *Schindler's List*, won both critical and popular acclaim. However, again like *Schindler's List*, it was also heavily criticized, but not because it was a bad movie. Like *Schindler's List* it was not cinematically unsound. The criticism came mainly because of Benigni's use of comedy to tell of an Italian Jewish family's experiences of persecution during the Holocaust. While this strategy worked superbly in highlighting the inconsistencies and sheer stupidity of racist antisemitism, it failed to work in the context of a mythical concentration camp, where Guido keeps his son Giosué alive by making the entire experience a game.

Although not nearly as successful at the box office as *Life Is Beautiful*, two more Holocaust movies that also contain strong comic elements were released in 1999. In *Jakob the Liar* – a remake of a 1977 East German movie – Robin Williams plays a café owner who invents fictitious radio reports of Allied advances to cheer up his fellow ghetto inhabitants. In *Train of Life*, an entire Jewish community creates a mock Nazi deportation train, which they ride through Nazi-occupied Europe to Palestine.

In many ways, these three movies share similarities with *Schindler's List*. All offer exceptional tales. *Schindler's List* shows us the exceptional story of 1,100 Polish Jews who were saved, rather than killed, during the Holocaust. *Life Is Beautiful* shows us the exceptional story of a boy who survived a concentration camp, rather than being killed. *Jakob the Liar* shows us the exceptional story of a ghetto that was liberated, rather than liquidated. *Train of Life* shows us the exceptional story of a 'deportation' train that took Jews to freedom, rather than to a death camp. All in their own way skirt the horrors of the Holocaust and offer us something much more palatable in its place. This is the celebration of survival that is so central to Spielberg's *Schindler's List* and that is perhaps one of the movie's greatest (and worst) legacies.

In all three movies, survival is celebrated not as a chance occurrence, but, like in *Schindler's List*, as the result of one man's [sic] – or community's – ability to make a difference. In *Schindler's List* it is the 'Righteous Gentile' Oskar Schindler who saves 1,100 Jews. In *Life Is Beautiful* it is the savvy Guido who saves his son. In *Jakob the Liar* it is Jakob who saves the lives of those in the ghetto with him. In *Train of Life* it is the ingenious community that bluffs the Nazis by building a deportation train that takes them to freedom rather than destruction. The message is essentially the same. We can, through cunning, goodness and ingenuity, defeat the Holocaust and bring about salvation.

In *Life Is Beautiful* and *Jakob the Liar*, there are, as in *Schindler's List,* strong references to Christ-like imagery. In both, the main character dies in securing salvation. However, any sense of sorrow is tempered by the joy of survival. After witnessing the destruction of Guido's off-screen death in *Life Is Beautiful*, we experience the redemption of Giosué's closing words, 'We won.' Not only is there closure, but it is a *redemptive* closure. And yet the Holocaust resists both.

As I note in Chapter 1, the redemptive closure of the 'happy ending' was chosen for both the stage and screen adaptations of Anne Frank's diary. The recent rewriting of the stage play of the *Diary of Anne Frank* has, however, changed not simply the ending, but also the earlier editing out of Anne's interest in her own sexuality. In the new stage play, the phrase that has become Anne's mantra – 'I still believe in spite of everything that people are really good at heart' – has been placed back into its original context within the diary. And the play ends with Otto Frank recounting the last time that Anne was seen in the camp by her friend Hanneli: 'naked, her head shaved, covered with lice. I don't have anybody anymore, she weeps.'[16]

However, despite these specific welcome changes to the play – one of the most dominant representations of the Holocaust – there remains a tendency for redemptive figures like Anne Frank to provide the discourse by which the Holocaust is viewed. The late 1990s rash of 'Holocaust' movies not only perpetuates that, but takes it to even greater lengths. As I have suggested in *Selling the Holocaust*, such attempts at redemption are not only inappropriate, but potentially dangerous. Swallowing a sugar-coated 'Holocaust' may be little more than swallowing a placebo. I wrote this book in the hopes that such sugar-coating would not only be acknowledged, but also questioned.

The sugar-coating of the 'Holocaust' was spoken of by survivor Sally Grubman, whose words I came across when reading Hank Greenspan's incisive reflections on a lifetime of speaking with Holocaust survivors. Grubman's satisfaction with seeing a greater interest in the Holocaust than when she first arrived in the United States was tempered with uncertainty over the tendency to prefer happy to sad stories. Her words from the late 1970s are still very much relevant (if not more relevant) today:

> There is a tremendous interest in the Holocaust that we didn't see when we came.... I see an awakening of consciousness, but also some confusion about the reality. American Jewish teachers invite me into their classrooms to speak, but they do not want me to make the Holocaust a sad experience.

They want me to turn us into heroes and create a heroic experience for the survivors. There is this book they use, *The Holocaust: A History of Courage and Resistance*, but the Holocaust was never a history of courage and resistance. It was a destruction by fire of innocent people, and it's not right to make it something it never was.[17]

Tim Cole
Washington, DC
March 16, 2000

## Notes

1. Janofsky, M., 'Increasingly, Political War of Words Is Fought with Nazi Imagery,' *New York Times* (23 October 1995) p. A12, cited in Shandler, J., *While America Watches. Televising the Holocaust* (Oxford, 1999) p. xiii.

2. ibid., p. 253.

3. ibid.

4. Novick, P., 'Holocaust Memory in America' in J. E. Young (ed.), *The Art of Memory. Holocaust Memorials in History* (New York, 1994) p. 162.

5. Flanzbaum, H., 'Introduction' in H. Flanzbaum (ed.), *The Americanization of the Holocaust* (Baltimore, 1999) p. 12.

6. Garland, A., *The Beach* (London, 1997) pp. 172–3.

7. Novick, P., *The Holocaust in American Life* (New York, 1999) p. 144.

8. ibid., p. 10.

9. ibid., p. 152.

10. ibid., p. 152.

11. ibid., p. 207.

12. ibid., p. 208.

13. ibid., p. 7.

14. Cesarani, D., 'History on Trial,' *Guardian* (18 January 2000) Section 2, p.2.

15. Novick, p. 261.

16. Cited in Hammelburg, B., 'A Fresh Look at "Anne Frank" In Search of the Historical One,' *New York Times* (30 November 1997) Section 2, p.4.

17. Cited in Greenspan, H., *On Listening to Holocaust Survivors. Recounting and Life History* (Westport, Conn., 1998) pp. 44–5.

PROLOGUE

# The Rise (and Fall?) of the Myth of the 'Holocaust'

It is a simple fact that in New Haven, the Jewish community of 22,000 spends about ten times as much money on the Holocaust memorial as it does on all the college students in New Haven. I think that is shocking ... The community is saying: 'We have money for Holocaust, and that's all' ... It seems to me the Holocaust is being sold ...[1]

At the end of the twentieth century, the 'Holocaust' is being bought and sold. $168 million was donated to pay for the building of the United States Holocaust Memorial Museum on a plot of Federal Land in Washington, DC. Millions of dollars more have financed memorial projects throughout the United States, ranging from the installation of Holocaust memorials to the establishing of University chairs in Holocaust Studies. Steven Spielberg's 1993 movie *Schindler's List* netted over $221 million at foreign box offices and seven Academy Awards. In short, '*Shoah** business' is big business.

And yet, as the above comments of Rabbi Arnold Wolf reveal, there is some disquiet over the priority accorded to the 'Holocaust' within the American Jewish community. That priority within American Jewish circles, and the more general contemporary obsession with the 'Holocaust', are indeed relatively recent phenomenon. Within the American Jewish community – where '*Shoah* business' is the biggest business – there was a noticeable time-lag between the end of the war and the emergence of the 'Holocaust' as the central community myth. Nathan Glazer in his definitive book on *American Judaism*, expressed surprise – with the benefit of hindsight – in his 1972 second edition that 'the two greatest events in modern Jewish history,

* The Hebrew term for the Holocaust.

the murder of six million Jews by Hitler and the creation of a Jewish State in Palestine, had had remarkably slight effects on the inner life of American Jewry up until the mid-fifties'.[2]

In the immediate aftermath of the Second World War, those Jewish survivors who arrived in Britain, Israel, Canada and the United States tended to remain silent about their experiences. Silence was a shared reaction to the trauma of the events which were 'too close, too painful to be confronted'.[3] In part, this may have been a 'natural' collective reaction of suppression. 'Consequently' – suggests Edward Linenthal in his book on the history of the Holocaust museum in Washington, DC – 'the Holocaust had not been constructed as a discrete "event", because the motivation to forget was too strong for survivors, perpetrators, and bystanders, the implications of what had happened were too threatening for public analysis, and the under-lying guilt for not having done more was too great among some Americans, Jews and non-Jews alike'.[4]

In that context of forgetting, academic interest in the Holocaust was as limited as popular interest. Perhaps the most authoritative Holocaust scholar, Raul Hilberg, has written about the lonely task that research on the Holocaust was when he first began in 1948.[5] His ground-breaking scholarly work *The Destruction of the European Jews* – undoubtedly the single most important academic text on the Holocaust – was rejected by publisher after publisher, and was only eventually published in 1961 after being subsidised by a survivor family.[6] It was only in the 1960s and 1970s that the nature of the Holocaust began to be grasped by both the academic community and the general public in the United States and Europe.

From a relatively slow start, we have now come to the point where Jewish culture in particular, and Western culture more generally, are saturated with the 'Holocaust'. Indeed the 'Holocaust' has saturated Western culture to such an extent that it appears not only centre stage, but also lurks in the background. This can be seen in the remarkable number of contemporary movies which include the 'Holocaust' as plot or sub-plot. As the novelist Phillip Lopate – who like Rabbi Wolf, has questioned the 'Jewish preoccupation with the Holocaust'[7] – is prompted to ask: 'where would the contemporary European art film be without the Holocaust? As a plot device it is second only to infidelity'.[8] And yet it is not simply the European art film which offers us a filmic 'Holocaust'. In the last two decades, the 'Holocaust' has come to Hollywood.

The 'Holocaust' is so familiar that we don't even need to hear the word spoken; the sight of tattooed numbers triggers a whole stock of mental images. In the Academy winning film *Shine*, it is even enough for David's father to roll up his sleeve and we realise that a number is tattooed on his arm. This is sufficient for us to relate the behaviour of this Jewish family in the present to a 'Holocaust' past. And yet – as a story recounted by Dorothy Rabinowitz reminds us – tattooed numbers on someone's arm meant little in 1950s America. She tells of a survivor at a dinner dance in San Francisco who

> ... noticed one man in the room staring curiously at her from time to time; finally he came over, introduced himself, and confessed that he had seen the numbers on her arm. 'I was wondering, ' he said, 'why you were wearing your laundry numbers on your arm?' What were they really, he wanted to know, some sort of decoration? I told him no, that's my telephone number.[9]

Such an exchange is inconceivable in contemporary America. The image of tattooed numbers has become one of several which have come to represent the 'Holocaust'. It is an image which appears not only in the movies, but also towards the end of the permanent exhibition in the United States Holocaust Memorial Museum in Washington, DC. Here, opposite a pile of shoes, hangs a number of photographs of tattooed arms taken at a meeting of survivors held in Los Angeles in 1991. And even if someone in contemporary America was to be unaware of the significance of these tattooed numbers, it is unlikely that a survivor would seek to explain them away as simply their telephone number. From a position of relative ignorance about the Holocaust on the part of non-survivors and relative silence about the Holocaust on the part of survivors, the Holocaust has emerged – in the Western World – as probably the most talked about and oft-represented event of the twentieth century.

This book seeks to explore how and why this is the case. It is therefore not so much a book about the historical event we call the Holocaust, but rather a book about the emergence of the myth of the 'Holocaust' over the last three decades. Taking three people – Anne Frank, Adolf Eichmann and Oskar Schindler – and three places – Auschwitz, Yad Vashem and the United States Holocaust Memorial Museum – by way of a focus, I want to examine how and why the myth of the 'Holocaust' has emerged in Europe, Israel and the United States. Rather than this 'myth' being homogenous, it is possible to discern shifting concerns and meanings over both time and space.

I admit that 'myth' is a highly problematic term, given that it has been used by those who suggest that the 'Holocaust' is little more than war-time atrocity stories and post-war Jewish propaganda.

However, by using the term 'myth' I do not suggest – as the so-called revisionists and Holocaust deniers do – that six million Jews were not murdered during the course of the Second World War, many of them by gassing. The historical reality is that around six million Jews *were* murdered in Second World War Europe. I would echo Liebman and Don-Yehiya's words – who also use the term 'the Holocaust myth' in their study of Israeli Civil Religion – that 'by labelling a story a myth we do not mean it is false'. Rather, 'a myth is a story that evokes strong sentiments, and transmits and reinforces basic societal values'.[10]

The term myth of the 'Holocaust' – for all its problematic connotations – is useful for distinguishing between the historical event – the Holocaust – and the representation of that event – the myth of the 'Holocaust'. It is a distinction noted by the writer Lawrence Langer who points out that 'the two planes on which the event we call the Holocaust takes place in human memory – the historical and the rhetorical, the way it was and its verbal reformation, or deformation, by later commentators'.[11] Lopate goes further than Langer and admits, 'in my own mind I continue to distinguish, ever so slightly, between the disaster visited on the Jews and "the Holocaust". Sometimes it almost seems that "the Holocaust" is a corporation headed by Elie Wiesel, who defends his patents with articles in the Arts and Leisure section of the *Sunday Times*'.[12] While perhaps not being as cynical as Lopate, I think he is right to point to the emergence of something which appears to have a life of its own. The myth of the 'Holocaust' may have drawn on the historical Holocaust, but it now exists apart from that historical event.

This emergence of the myth of the 'Holocaust' has parallels with the emergence of the 'Myth of the War Experience' in post – First World War Europe, a term introduced by the historian George Mosse.[13] Historian Jay Winter describes how the mass slaughter of the First World War impacted upon both society and culture to the extent that 'Europeans imagined the post-war world as composed of survivors perched on a mountain of corpses' and questions of 'how to relate to the fact of mass death, how to transcend its brutal separations and cruelties, were universal dilemmas'.[14] In this context of trying to make sense of the past, Mosse argued that 'the reality of the war experience came to be transformed into what one might call the Myth of the War Experience, which looked back upon the war as a meaningful and even sacred event'.[15] And just as the First World War experience was transformed into the 'Myth of the War Experience', so – it seems to me – the Holocaust has been transformed in the last fifty years into the myth of the 'Holocaust'. That transformation has been undertaken in response to the sheer horror of the mass murders, to meet contemporary needs and as an attempt to find meaning in the murder of six million Jews.

Mosse examines the construction of the 'Myth of War Experience' in terms of the defeated nation-state drawing meaning from the meaninglessness of the war through a process of sanctification. And while there have been Jewish attempts to draw meaning from the meaningless of the Holocaust through a process of sanctification in Israel, it is in the United States that the myth of the 'Holocaust' has been particularly important during the last two decades. Thus the myth of the 'Holocaust' has emerged within an international context, rather than simply in the context of the political nation-state. Moreover, while Jews have played a crucial role in transforming the Holocaust into the myth of the 'Holocaust', the 'myth' is one embraced by Jew and non-Jew alike. Indeed, as Wolf's comments at the beginning of this chapter make clear, some of the strongest critiques of the mythical status of the 'Holocaust' come from within the Jewish community. At the end of the twentieth century, the myth of the 'Holocaust' cannot be restricted to a purely Jewish ethnic marker. As Linenthal argues, 'On April 22, 1993, the Holocaust became an event officially incorporated into American memory' when US President Bill Clinton opened the United States Holocaust Memorial Museum as the Holocaust museum 'for *all* Americans'.[16]

The United States Holocaust Memorial Museum, at the heart of the Mall in Washington, DC, represents the official face of the myth of the 'Holocaust' within contemporary America, but it is not the only expression of remembrance. More or less every large city in the United States has its own Holocaust memorial, and a number of cities have major Holocaust museums. In some way, that response parallels the erecting of stone monuments and plaques in almost every village, let alone every town, in Britain after the First World War. And yet, as we stand at the end of the twentieth century, the 'Myth of the War Experience' (of the 1914–18 war) described by Mosse appears rather distant, and the war memorials which dot the British landscape have come to mean less and less to each new generation. There is a sense, perhaps, in which the immortalisation of memory in stone leads toward a process of distancing and forgetting. Rather than memory being alive and fluid, it becomes dead, fixed, and forgotten. As the literary scholar Andreas Huyssen points out

> ... the promise of permanence a monument in stone will suggest is always built on quicksand. Some monuments are joyously toppled at times of social upheaval; others preserve

memory in its most ossified form, either as myth or as cliché. Yet others stand simply as figures of forgetting, their meaning and original purpose eroded by the passage of time.[17]

As First World War memorials and memory have become increasingly peripheral, so it is possible to envisage something similar happening to the remembrance of the Holocaust. We will, perhaps, stand at the end of the twenty-first century and look upon the myth of the 'Holocaust' as largely irrelevant to the present and live lives surrounded by Holocaust memorials which have become meaningless.

From today's perspective, such a diminishing power of the myth of the 'Holocaust' appears unlikely. 'Holocaust' sites and museums are enormous tourist attractions, pulling in millions of visitors a year. The United States Holocaust Memorial Museum in Washington, DC, alone attracts over two million visitors each year, and even the Holocaust Memorial Center in West Bloomfield, Michigan, can boast that it is Michigan's number one tourist attraction. It is rare to read a newspaper in Britain or America – especially the Sunday papers – for more than a month without spotting a 'Holocaust' story about Nazi gold, Swiss bank accounts' or a review of the latest film/book/play/exhibition on a 'Holocaust' theme. In the words of the Jewish historian Yaffa Eliach, 'There is no business like *Shoah* Business'.[18]

And yet, I want to suggest that there was nothing inevitable about us finding ourselves in that situation, and therefore there is nothing inevitable about being in the same situation in fifty or a hundred years' time. Historians – of all people – tend toward scepticism when anyone suggests that things won't change all that much. We look back and see change everywhere, and therefore we are the last people to argue that things are likely to remain the same. We aren't prophets – at least, if we are, we aren't very good ones – but we are healthily suspicious about anything which makes a claim for permanence. In this book I am not writing as a prophet, but as a historian who suggests that the 'Holocaust' has become a central cultural icon in the West for a number of reasons, and that it may well not be so central in years to come. Rather than being an inevitable feature of contemporary life, the myth of the 'Holocaust' is a myth which quite obviously has a history of 'rise' and thus may well also have a history of 'fall'. While this book is primarily about the 'rise' of the myth of the 'Holocaust', there is a sense in which it is also about the 'fall' of that myth. After all, this myth, which has emerged in particular places at particular times for particular reasons, is a historical construct and not a given. In looking back to the time before the 'myth' emerged, it becomes all the more possible to imagine a time when the 'myth' will have disappeared.

## The rise of the myth of the 'Holocaust'

'In the beginning there was no Holocaust', writes Hilberg. 'When it took place in the middle of the twentieth century, its nature was not fully grasped'.[19] While the Holocaust was perpetrated in Europe during 1941–45, it was not really until the early 1960s that anything like widespread awareness of the 'Holocaust' began to emerge. The word itself – which comes from the Greek translation of the Old Testament and literally means 'a sacrifice wholly consumed by fire; a whole burnt offering'[20] – was not really much used to refer to the mass murder of European Jews until the late 1950s. As one writer points out, 'in referring to their fate, one typically spoke, in the immediate post-war years, about the "catastrophe", or perhaps the "disaster".'[21] The *Oxford English Dictionary* notes some 'contemporary references to the Nazi atrocities as a "holocaust" ' during the 1940s, and it dates 'the specific application by historians' to the 1950s'.[22] The word itself did not appear in the *New York Times* until 30 May 1959, and interestingly was not used at all by Hilberg in his classic *The Destruction of the European Jews*.[23] Indeed, it was not really until the 1960s that the term began to be used with anything like regularity in the United States and Britain, making it into the 1972 publication *The Barnhart Dictionary of New English Since 1963*, as a word referring to 'the destruction of European Jewry in World War II'.[24] Yet 'Holocaust' is a word which is now both widely used and widely recognised, with a series of surveys in the early 1990s suggesting that around 95 percent of Americans have heard of the term and 85 percent claim to know what it means.[25] 'Holocaust' is both a word which has entered into our vocabulary and an event which has entered into our consciousness.

Perhaps more than anything else, it was the capture of Adolf Eichmann by Israeli Secret Service personnel in May 1960, and his subsequent trial in Jerusalem in 1961, which first awoke popular interest in the Holocaust. From the start it was clear that the trial was not simply about Eichmann. It was a trial concerned with the *Shoah*, and was a self-conscious attempt to bring awareness of the massacre of six million European Jews to both native-born Israeli youth and the wider world. For the latter, the Eichmann trial was to act as evidence of the ultimate expression of antisemitism and a reminder that this was never to happen again. For the former, the

Eichmann trial was intended to provide the opportunity both to begin to understand the Holocaust and in some ways identify with its victims.

It seems rather surprising from the perspective of the present, that in 1960-61 the Israeli government saw the need to educate Israeli youth about the Holocaust. However, this decision marked a change in Israeli attitudes, which up until then had been characterised by distinct ambiguity. The early years of Israeli state-building were marked by a reticence in talking about the Holocaust, which was an event seen by 'early statists like David Ben-Gurion ... as the ultimate fruit of Jewish life in exile' and therefore 'represented a diaspora that deserved not only to be destroyed, but also forgotten'.[26] While 'the state ... recognised its perverse debt to the Holocaust',[27] this sense of ambiguity resulted in effectively a veil of silence up to the time of Eichmann's trial. In 1961 that silence was broken as survivor after survivor took to the witness stand in the Jerusalem courtroom and spoke of their Holocaust experiences.

It is ironic to think that in some ways Eichmann, who was a central player in perpetrating the Holocaust, also played a part in the emergence of the myth of the 'Holocaust'. He did the former from his desk in Section IV of the Reich Security Head Office, and the latter from his bulletproof-glass encased dock in a Jerusalem courthouse. In both cases he was a pawn of more major players – Hitler and Himmler on the one hand, and Israeli Prime Minister Ben-Gurion on the other. His arrest – in controversial circumstances – and trial can be seen as ushering in a new awareness of the 'Holocaust' in the public domain. James Young, a literary scholar, suggests that with this renewed exposure, the 'Holocaust' became an 'archetype', 'an independent icon', 'a figure for subsequent pain, suffering, and destruction'[28] and 'began to inform all writers' literary imagination as a prospective trope'.[29] Thus he points out that in the poems 'Mary's Song', 'Lady Lazarus' and 'Daddy' written at the end of 1962, Sylvia Plath uses the 'Holocaust' to express her own despair after discovering her husband's infidelity.

From the day that Eichmann's arrest was announced to the astonished Israeli parliament, a host of 'instant biographers'[30] started writing on Eichmann. A bibliography on the trial compiled in 1969, reveals that more than a thousand works had been written on Eichmann and his arrest and trial, and that Hannah Arendt's book on the trial alone had resulted in over 250 reviews.[31] This torrent of publications ranged from the scholarly to the sensational, making clear that the trial had sparked debate and focused attention on this period of history.

However, writing about Eichmann did not necessarily mean writing about the Holocaust. Indeed for Hannah Arendt – whose trial reports for the *New Yorker* had a dramatic impact in America – writing about Eichmann was more about totalitarianism. In the context of the Cold War, this Eichmann – characterised by the 'banality of evil' – stood as the archetypal 'desk killer' in the pay of totalitarianism. Thus in the United States, Eichmann came to symbolise far more than simply *the* 'Holocaust' perpetrator. When American anti-Vietnam War protesters daubed his name on banners, they were thinking of 'the issue of individual conscience: whether the individual had a duty to refuse obedience to a system which perpetrated crimes against humanity' rather than the Holocaust.[32] And when Eichmann's name was used in the context of Stanley Milgram's controversial experiments into the relationship between authority and acts of cruelty – which were seen as proof that the 'latent Eichmann'[33] lay hidden within most of us – the reference was far from Holocaust specific. The complicity of Eichmann which was revealed in Jerusalem became – in the United States in particular – a universal object lesson.

A similar universalising of Eichmann can be seen to have taken place in West Germany. There is a sense in which in 1961 the silence in West Germany over the Nazi past was broken as witnesses spoke out in Jerusalem. The deliberate overlooking of the recent past in post-war Germany was questioned by radical youth engaged in generational struggle, who started to ask an entire generation the questions asked of Eichmann in Jerusalem. However, these questions lost their specificity when, by the end of the 1960s and early 1970s, the new-left broadened their attack into one over American involvement in Vietnam and the position of the Palestinians in Israel. The questioning in Germany became less about the 'Holocaust' than about the perceived faults of capitalism and the establishment.

Thus while the arrest and trial of Adolf Eichmann at the start of the 1960s did do much to bring the 'Holocaust' as a specifically Jewish tragedy to public attention in Israel, there was a greater time-lag elsewhere. I think that the theologian Jacob Neusner is right to suggest that it was not until the late 1960s that the myth of the 'Holocaust' emerged within the Jewish community in the United States. His argument is that in 1967 American Jews took hold of the Holocaust in direct response to the geo-political situation in Israel, and created 'the American Judaism of Holocaust and Redemption'. This – Neusner suggests – involved 'the transformation of the mass murder of European Jews into an event of mythic and world destroying proportions'.[34]

10

In mid 1967 it seemed that Israel's very existence was threatened, raising fears that what had happened before was about to happen again. The Holocaust provided the most obvious parallel to the precarious situation faced by the new Jewish state. The Jews who had been threatened with extinction in the 1940s were once again threatened with extinction. In the United States in particular, the parallelism of the 1940s and 1967 had a powerful impact upon a Jewish community which had in many ways kept silent about the Holocaust for the last two decades. In 1967 that silence was broken as American Jews visited the recent past.

However, during 1967 a position of Israel under threat was turned round with Israeli victory in the Six-Day War. It is the euphoria of victory – with Israeli troops arriving at the Temple Wall in Jerusalem – which Neusner sees to be even more significant than the dark days when it seemed that Israel would be defeated. In the aftermath of the Israeli victory, the 'Holocaust' provided an unexpected antithesis to the contemporary situation in Israel, rather than a doom-laden parallel to the contemporary situation in Israel. Neusner suggests that after Israeli victory it became safe to reflect on the 'Holocaust' and bring that period to a sense of completion. Indeed Neusner goes so far as to suggest that

> ... the extermination of European Jewry could become *the* Holocaust only on 9 June [1967] when, in the aftermath of a remarkable victory, the State of Israel celebrated the return of the people of Israel to the ancient wall of the Temple of Jerusalem. On that day the extermination of European Jewry attained the – if not happy, at least viable – ending that served to transform events into a myth, and to endow a symbol with a single, ineluctable meaning.[35]

Deborah Lipstadt, an historian, argues in very similar terms, pointing to the importance of the 'redemptive victories of the Jewish State' in shattering 'the silence of the previous decades' over the Holocaust within American Jewry. Like Neusner, she suggest that 'now that the Holocaust was "history" and not "probability", it could be confronted'.[36]

Whereas Neusner and Lipstadt see the emergence of the 'Holocaust' in American Jewish consciousness during 1967 in terms of the closure (happy ending) offered by Israeli victory, Norman Finkelstein has controversially claimed that the motivation was solely political. Like Neusner and Lipstadt, he notes that in the wake of Israeli victory, American Jewish intellectuals 'suddenly discovered the Nazi genocide', and what had been 'a tiny cottage industry before 1967' was transformed as 'Holocaust studies began to boom'. However, 'this was not a coincidence. Basking as they were in Israel's reflected glory, American Jews had also to contend with increasing censure of its repressive policies. In these circumstances the Nazi extermination proved politically useful ...'

Thus Finkelstein claims that American Jews 'seized upon and methodically marketed' a 'Zionist account of the Nazi holocaust' precisely 'because it was politically expedient'.[37] According to this 'Zionist account', he suggests, 'the Nazi genocide marked ... the ineluctable culmination of Gentile anti-Semitic hatred' and therefore 'the Nazi extermination both justified the necessity of Israel and accounted for all hostility directed at it: the Jewish State was the only safeguard against the next outbreak of homicidal anti-Semitism and, conversely, homicidal anti-Semitism was behind every attack on, or even defensive manoeuvre against the Jewish state'.[38]

It would be simplistic, however, to see the emergence of the Holocaust in America in the aftermath of 1967 as simply a tool in the hands of Zionism. As journalist Judith Miller argues

> ... there was nothing *inherently* exploitative in the Jewish push for monuments, memorials, and public tributes to the period of their most intense suffering. *But* the linkage of the Holocaust with campaigns to raise money and enhance support for the State of Israel marked the beginning of serious abuse and misuse of the Holocaust.[39]

Miller is right to acknowledge that while 'American Jews discovered that the Holocaust could be used as a weapon not only for garnering sympathy at home, but also for insisting on unquestioning support for Israel abroad', it is mistaken to see the emergence of the myth of the 'Holocaust' as wholly political. After all, the 'Holocaust' can be seen to be emerging in both non-Jewish as well as Jewish America. Moreover, the American telling of the 'Holocaust' – while often containing Zionist elements – differed quite radically from the Israeli version.

I think that Neusner and Lipstadt's suggestion that the 'Holocaust' could only emerge once there was a sense of closure is more persuasive than Finkelstein's political explanation. Zionism could provide that 'happy ending', but there were in fact a number of alternative happy endings that emerged both before and after 1967. What all of these have in common is a sense of discerning meaning in the historical event which has become known as the 'Holocaust'. And it is this sense of seeking to find meaning in this event which warrants the use of the term the myth of the 'Holocaust'.

The 'Zionist' myth of the 'Holocaust' was – as Finkelstein recognises – important, but it was far from the only meaning given to the murder of Europe's Jews by American Jews at the end of the 1960s and into the 1970s. Perhaps more importantly, the 'Holocaust' was emerging as one of the – if not *the* – primary ethnic markers for the American Jew. The historian Michael Berenbaum argues that 'in the seven years between the Six Day War [1967] and the Yom Kippur War [1973], the Holocaust became a central part of Jewish consciousness'.[40] Yet this shifting concern needs to be seen not simply in the context of what was happening in Israel, but also in the context of what was happening in America. In a period during which ethnic assertion reversed the earlier process – experienced by all ethnic minority groups in the United States – of assimilating in silence, American Jews discovered the 'Holocaust'. It was an event made all the more attractive by fitting into the popular American model which shapes ethnic distinctiveness around a history of victimhood.

It is in this context that NBC's nine-and-a-half-hour 1978 TV miniseries *Holocaust* became to American Jews what the 1977 TV show *Roots* was to African-Americans.[41] The parallel is one noted by Yosefa Loshitzky, a scholar of Holocaust films, and seen as pointing to 'the new status of victimhood in American society'.[42] *Holocaust* became required viewing for American Jews, with the Jewish monthly magazine *Moment*, suggesting 'that for Jews, the watching [of *Holocaust*] has about it the quality of a religious obligation'.[43] This nine-and-a-half hour TV representation of the 'Holocaust' played a part in cultivating 'the idea that being Jewish is primarily an ethnic rather than a religious category and that Jewish identity can be affirmed through the Holocaust'.[44] As a 1989 American Jewish Committee survey discovered, while only 46% of American Jews said that it was important to practice Jewish rituals, 85% said that the Holocaust was important.[45] There is little question that in the 1970s and 1980s the 'Holocaust' assumed a critical role in self-definition as Jewish.

However, to see the myth of the 'Holocaust' simply as a Jewish ethnic marker and as part and parcel of an 'American Judaism of Holocaust and Redemption', fails to explain why the 'Holocaust' has emerged as an icon for the non-Jewish imagination as well. At the end of the twentieth century, the 'Holocaust' is central to modern consciousness. The TV mini-series had a considerable impact in non-Jewish America. It wasn't simply American Jewry who was tuning in with almost religious devotion. The NBC mini-series was watched by a total of more than 120 million Americans over four consecutive evenings in April 1978. Indeed, such was its impact on the nation as a whole that the series' opening night – Sunday 16 April – became known as 'Holocaust Sunday'.[46] The soap-opera style of portraying the 'Holocaust' through the experiences of one imaginary family – the Weiss family – captured the public imagination with the *Anti-Defamation League Bulletin* noting that 'four days in April saw greater awareness of the Holocaust, and its significance, than in three decades preceding'.[47] It was this TV show, above anything else, which turned the term into a 'household' name in the United States.[48]

*Holocaust* also had a significant impact in Europe. When it was screened in West Germany in 1979, it attracted 14 million viewers[49], prompting many to see it as a turning-point in German history. For example, the film historian Ilan Avisar claims that 'Green's film practically introduced the Holocaust into the public discourse of modern Germany'.[50] In France, the wartime murder of Jews ceased to be known as 'genocide' and became instead known as the 'Holocaust'.[51]

That the 'Holocaust' had a resonance beyond Jewish America can be seen in the United States in the aftermath of the showing of the mini-series. Less than two weeks after *Holocaust* had been aired, President Jimmy Carter announced the formation of a Presidential Commission to recommend a national Holocaust memorial. While this can be seen as both a gesture towards American Jewry and Israel after Carter's expressed support for the legitimacy of Palestinian rights to a homeland and approval of the sale of F15 aircraft to Egypt and Saudi Arabia, the result of the setting up of the Commission was to bring the 'Holocaust' officially to the heart of American government. The 'Holocaust' assumed a central place within American identity.

The emerging significance of the myth of the 'Holocaust' for non-Jewish – as well as Jewish – America is reflected upon by Hilberg. He was surprised at the take up of a course on the Holocaust which he started teaching in the 1970s by both Jewish *and* non-Jewish students. For the latter in particular, Hilberg suggested that 'after the disorientation of Vietnam they wanted to know the difference between good and evil. The Holocaust is the benchmark, the defining moment in the drama of good and evil' and that 'against this single occurrence, one would assess all other deeds. And so, memorialisation began in earnest, that is to say it became organised'.[52]

In the United States particularly, the 1980s and 1990s have witnessed massive interest in the 'Holocaust', expressed through numerous acts of such 'organised memorialisation'. This two-decade process of memorialisation culminated in 1993 being dubbed 'the year of the Holocaust'. With the opening of the United States

Holocaust Memorial Museum and first screening of Spielberg's *Schindler's List*, it seemed that the 'Holocaust' had become as American as apple pie. The 'Holocaust' was now both on the Mall in Washington, DC, just a few hundred feet away from the Washington Monument, as well as being filmed by Hollywood's most successful producer.

The result of this interest in the United States has been the 'Americanisation of the Holocaust'. This process has seen the reshaping of the 'Holocaust' into a story participating 'in the fundamental tale of pluralism, tolerance, democracy, and human rights that America tells about itself'[53]. As the 'Holocaust' became an export product to America, the centre of gravity of the myth of the 'Holocaust' shifted from Europe – and to a lesser extent Israel – to the United States. The 'Holocaust' is now considerably less important in Europe where it physically took place than it is in America where it has been embraced as a statement of faith.

There is something surprising about this adoption of what is in many ways someone else's history. It is – as Berenbaum suggests – slightly incongruous for American Jews to talk of Jewishness in terms of 'Holocaust' and 'Israel', when 'the overwhelming majority of American Jews are neither survivors nor the children of survivors, and all American Jews have chosen not to be Israelis'.[54] And it is perhaps even more incongruous that – as Jeffrey Shandler points out – it is the 'Holocaust' which has emerged as 'a master paradigm in American consciousness' (non-Jewish as well as Jewish) despite the fact that it neither took place on American soil nor involved most Americans.[55]

An event in European history has become a sort of adopted part of American history. Yet the fact that the Holocaust is a European – rather than American – event has, it would seem, added rather than detracted from its attractiveness to an American audience. It is sufficiently 'foreign' and distant over both time and space to be relatively unthreatening. Indeed it has been suggested that 'the popular American fascination with the Holocaust may function as a "screen memory" in the Freudian sense, covering up a traumatic event – another traumatic event – that cannot be approached directly ... the fascination with the Holocaust could be read as a kind of screen allegory behind/through which the nation is struggling to find a proper mode of memorialising traumata closer to home'.[56] Allowing a foreign trauma to take up a central position means that national traumas may be dealt with in the shadows, or ignored. The implication is that contemporary fascination with the 'Holocaust' is simply a cover for 'events as distant as the genocide of Native Americans or as recent as the Vietnam War'.[57] Thus, the contemporary fascination with the

'Holocaust' may in reality be less about a concern with the Holocaust than about other, more internal matters.

Whatever the explanation – and there are surely many – there is little doubt that at the end of the twentieth century the 'Holocaust' is being made in America. The result – a number of critics have suggested – is that a process of trivialisation is taking place. Writers have pointed to the transformation of 'Europe's most searing genocide ... into an American version of kitsch',[58] and that a process of 'gentrification'[59] of the Holocaust is taking place over the course of the last two decades. And they are surely right to signal that there is plenty of 'Holocaust' trivia around at the end of the twentieth century. As Finkelstein notes, 'a veritable Holocaust industry has sprung up. The recent publication of a Holocaust cookbook [in 1996 in New York] – to rave notices, no less – points up the marketing possibilities of Holocaust kitsch'.[60]

The response of creating kitsch is one which Mosse signalled when he examined the reaction of Europeans to the horrors of the First World War. He suggested that they reacted to war in two 'radically different' ways: sanctification – which characterises for Mosse the making of the 'Myth of the War Experience' – and trivialisation. This trivialisation of the war experience was the response of 'those who had stayed at home or were too young to have fought', who 'distorted and manipulated at will' the realities of war, much to the horror of the veterans.[61] Thus, the wartime division between the front and home-front continued after the war along the lines of a division between these different attempts at sanctification and trivialisation. Sanctification was a way of giving meaning to the war, while trivialisation involved 'cutting war down to size so that it would become commonplace instead of awesome and frightening'. Through the process of 'trivialisation'

> ... the reality of war was disguised and controlled, even if it was not transcended ... Trivialisation was one way of coping with war, not by exalting and glorifying it, but by making it familiar, that which was in one's power to choose and to dominate. Trivialisation was apparent not merely in kitsch or trashy literature but also in picture postcards, toys and games, and battlefield tourism.[62]

Mosse's division between those with direct experience of the past event and those with none may provide us with a useful framework to adopt when thinking about the representation of the 'Holocaust' in the past three or four decades. It is too simple to suggest that the response of the Holocaust survivor has always been to opt for 'sancti-fication', while the non-survivor has always opted for 'trivialisation'. There are too many exceptions to justify the use of such a clear cut division between the responses of the survivor and the second or third generation. However, Mosse's distinction is useful in pointing to the kind of differences of opinion in how to represent the 'Holocaust' articulated by for example the 'purist' Elie Wiesel – who acts as a self-appointed spokesman-of-sorts for the survivor generation – and the third-generation movie director Steven Spielberg.

Elie Wiesel – who has been particularly outspoken in his criticism of what he sees to be the trivialisation of a sacred event – has written of the impossibility of representing the Holocaust. He claims that 'whoever has not lived through the event can never know it. And whoever has lived through the event can never fully reveal it'[63] and famously asserts that in his own writing of this event, he writes to denounce writing. For Wiesel, therefore, there is something unap-proachable and unknowable about this past. In particular, he sees Auschwitz – where he was taken as a teenager in 1944 – to be 'a kingdom of night' which is so 'other' as to be beyond imagination. For Spielberg, however, Auschwitz is not simply a place which can be imagined, but a place which can be reconstructed as a 'Holocaust' movie set. In taking his cameras into the reconstructed gas chambers of Auschwitz, Spielberg demonstrates the distance in reflecting upon this event which lies between him and Wiesel. That distance is in some ways the distance between the first generation of 'Holocaust' survivors, and the second and third generations who are the cultural producers and consumers at the end of the twentieth century.

Regardless of Wiesel's concerns, not only is it possible to buy a 'Holocaust' cookbook in the 1990s, but it is also possible to 'consume' the 'Holocaust' equivalents of the 'kitsch or trashy literature ... picture postcards, toys and games, and battlefield tourism', which Mosse points to as the products produced in the aftermath of the First World War. In the aftermath of the Holocaust, trashy literature, picture postcards, toys and games and death camp tourism are wide-spread. The 'Holocaust' has been visited by the comic superhero Superman, who 'travels back in time and witnesses the horrors of the Holocaust in Nazi-occupied Poland' and utters the words 'I'm not one to interfere with the governments of the world, but I just can't turn a blind eye and let these fascist bullies exterminate everyone they don't like'.[64] It has been the theme of an Israeli TV 'Holocaust Quiz, shot "on location" in Poland ... participating in it were Jewish boys and girls who were asked questions about what took place in the camps, and they were awarded two points for each correct answer. Applause was not allowed because it was judged to be in bad taste and to "desecrate the memory of the victims".'[65] And it is – as I explore in this book – the focus of a type of tourism that is on the increase. Each year tourists flock Auschwitz, Anne Frank House, Yad Vashem, the museums in Washington, DC, Dallas, Houston and buy postcards (to send to friends at home with the message 'Wish you were here'). At the end of the twentieth century the 'Holocaust' is being consumed. When in Washington, DC, we 'consume' the 'Holocaust' on offer at the United States Holocaust Memorial Museum; when in Amsterdam we 'consume' the 'Holocaust' on offer at the Anne Frank House and when in Kraków we 'consume' the 'Holocaust' on offer at the State Museum at Auschwitz. And then it is on to yet another stop.

Seeing as we were visiting friends in Amsterdam for the weekend, we followed the logic of 'Holocaust tourism' and decided to walk along Prinsengracht in search of the Anne Frank House. We knew we were there when we saw the line of people who – like us – looked unmistakably like tourists. And standing in that line we recognised a number of faces from our plane that morning. Obviously quite a few others had done what we had done. They – like us – had taken the train into Amsterdam from the airport, found where they were staying, eaten some lunch, and then walked to the first tourist attraction on the Amsterdam itinerary – the Anne Frank House. So here we all were, shuffling along in a line which stretches back – even on that Friday afternoon – round the corner. This line gradually creeps closer and closer to the sales desk where our admission money is taken, and we climb the stairs – still walking in this seemingly never ending line of tourists – to the house where Anne lived.

We shuffle around like this through the front-house where the helpers worked. Two little girls who are clutching a copy of Anne Frank's diary under their arms pause and smile for their father who takes a photograph of them standing in front of the bookcase which hides the stairs into the Secret Annexe. We all pause, and then once the camera has been packed away, continue to 'follow the leader' into the Secret Annexe. We walk through the unfurnished rooms – the furniture was confiscated when the Secret Annexe was discovered in 1944 – and into Anne's rooms with its collection of pictures of filmstars on the walls. It is here that we walk the slowest. And then the pace quickens and we go up through the top floor of the Secret Annexe and into the attic of the neighbouring house. Here we see the 'Holy Book' – Anne's first diary, and the last page written by Anne – a small exhibition about the diary and Anne's death in Bergen Belsen, and then shuffle down to the gift shop where I buy postcards of the 'Bookcase (open)' and the 'Bookcase (closed)' because I didn't have my photo taken standing in front of this particular bookcase clutching my copy of Anne Frank's diary, but I wanted to consume all the same.

Judging by the crowds of tourists at the Anne Frank house on a Friday afternoon in August 1998, historian Yehuda Bauer is right to reflect that 'contrary to warnings by many writers and historians, the Holocaust is not receding into the background; quite the contrary.' Rather, as Bauer continues,

> Whether presented authentically or inauthentically, in accordance with the historical facts or in contradiction to them, with empathy and understanding or as monumental kitsch, the Holocaust has become a ruling symbol in our culture. I am not sure whether this is good or bad, but it seems to be a fact.[66]

And it is that fact – that the 'Holocaust' has emerged as nothing less than a 'ruling symbol in our culture' – which is the theme which I seek to explore throughout this book. By focusing on three people – Anne Frank, Adolf Eichmann and Oskar Schindler – and three places – Auschwitz, Yad Vashem and the United States Holocaust Memorial Museum – my aim is to consider both the period from the late 1940s through to the present day, and to consider Israel and America as well as Europe. However, I am the first to recognise that the choice of these people and places does leave some noticeable absences. In particular, I devote relatively little space to the representation of the 'Holocaust' in Germany, preferring instead to reflect at greater length upon Israel and the United States. In large part this is motivated by a belief that those two countries, ironically, have been much more instrumental in creating the myth of the 'Holocaust'.

As I consider the representation of Anne Frank, Adolf Eichmann and Oskar Schindler, and reflect upon the nature of Auschwitz, Yad Vashem and the United States Holocaust Memorial Museum, I have given some consideration to the categories raised by Bauer. Thus I have pointed out what I consider to be 'inauthentic', historically inaccurate and 'kitsch' representations of the 'Holocaust'. However, my aim in doing this has not been to rank 'Holocaust' movies or museums in any sort of order of personal preference, or historical accuracy. Rather my aim in critically assessing the myth of the 'Holocaust' on offer in a particular movie or museum is to ask first how, and second why, the 'Holocaust' has emerged as a dominant icon at the end of the twentieth century. No doubt, as you reflect on the movies and museums that I am commenting on in this book, there will be times when we disagree. There can, however, be little disagreement over the fact that the 'Holocaust' has emerged as an icon in the West. And it is perhaps worth going further than Bauer, and at least ask whether the centrality of the myth of the 'Holocaust' at the end of the twentieth century is a good or a bad thing.

# Part I
# PEOPLE

# 1

# Anne Frank

At the end of the twentieth century, Anne Frank is ubiquitous. She is simultaneously 'the Holocaust's most famous victim'[1], 'the most famous child of the twentieth century'[2], and 'her face with the sad shy smile is one of the icons of this century, a present-day Mona Lisa'.[3] Since the 1950s Anne Frank's name has been attached to a day, a week, a rose, a tulip, countless trees, a whole forest, streets, schools and youth centres, and a village. Her diary has been translated into more than 55 languages, has sold over 24 million copies worldwide and is *the* canonical 'Holocaust' text. In 1997, there were more than 700,000 visitors to the Amsterdam house which was the Frank family's hiding place during the war, among them the American First Lady Hillary Clinton and the 1970s pop group the Bee Gees.

And yet, it is perhaps rather surprising that it is Anne Frank's diary which has assumed the status of 'Holocaust' text *par excellence*. It is after all, only one amongst many 'Holocaust' diaries to survive the war. Moreover, in the text of *The Diary of Anne Frank*, the implementation of the 'Final Solution of the Jewish Question' plays a somewhat peripheral role. The 'Holocaust' is essentially the context within which the diary is written, rather than the central focus. In the words of Anne's father – Otto Frank – in a letter of 1952, the diary 'is not a warbook. War is the background. It is not a Jewish book either, though Jewish sphere, sentiment and surrounding is the background'.[4]

Unlike the ghetto diary written by – for example – Avraham Tory in Vilna,[5] Anne's diary – written in hiding in Amsterdam – does not describe the unfolding of the Nazi persecution of the Jews in depth. Aside from detailing the nature of Hitler's anti-Jewish laws in the entry for 20 June 1942, specific references in the diary to the activities of the Nazis are restricted to the few snippets of information gleaned from radio reports or Dutch 'Christian' visitors. Anne herself writes in her entry for 28 March 1944: 'I could write a lot more about politics, about the news bulletin early this morning, about Miep's and Bep's questions and so on and so forth, but I have heaps else to tell you today.'[6] The 'heaps else' relate to the relationships within the annexe in general, and her relationship with Peter in particular. It is this developing relationship between two adolescents which dominates the diary. The Holocaust is merely the setting within which this relationship evolves, and the reason why both of them find themselves in hiding together.

When Anne does make specific references to events going on outside of the annexe, they are subsumed by the concerns of an adolescent girl living with seven other people, one of whom she is growing to love. On 31 March 1944 she writes briefly of the German occupation of Hungary where 'there are still a million Jews ... so they too will have had it now', and at more length of the birthday presents given to Peter's father, and her developing relationship with Peter himself:

> The chatter about Peter and me has calmed down a bit now, he's coming to fetch me this evening, nice of him don't you think, because he finds it such a bore himself! We are very good friends, are together a lot and discuss every imaginable subject. It is awfully nice never to have to keep a check on myself as I would have to with other boys, whenever we get onto precarious ground. We were talking, for instance, about blood and via that subject we began talking about menstruation etc. He thinks we women are pretty tough, seeing that we can stand up to losing 1 to 2 litres of blood. He thinks I'm tough as well. I wonder why?[7]

Nonetheless, Anne Frank's diary has become the central 'Holocaust' text. It is Anne's diary – rather than someone else's – which has become the 'Holocaust bible', and this despite (or perhaps precisely because of) being 'one of the "easiest" and most antiseptic works of Holocaust literature'.[8] It is this book above all others which is the most widely read 'Holocaust' text, and yet as Alvin Rosenfeld suggests, 'to limit one's understanding of the Holocaust to such a book as Anne Frank's diary is to grasp only the most preliminary outline of the coming war against the Jews'.[9]

From the perspective of the present it is easy to assume that *The Diary of Anne Frank* was in some ways destined to worldwide popularity because of the remarkable maturity of Anne's writing.

However, Anne Frank made an inauspicious start as a 'contemporary cultural icon'[10] in the years immediately after the end of the war. Despite its later phenomenal success, the early post-war attempts of Anne's father Otto – the only survivor from the 'secret annexe' – to get her diary published, were unsuccessful. Anne's diary was rejected by at least four leading Dutch publishers, before finally being published by Uitgeverij Contact in a limited print run of 1, 500 copies in June 1947. Annie Romein, who showed a copy of the diary to the Dutch publishers Querido in 1946, saw their rejection of the manuscript to be a result of 'the certainty [which] prevailed there at the time that interest in anything to do with the war was stone cold'.[11] And yet reading the diary had made a profound impact upon her historian husband, Jan Romein. It was he who referred to the diary – although not by name – for the first time in print, in an article published in the newspaper *Het Parool* on 3 April 1946. There he recounted reading a diary written by a thirteen-year-old Jewish girl who had been in hiding with her parents and older sister for two years before being arrested by the Gestapo and dying in a German concentration camp shortly before liberation. Writing in the context of the start of the war crimes trials, Jan Romein claimed that 'this apparently inconsequential diary by a child, this *"de profundis"* stammered out in a child's voice, embodies all the hideousness of fascism, more so than all the evidence at Nuremberg put together'.[12] It was primarily as a result of this article that the publisher Contact expressed an interest in the diary.

However, it would be wrong to suggest that there was anything like a straight line between the publication of *The Diary of Anne Frank*, in Dutch *Het Achterhuis*, by Contact in 1947, and this 'apparently inconsequential diary by a child' becoming a central icon in the myth of the 'Holocaust' some fifty or so years later. The diary was moderately successful in the Netherlands, and went through six Dutch editions in three years, but this remained a relatively slow start. Indeed, almost five years separated the printing of the sixth (July 1950) and seventh (April 1955) editions of *Het Achterhuis*.[13]

From 1957 onwards, the popularity of the diary increased rapidly in the Netherlands: three editions were published in 1955, three more in 1956, a further nine in 1957 and five in 1958.[14] In 1957 the decision was made not to demolish Prinsengracht 263 and it opened to the public in 1960. This renewed interest in Anne Frank and her diary in the Netherlands was stimulated by the opening of the Broadway play based on the diary there on 27 November 1956, meaning it 'came about "via an international detour".'[15] For Anne Frank to become famous in the Netherlands, she had to be taken to

America in 1952, and then taken back to the Netherlands in 1956. Arguably the 'Anne Frank' who returned to the Netherlands in the mid-fifties was not the same 'Anne Frank' who had been taken across the Atlantic four years previously. 'Anne Frank' had been 'Americanised', and her story reshaped and repackaged.

Although the original manuscript of the diary is written in Dutch, when Anne and her family were in hiding in wartime Amsterdam, the Frank family were German Jews. Anne had been born in Frankfurt on 12 June 1929. Thirteen years later – when one of her birthday presents was a red and white checked autograph album, which became the first book in which Anne wrote her diary – she was living in a suburb in southern Amsterdam. The family had moved from Germany to Amsterdam at the end of 1933, after the Nazi rise to power. Amsterdam was well known to Otto Frank, who had travelled there on business during the early to mid 1920s. It was, therefore, in many ways a natural place to take his family when Otto started to consider emigrating. He arrived in the middle of 1933 to establish a Dutch branch of the pectin manufacturers Opekta-Werke, on the recommendation of his brother-in-law who headed the Swiss Opekta subsidiary. In December 1933, his family joined him in their second floor apartment at Merwedeplein 37, although Anne did not arrive in Amsterdam until February – or possibly March – 1934.[16]

It was in this apartment that Anne wrote her first diary entries in June 1942. However, less than a month later the family moved into the building which was to become associated with her name – Prinsengracht 263 – where Otto Frank had moved his offices and warehouse in December 1940. After the issuing of call-up notices for German Jews at the beginning of July 1942, the family went into hiding in the 'secret annexe' at the rear of the office building. The original plan to go into hiding on 16 July was brought forward by ten days as a result of the call-up papers. For a little more than two years, the 'secret annexe' was home to Anne, her sister Margot, her father and mother Otto and Edith, Mr and Mrs van Pels and their son Peter (2 years older than Anne) and the dentist Dr Friedrich Pfeffer (who moved in at the end of 1942). Herman van Pels and his family, and Pfeffer had been family friends for a number of years.

While Anne and her sister Margot had both been born in Germany, they had moved to Amsterdam as young girls and, in reflecting on her identity in her diary, Anne no longer saw herself as German. On 9 October 1942, news of German shootings of hostages led her to comment: 'Nice people the Germans and to think that I am really one of them too! But no, Hitler took away our nationality long ago, in fact Germans and Jews are the greatest enemies in the world'.[17] And in her 'Prospectus and Guide to the "Secret Annexe"' Anne had specified that 'it is strictly forbidden to listen to German news bulletins', and that 'German [radio] stations are only listened to in special cases, such as classical music'. As far as 'use of language' went, 'all civilised languages are permitted, therefore no German! ... No German books may be read ...'[18]

Anne considers her Jewishness perhaps nowhere more so than in a passage written after the shock of another break-in:

> We have been pointedly reminded that we are in hiding, that we are Jews in chains, chained to one spot, without any rights, with a thousand duties. We Jews mustn't show our feelings, must be brave and strong, must accept all inconveniences and not grumble, must do what is within our power and trust in God. Sometime this terrible war will be over. Surely the time will come when we are people again, and not just Jews!
>
> Who has inflicted this upon us? Who has made us Jews different from all other people? Who has allowed us to suffer so terribly up till now? It is God that has made us as we are, but it will be God, too, who will raise us up again. If we bear all this suffering and if there are still Jews left, when it is over, then Jews, instead of being doomed, will be held up as an example. Who knows, it might even be our religion from which the world and all peoples learn good, and for that reason and that reason only do we have to suffer now. We can never become just Netherlanders or just English or any other nation for that matter, we will always remain Jews, we must remain Jews, but we want to, too.[19]

Yet it is clear that while identifying herself as a Jew, Anne also identified with the Netherlands, writing of 'our beloved queen',[20] and of her desire to 'become Dutch! I love the Dutch, I love this country, I love the language and want to work here'.[21] However, news of growing antisemitism in Dutch circles and the possibility that Jewish immigrants may be forced to leave the Netherlands after the war, caused Anne to reflect on her relationship with her adopted country:

> I hope one thing only, and that is that this hatred of the Jews will be a passing thing, that the Dutch will show what they are after all, and that they will never totter and lose their sense of right, for this is unjust! And if this terrible threat should actually come true, then the pitiful little collection of Jews that remain in Holland will have to leave. We, too, shall have to

move on again with our little bundles, and leave this beautiful country, which offered us such a warm welcome and which now turns its back on us. I love Holland. I who, having no native country, had hoped that it would become my fatherland, and I still hope it will![22]

This Anne who distances herself from her German roots, and reflects upon her Jewishness in the pages of her diary, was made into someone else when she was exported. That reshaping of her identity can be seen first of all in the German translation of her diary. Originally intended for Anne's grandmother, who could not read Dutch, Anneliese Schutz's 1946 German translation of Otto Frank's typescript of the diary was published by Lambert Schneider Verlag in 1950. Anne's negative references to Germans were either toned down or removed entirely. Thus the rule in her 'Prospectus and Guide to the "Secret Annexe"' that 'German [radio] stations are only listened to in special cases, such as classical music' was left out of the German translation, and the rule 'Speak softly at all times, by order! All civilised languages are permitted, therefore no German!' became 'All civilised languages ... but softly'.[23] Anne's statement that 'there is no greater hostility than exists between Germans and Jews' was changed in the German translation into 'there is no greater hostility in the world than between these Germans and Jews!'[24] This last change was specifically justified by Otto Frank on the grounds that Anne, 'despite the great tribulations she had suffered as a result of the persecution of the Jews and which she felt so acutely despite her youth, by no means measured all Germans by the same yardstick. For, as she knew so well, even in those days we had many good friends among the Germans'.[25] The removal of anything which could be taken as anti-German was justified by *Der Spiegel* on the grounds that 'a book intended for sale in Germany ... cannot abuse the Germans'.[26]

In the process of publication, 'Anne' was stripped of more than simply any comments which could be perceived as 'anti-German'. There were clear attempts by Otto Frank and the early publishers not to compromise Anne and her mother's posthumous reputation. Thus the passages of sexual self-discovery were heavily edited, and the Anne who writes: 'Dear Kitty, There's no one in the world I've told more about myself and my feelings than you, so I might as well tell you something about sexual matters too',[27] was more or less silenced. No doubt, Anne's adolescent description of her vagina was seen to be inappropriate in the conservative context of the late 1940s and early 1950s.[28] The 'Anne Frank' who was published was not only seemingly disinterested in sex. She was also made into a teenager whose poor relationship with her mother was patched up through the editing of her most cutting and critical observations. It wasn't until the late 1980s that Anne was given back her sexuality and troubled family relationships, when *The Critical Edition* of *The Diary of Anne Frank* was first published in Dutch in 1986 and in English in 1989.[29] Within the last year, a further five pages of Anne's manuscript which reflect critically on the nature of her parent's marriage have come to light. These – it turns out – were removed from the original by Otto Frank shortly before his death in 1980, when he allowed the original diary to be studied so as to refute claims that it was a post-war fake.[30] The result of the editing of her father and the first publishers of the diary was to create a girl who was in many ways the perfect 'victim'. Not only was she young and female, but also 'innocent'.

It was arguably when this innocent 'Anne Frank' was exported to the United States that she underwent the greatest changes. These changes were to have a major impact upon the subsequent memory of Anne Frank, as it was in America that what may be termed as the 'myth of Anne Frank' was created. In 1952, Doubleday published the first English translation of the diary, which sold more than 45,000 copies in literally a matter of days. The diary went on to sell around 100,000 copies in the United States in its first year of publication, a figure matched only in Japan, where Anne Frank's diary came to stand as *the* book on the Second World War. In contrast, the Vallentine Mitchell edition published in Britain in 1952, while selling its initial print run of 5,000 in six months, was then 'seen to be coming to the end of its natural sales life' and thus was not automatically reprinted.[31] As in the Netherlands, it was not so much the publication of the diary in English that shaped the 'myth of Anne Frank', as the opening of the Broadway play on 5 October 1955 and the release of the Hollywood film in 1959. The 1955 play in particular was crucial in popularising Anne Frank, and creating the myth of 'Anne Frank'.

As early as June 1952, American journalist and novelist Meyer Levin had suggested in a review of the diary, recently published under the title *Anne Frank: The Diary of a Young Girl*, that the book should be made into a play and film.[32] He persuaded Otto Frank that he was the best person to write the stage play, and had completed the script by October. However, this script was turned down by the first two producers Levin and Frank approached, and subsequently by a further fourteen. Ultimately, the script of the play was written not by Levin, but by a husband and wife script-writing team from the MGM studios in Hollywood, Albert and Frances (Goodrich) Hackett. They went through multiple draftings in consultation with Otto Frank, the producer Kermit Bloomgarden, the director Garson Kanin and the playwright Lillian Hellman, before producing a final script which previewed at the Walnut Theatre in Philadelphia before opening on Broadway – at the Cort – on 5 October 1955. The play was acclaimed by the critics, and subsequently went on to win a number of prestigious theatre awards. It ran for 717 performances in the 1000-seater Cort theatre alone and then in nearly every major city in the United States.[33] Subsequently the Hacketts went on to write the screen-play for the Twentieth-Century Fox film version of the diary – directed by George Stevens – which premiered in 1959, and went on to win three Academy Awards.

However, the decision to stage the script written by the Hacketts was contested by Levin, who claimed breach of contract and took Otto Frank and Kermit Bloomgarden to court at the end of 1956, suing for $200,000 damages. Levin claimed that the Hacketts had used some of his material, and was awarded $50,000 damages by a New York State jury. This decision was later overturned by Judge Coleman of the New York State Supreme Court who argued that because both Levin and the Hacketts were working from the diary, similarities in the scripts were inevitable and that it was impossible to prove plagiarism. A settlement was finally agreed at the end of 1959 whereby Levin signed over all authorial rights to Otto Frank, receiving $15,000 in return.

Levin's disquiet was essentially over the script that the Hacketts had written. In particular, he claimed that they had removed the 'Jewishness' from Anne Frank's diary entries. They had ended up with a play – and later a movie script – universalising the tale of a girl who, because of her Jewishness, was in hiding.

In claiming this, Levin was making a valid point. There is not a shadow of doubt that, compared with the diary, the stage-play and movie-script downplayed Anne's Jewishness. Perhaps the clearest example of this is the editing for Broadway consumption of Anne's diary comments to Peter. In response to his despairing 'Look at us, hiding out for two years! ... Caught here, like rabbits in a trap, waiting for them to come and get us! And all for what? Because we're Jews! Because we're Jews!', Anne – in her diary – responds that 'we're not the only Jews that've had to suffer. Right down through the ages there have been Jews and they've had to suffer'. However, the Broadway Anne replies in far more universal terms: 'We're not the only people that've had to suffer. There've always been people that've had to ... Sometimes one race ... Sometimes another ... and yet ...'[34] Writer Lawrence Graver argues that this change came after the direct intervention of director Garson Kanin, who had told the

Hacketts that Anne's original words were 'an embarrassing piece of special pleading', and that:

> ... people have suffered because of being English, French, German, Italian, Ethiopian, Mohammedan, Negro, and so on. I don't know how this can be indicated, but it seems to me of utmost importance.
> The fact that in this play the symbols of persecution and oppression are Jews is incidental, and Anne, in stating the argument so, reduces her magnificent stature. It is Peter here who should be the young one, outraged at being persecuted because he is a Jew, and Anne, wiser, pointing out that through the ages, people in minorities have been oppressed. In other words, at this moment, the play has an opportunity to spread its theme into the infinite.[35]

Despite Kanin's perception of the Jewishness of the victims being incidental as far as the play was concerned, the historical reality was that Peter and Anne's Jewishness was very much the point. They were not hiding in a 'secret annexe' – 'caught here, like rabbits in a trap, waiting for them to come and get us!' – in Amsterdam, in 1944, because they were 'English, French, German, Italian, Ethiopian, Mohammedan, Negro, and so on', but because they were Jews. Their Jewishness was not incidental to the story, but absolutely central. However, in the mid-1950s for Kanin, the historical context of Amsterdam in 1944 was of far less importance than the context of contemporary America.

This was not an isolated example of the more universal and de-historicised message conveyed by the stage-play. Rather there was a conscious attempt to Americanise the story. The Hacketts justified their decision to have the song in the Hannukah scene sung in English on the grounds that a Hebrew song

> ... would set the characters in the play apart from the people watching them ... for the majority of our audience is not Jewish. And the thing that we have striven for, toiled for, fought for throughout the whole play is to make the audience understand and identify themselves ... to make them one with them ... to make them feel 'that, but for the grace of God, might have been I'.[36]

Their desire to present a universal message to as wide an audience as possible was something shared by Otto Frank himself, who wrote

that it 'was my point of view to try to bring Anne's message to as
many people as possible even if there are some who think it is a sac-
rilege and does not bring the greatest part of the public to understand'.[37]

The Hacketts – themselves not Jewish – wrote a play which would
make Anne's story of universal significance to audiences in 1950s
America. In doing this, they were starting with a text – *The Diary of
Anne Frank* – which was already relatively accessible to a non-Jewish
world. Written by a young, assimilated, middle-class Jew, the diary
has few references to specifically Jewish themes or culture. And I
think the very fact that the diary was penned by an assimilated Jew
goes a long way towards explaining the remarkable impact of the
work with a non-Jewish audience in the 1950s. It was *The Diary of
Anne Frank* which made an impact, and not another diary written
by a Jewish teenager in hiding in Western Europe – Moshe Flinker
– who like Anne, was captured and died in a concentration camp. In
*Young Moshe's Diary* we have a work written by someone whose
wartime experience parallels that of Anne very closely.[38] Yet, as
James Young has pointed out, while 'Moshe was reared in a religious home, a Zionist and, wrote his diary in Hebrew, Anne was
assimilated, non-Zionist, and wrote in Dutch'.[39] In the context of the
1950s, Moshe was too Jewish to be of popular significance. It was
the diary of the assimilated Anne, and the play which removed most
traces of Jewish specificity, which made a worldwide impact.

With the writing of the screenplay, the universal message of the
diary was stressed even more. As the film critic Elkan Allan commented: 'In transferring the tragedy to the screen George Stevens
concentrated on the universal humanitarian qualities of the piece
rather than on the particular ethnic problems of the heroes'.[40] What
is remarkable is that this was lauded by none other than the director of the Jewish Film Advisory Committee, John Stone. His words
reveal something of the relationship between the American Jewish
Community and the 'Holocaust' in the late 1950s:

> ... this screenplay is even better than the stage play. You have
> given the story a more 'universal' meaning and appeal. It
> could very easily have been an outdated Jewish tragedy by
> less creative or more emotional handling – even a Jewish
> 'Wailing Wall', and hence regarded as mere propaganda.[41]

It would be completely impossible even to imagine a person in a
similar position within the American Jewish community saying

such a thing thirty or forty years later. But in 1957, 'John Stone, too, voiced the apparent mood of the period'.[42]

But Stone was not simply reflecting the mood of universalism. He was also reflecting the ambivalence that American Jews felt towards the 'Holocaust' in 1957. The 1950s were – as I'm arguing throughout this book – a period when the myth of the 'Holocaust' had not yet emerged. And Stone's comments on the screenplay reflect that effective silence. In this period – prior to the emergence of the myth of the 'Holocaust' – 'Anne' gained a reputation not specifically as a 'Holocaust victim', but as a spokesperson of other causes. In the mid 1950s, America had little time for the 'Holocaust', being caught up in the early years of the Cold War and McCarthyism, and the beginnings of the challenge to segregation in the South. In this context, the liberal message of the Broadway 'Anne Frank' became, in film historian Judith Doneson's words:

> ... a symbol and a metaphor for events in the United States in the 1950s. We are not the only ones to suffer, says Anne, sometimes one race sometimes another. The persecution of the Jews and its results show what can happen when racism prevails, a warning to the American public with regard to blacks. The film also functions as a metaphor for the prevailing domestic political theme of the 1950s – the HUAC [House Committee on Un-American Activities] hearings. When the end came for Anne and the others in the secret annex, it was because someone informed on them ... In the sense that *The Diary of Anne Frank* reflected racial discrimination against blacks along with the danger posed by the informer, its message in the 1950s was a liberal one.[43]

Anne became the patron saint of liberalism. Thus a diary in which the Holocaust provided the context rather than the central theme was made into a play and a film which reflected the concerns of 1950s America much more than it reflected the Holocaust. It was not only the specifically Jewish references of the diary which were omitted from the play and the film, but also the relatively few specifically 'Holocaust' references. For example, Anne's comments on the deported Jews in her entry for 9 October 1942 – 'if it is as bad as this in Holland whatever will it be like in the distant and barbarous regions they are sent to? We assume that most of them are murdered. The British radio speaks of their being gassed'[44] – were omitted in the script written by the Hacketts. In effect, they had largely edited out the Holocaust.

By effectively separating the diary from its Holocaust context, it was possible to create a play and a film with a happy ending. On the stage, it is through re-reading excerpts from Anne's diary – which he discovers when he returns to the 'secret annexe' – that Otto Frank turns from a 'bitter old man' into a man filled with hope. And the audience experiences the same sense of 'redemption' as they follow the same journey. It is a contrived journey, which omits the few passages of horror and pessimism in the original diary, and ends with the ultimate in 'feel-good' endings. We walked from the theatre with Anne's last words, twice-repeated, ringing in our ears: 'In spite of everything I still believe that people are really good at heart', and Otto Frank's closing comment, 'She puts me to shame'.[45]

It is thus a play which ends 'not on a note of final gloom but of moral triumph'.[46] And it is clear that this was quite an intentional decision on the part of director Garson Kanin. He justified the upbeat ending on the grounds of not wishing 'to inflict depression on an audience ... I don't consider that a legitimate theatrical end'.[47] Interestingly, when the play opened in Israel a slightly different twist was put on the ending by the Habimach Theatre Group. Anne's optimistic words are questioned in effect, by the close of the Israeli version of the play, which has Otto Frank shaking his head and repeating to himself 'I don't know, I don't know'.[48] This questioning of Anne's optimism was considered by George Stevens for the ending of the 1959 movie based upon the Hackett's play. At a preview in San Francisco, an alternative ending was shown which portrayed Anne 'in a concentration camp uniform swaying in a numb miasmic fog'. However, this ending 'was deemed too tough in audience impact and against 20th – [Century] Fox's desire to have the film considered "hopeful" despite all'.[49] Thus the movie finishes with Otto's words 'for two years we've lived in fear; from now on we'll live in hope' and the imagery of a cloud studded sky, complete with birds that speak of final freedom for Anne.

Hollywood – like Broadway – opted to give 'Anne Frank' a happy and hopeful ending, rather than death from sickness in the overcrowded filth of a Bergen-Belsen barrack. Both effectively evaded the Holocaust. Far from being a first encounter with the event which was becoming known as the 'Holocaust', the play and the film based on Anne's diary shied away from dealing with the issues raised by the murder of Anne in 1944 simply because she was a Jew. As Langer suggests,

> ... an audience coming to this play in 1955, only a decade after
> the event, would find little to threaten their psychological or

emotional security. No one dies, and the inhabitants of the annex endure minimal suffering. The play really celebrates the struggle for harmony in the midst of impending disruption, thus supporting those values which the viewer instinctively hopes to find affirmed on the stage.[50]

As numerous critics have noted, the decision to end the play and film with Anne's catch phrase 'In spite of everything I still believe that people are really good at heart' was wholly unsuitable. These words are – for Langer – 'the least appropriate epitaph conceivable for the millions of victims and thousands of survivors of Nazi genocide',[51] and he is surely right to draw such a conclusion. In the play and film, these words – 'In spite of everything I still believe that people are really good at heart' – are not simply de-coupled from Anne's subsequent death in Bergen-Belsen and thus from the Holocaust, but also from their context within the diary itself. When Anne wrote these words, it was in a passage which combines optimism and pessimism:

It's really a wonder that I haven't dropped all my ideals, because they seem so absurd and impossible to carry out. Yet I keep them, because in spite of everything I still believe that people are really good at heart. I simply can't build up my hopes on a foundation consisting of confusion, misery, and death. I see the world gradually being turned into a wilderness, I hear the ever approaching thunder, which will destroy us too, I can feel the sufferings of millions and yet, if I look up into the heavens, I think that it will all come right, that this cruelty too will end, and that peace and tranquillity will return again.[52]

The 'Anne Frank' made in America in the 1950s is not allowed a hint of pessimism expressed in this entry, but only speaks optimistically of an enduring belief in human goodness in spite of everything. The Broadway and Hollywood 'Anne Frank' is not even the Anne in the 'secret annexe', let alone the Anne in Bergen-Belsen. Rather, she is a creation who comes and offers reassurance that the central tenet of liberalism – that humans are essentially good – is still valid. As the psychotherapist Bruno Bettelheim suggests, Anne's 'moving statement about the goodness of men [sic.] releases us effectively of the need to cope with the problems Auschwitz presents ... If all men [sic.] are good at heart, there never really was an Auschwitz; nor is there any possibility that it may recur'.[53]

Yet, there was a place called Auschwitz where Anne's mother and Mr Van Pels both died, and a place called Bergen-Belsen where Margot and Anne both died. And these places – Auschwitz and Bergen-Belsen – are a fundamental challenge to the very basis of liberalism. Liberalism's assumption of human goodness comes face-to-face with the gas chambers of Auschwitz-Birkeneau and is found wanting. As historian Steven Beller argues, the very crux of historical writing which attempts to understand why Europe's Jews were murdered, is motivated by this disquiet on the part of liberalism. After all, he suggests,

> ... for a certain brand of conservative the Holocaust is a horrific event, but it just goes to show how bestial men [sic.] are under the surface ... Man is a Fallen Being, and the Holocaust proves it ... But for those within the liberal world, broadly defined, whose foundation is a belief in the basic goodness of human beings, and their ability to tell right from wrong, the Holocaust ... is an awful conundrum.[54]

*None* of that conflict emerges in the play and movie of Anne Frank's life. Rather, they leave us with the sense that liberalism has been tested *and* vindicated by Anne. However, unlike the Broadway and Hollywood 'Anne Frank', the historical Anne's life does not end with the words 'In spite of everything, I still believe that people are really good at heart'. The reality is that 'the diary is incomplete, truncated, broken off – or rather, it is completed by Westerbork ... and by Auschwitz, and by the fatal winds of Bergen-Belsen'.[55]

If Anne had survived Bergen-Belsen, I wonder what she would have chosen to end her story with, if she had even wished that story to be told. Her choice may well not have been that of the writers of the play and the movie. They chose to evade the troubling reality of Auschwitz and Bergen-Belsen, and instead to fall back upon 'the most conventional of responses about "man's inhumanity to man", the "triumph of goodness over evil", the eternal verities of "the human spirit", and other such banalities'.[56] And in the process, as Rosenfeld suggests, 'the harshness of history was left behind, and in its place softer, more acceptable images of a young girl's gaiety and moral gallantry came to the fore'.[57]

While it is in the play – and subsequent movie – that 'Anne Frank' was primarily made into a heroic icon whose goodness somehow transcended and triumphed over the evil of Nazism, there are signs of this optimism in the initial reception of Anne's diary. Even Meyer Levin, who was to later challenge the Hackett's script for presenting a universal 'Anne Frank', wrote in his *New York Times* review (1952) of Anne's diary that it was 'so wondrously alive, so near, that one feels overwhelmingly the universalities of human nature'. His tone was markedly different in a review for the Jewish *Congress Weekly* (1952), where he described the book as 'without doubt the most important human document to have come out of the great catastrophe ... The holocaust at long last comes home, and our defences are shattered. We weep.' Yet non-Jewish America was not ready for the 'Holocaust' – and indeed Jewish America was hardly ready – so in the *New York Times*, the diary was – according to Levin – 'a warm and stirring confession', 'no lugubrious ghetto tale, no compilation of horrors' and a book 'that simply bubbles with amusement, love, and discovery' and expresses 'a poignant delight in the infinite human spirit'.[58] Levin's words were typical of the early response to the book in the United States, which was characterised by 'the tendency to idealise her story',[59] and make it into little more than a message of hope.

The dehistoricisation and universalisation of the diary was therefore not unique to the Hacketts' stage and film scripts. They were certainly the most influential – given their impact – but they fitted broadly within the strand of what everyone else in 1950s America was doing with the diary. In her ghost-written introduction to the American edition, Eleanor Roosevelt noted that the diary makes us 'shockingly aware of war's greatest evil – the degradation of the human spirit', yet 'at the same time ... makes poignantly clear the ultimate shining nobility of that spirit'.[60] A similarly triumphant Anne was presented by Anne Birstein and Alfred Kazin in their introduction to *The Works of Anne Frank* published in 1959, where they reflected that Anne's bedtime prayer – 'I thank you God, for all that is good and dear and beautiful' – was 'perhaps ... Anne's last prayer in hiding. Perhaps when she went to bed on the night of August 3, 1944, her last thought was of her own blessedness: her youth, her strength, her love for all the people and the growing things around her, her closeness to God, who had provided them all'.[61] Rosenfeld cynically comments 'Perhaps'.[62]

It was this universal 'Anne Frank' who was exported back to Europe, when the stage-version of the diary opened in Gothenburg in August 1956. In October, the play opened in West Germany, being performed in West Berlin, Dresden, Düsseldorf, Hamburg, Karlsruhe, Aachen and Konstanz, before travelling to Vienna and then Zurich. In November, the play was shown in the Netherlands for the first time. As had been the case in the United States, the play was widely acclaimed in Europe. Perhaps nowhere was the impact greater than in Germany, where the newspaper *Trouw* pronounced in a headline:

'Anne Frank's diary conquers Germany'.[63] The German press 'reported very mixed reactions: at the end of the performance there would be complete silence for a long time and the audience would leave the theatre quietly and "with feelings of shame"; or there would be prolonged applause'.[64] The response amongst young people was particularly marked, with the setting up of Anne Frank clubs, and a march of around two thousand young Germans in 1957 to Bergen-Belsen organised by the Hamburg Society for Christian and Jewish Co-operation. On the back of the success of the play, the diary was reprinted a total of eighteen times and sold over 700,000 copies in Germany in the next five years.

Encountering the universal 'Anne' – stripped of much of her Jewishness and her 'Holocaust' context – presented in the play, however, did not necessarily equate to coming to terms with the past. Norbert Muhlen noted in the *Anti-Defamation League Bulletin*, 'many young Germans identify with Anne Frank, see in her the prototype of all youth – helpless, imprisoned, at the mercy of elders, defiant of the outside world and terrified within. And the persecution and murder of Jews seems to them to be merely a peculiar external circumstance – secondary in importance to the personal tragedy of the heroine ...'[65] One critic in *Theatre der Zeir* captured this sense of identification with a universal 'Anne', writing, 'we see in Anne Frank's fate our own fate – the tragedy of human existence *per* se'.[66] Moreover, the liberal 'Anne Frank' who was remembered for her words 'in spite of everything I still believe that people are really good at heart' offered – in Rosenfeld's words – 'a ready-at-hand formula for easy forgiveness'. He goes on to suggest that the success of the Broadway 'Anne Frank' in Germany was therefore perhaps not so much 'her triumphant home-coming to the country that first expelled and then killed her', but rather 'the triumph of Anne Frank's former countrymen over her. In her name, they have, after all, forgiven themselves'.[67]

The opening of the play in the Netherlands had a similarly dramatic impact. As has been noted, on the back of the popularity of *Het Achterhuis*. Anne's hiding place – Prinsengracht 263 – was rescued from demolition and opened to the public in May 1960. There were 9,000 visitors in that year. By 1970 the annual number of visitors had risen to 182,000, by 1980 to 330,000, and by 1990 to around 600,000. It has become a near compulsory site of pilgrimage for Dutch schoolchildren, as well as the hundreds of thousands of tourists passing through Amsterdam. As James Young notes, prior to the opening up of Eastern Europe, it was 'the most likely introduction to the Holocaust for young Americans travelling abroad',[68] along with the concentration camps situated in the former West Germany.

Those increasing visitor statistics reflect the increased interest in the 'Holocaust' over the last three decades, and the growth of 'Holocaust' tourism. As the myth of the 'Holocaust' emerged during the 1960s, and particularly the 1970s and 1980s, there is a sense in which the universal 'Anne Frank' created in the 1950s was given back both her Jewishness and 'Holocaust' context. Rather than merely being a universal symbol, 'Anne Frank' became the symbol of the 'Holocaust' victim: not only the symbol of the six million Jewish victims of Nazism, but specifically the symbol of the 1 to 1.5 million Jewish children who were killed. Her memory has, therefore, been reshaped in the context of renewed interest in the 'Holocaust', and her status as Jewish victim restated. It is as Jewish victim *par excellence*, and particularly as representative of the child victims of the Holocaust, that Anne Frank's name has been attached to street names, and specifically schools and youth centres, throughout Europe and the United States.

In large part, 'Anne Frank' was given the role of the 'Holocaust' victim from the 1960s onwards precisely because she was someone who had already gained a reputation. By the time that interest in the 'Holocaust' grew, Anne – by dint of her established reputation – offered herself as the ideal symbol of 'Holocaust' victimhood. That she was not only a child, but a young girl – stripped of her sexuality – added to her appeal. And yet the irony is that her reputation had been gained in the 1950s precisely because of the relative peripherality of the 'Holocaust' in her diary and her middle-class, assimilated Jewishness. And yet from the late 1960s onwards, this Anne – assimilated and someone who rarely mentioned the events of the 'Holocaust' in her diary – was cast as *the* Holocaust victim and her diary as *the* Holocaust text.

In the last three decades, 'Anne Frank' has become not simply the representative 'Holocaust victim', but – in James Young's words – 'a two-sided metonymy for both Jewishness and Holocaust'.[69] He cites the author Philip Roth as an example, who puts Anne Frank's name on the lips of aspiring novelist Nathan Zuckerman in *The Ghost Writer*. Nathan seeks to prove his Jewishness to his family, who are upset by what they see to be his use of unflattering Jewish characters in his writing. He fantasises that a girl he meets is Anne Frank, and imagines taking her home to Mom and Dad.[70] To marry 'Anne Frank' is for Zuckerman the ultimate proof of Jewishness. You can't get more Jewish than that! These references to 'Anne Frank' in Roth's 1979 novel only work because the universal, liberal 'Anne Frank' has been placed back within a Jewish and 'Holocaust' context during the last three decades.

However, the message of the universal, liberal 'Anne Frank' created in 1950s America remains a potent one. 'Anne Frank' may have been given back her Jewishness and fitted back into the context of the 'Holocaust', but she still remains a powerful universal symbol. In the United States Holocaust Memorial Museum a 'Holocaust Anne' features as a symbol of both the Final Solution in Western Europe and the fate of 'the hundreds of thousands of Jewish children who died in the Holocaust', but the universal Broadway and Hollywood 'Anne' is also present. On the museum's second floor, where the section of the permanent exhibition dealing with 'The Final Solution' begins, it is the diary entry of July 15, 1944 – 'I still believe that people are really good at heart, I … can't build up my hopes on a foundation consisting of confusion, misery and death' – which has been chosen for use. The 'Anne Frank' as exhibited in Washington, DC, reflects the layers of meaning that have been given to her over the course of the last four decades. Thus the up-beat 1950s 'liberal Anne' who still believes 'that people are really good at heart' is there alongside the 1980s 'Holocaust Anne' who is described in the book which acts as a *de facto* museum catalogue, as 'one of the many German Jewish children forced out of their homes'.[71] Before we are taken through the ghettos of Eastern Europe, into the railway car, under the gateway of Auschwitz and into the 'Concentration Camp Universe', we meet Anne Frank's face. And this Washington 'Anne' is one who is represented both as 'an emblem of lost potential' and a beacon of hope. Rather than leaving a Broadway theatre with her comforting words that 'people are really good at heart', at Washington, DC, we read those same words before we are taken to a virtual 'Auschwitz' (where Anne was taken in 1944). Those words therefore provide us with a familiar framework with which to interpret that which we are about to encounter. Like Anne, we go to Auschwitz still believing – 'in spite of everything' – 'that people are really good at heart'. At Washington, DC, the universal, liberal 'Anne' made in 1950s America lives alongside the Jewish, Holocaust 'Anne' made in contemporary America.

That mixture of Jewish and 'Holocaust' specificity and more universal liberal themes can also be seen in the exhibition mounted in the Anne Frank House in Amsterdam when it reopened to the public in 1971. In the context of the emergence of the myth of the 'Holocaust', the exhibition focused on the history of Nazi Germany and the persecution of the Jews through the person of 'Anne Frank' the 'Holocaust' victim. However, this was not the only 'Anne' on display. In examining 'current centres of discrimination and persecution', the exhibition drew universal lessons from a universal 'Anne Frank'. This drawing of 'universal' lessons has become a central aspect of the Anne Frank Stichting, and its sister organisations, The Anne Frank Center, USA, and the Anne Frank Educational Trust in the UK, as can be seen from the claim made by the director of the Anne Frank House, Hans Westra, that 'the memory of Anne Frank is directly related to a concern for preserving freedom and maintaining human rights and a pluralistic and democratic society'.[72] Thus, visiting the Anne Frank House has become not only – and perhaps not primarily – a way of learning about the 'Holocaust', but also a way of learning about human rights, apartheid, the Vietnam War and racism. It has perhaps become not so much a site of 'Holocaust tourism', as a site of 'liberal tourism'.

That 'liberal' message of the 'Universal Anne' was exported worldwide by the Anne Frank Stichting through the travelling exhibition 'Anne Frank in the World 1929-45' which was visited by around 7 million people in 40 countries between 1985 and 1996. It was an exhibition which quite self-consciously sought to draw lessons from the story of 'Anne Frank', by asking the question 'had Anne Frank – an ordinary young Jewish girl – lived next door, could she have counted on us for help during the Nazi occupation?'[73] In October 1996 the Anne Frank Stichting launched a new travelling exhibition 'Anne Frank: A History for Today', which 'aims to stimulate visitors to analyse the significance of tolerance, human rights and democracy ... by telling the life story of Anne Frank from the perspective of the Frank family and by outlining the history of the Holocaust through other contemporary witnesses'. Visitors are encouraged 'to think about parallels and differences in events then and now'.[74]

While the two exhibitions do share a large number of common features, the one updated for the 1990s is much more focused on the Holocaust – no doubt in part fuelled by the success of *Schindler's List*. It is an exhibition characterised by both a reassertion of Anne's Jewishness, and a tendency towards her 'universalisation'. Perhaps this universalisation is seen nowhere more clearly than the citing – apparently approvingly – of the words of German President Roman Herzog:

On 11th April she wrote in her diary: 'One day this terrible war will be over. The time will come when we'll be people again and not just Jews!' In place of 'not just Jews', Anne Frank could also have written: not just Gypsies, not just Christians, not just trade union members, not just Socialists, not just the handicapped, not just this or that minority. It is our responsibility to see that people are never again divided up and selected in this way'.[75]

These are words strikingly similar to those of director Garson Kanin in 1954, justifying the universalising of the Broadway 'Anne Frank'. And yet the historical reality is that Anne Frank could not simply have written something else in place of the word 'Jews'. As mentioned earlier, the Frank family, the van Pels family and Fritz Pfeffer would not have been sought out, arrested, and deported from a hiding place in Amsterdam in 1944 if they had been 'Christians', 'trade union members', 'Socialists', 'the handicapped' or members of 'this or that minority'. Only Gypsies and Jews were rigorously persecuted wherever they were in Europe, with this persecution being more widespread in the case of Jews. Anne, Margot, Edith Frank, the van Pels family and Fritz Pfeffer died in 1944-5 *because* they were Jews. In a search for universal lessons, it is all too easy to misrepresent the past as Herzog does.

Drawing lessons from the past is rather problematic. It is easy to project the lessons demanded by the present back into the past, and rewrite it in such terms. The contemporary lesson of tolerance demands that Anne's words be rewritten to include members of 'this or that minority', and yet that makes a mockery of the historical reality. When the lessons become more important than the history, the tendency is for the complexity of the past to be reduced to a number of rather banal statements designed merely to meet the needs of the present. That is one of the great dangers with the 'Holocaust'. Given its mythical status, the 'Holocaust' risks becoming a popular past used to serve all sorts of present needs. In particular, the needs of contemporary liberalism tends to latch onto a powerful tale in the past and universalise it so as to produce a set of universal lessons.

It is ironic that the 'Holocaust' has been seized by liberalism as the liberal tale *par excellence*, from which any number of lessons relating about the dangers of discrimination, racism and antisemitism can be – and are – drawn. The 'Holocaust' has becomes a central anti-icon of a liberalism which worships pluralism and relativism. If you don't have pluralism, you have the Holocaust, emerges as the catch phrase of an 'Anne Frank' liberalism which draws neat – if somewhat banal – lessons from the past. And yet the irony is that the Holocaust stands as the greatest imaginable challenge to this 'Anne Frank' liberalism which proclaims 'in spite of everything I still believe that people are really good at heart'. If there is one lesson that can be drawn from the Holocaust it is precisely that the optimism of Anne Frank was woefully misplaced.

It may be comforting to think that by encouraging school children to read *The Diary of Anne Frank* and learn about the 'Holocaust', we can put an end to intolerance and discrimination. Yet if we ask ourselves 'had Anne Frank – an ordinary young Jewish girl – lived next door, could she have counted on us for help during the Nazi occupation?' and simply answer 'yes', we betray a lack of humility which confrontation with the Holocaust demands. When faced with what 'ordinary' men and women did to other 'ordinary' men and women because of their Jewishness, what other response is there but 'I just don't know'. It is too easy to say 'yes' and thereby set up self-righteous categories of 'us' and 'them', meaning 'we' would have helped, but 'they', the 'racists', the 'intolerant', the 'prejudiced', the 'nationalists', would not have done so.

The reality was that the girl-next-door – Anne Frank – was helped by some ordinary people, but betrayed and captured by other equally ordinary people. It is impossible to claim with any certainty that we would have been the former rather than the latter. And yet, liberalism claims the moral high-ground of the former for itself, as does – to a certain extent – Dutch national pride. Anne Frank 'has been canonised by the Dutch', enabling them 'to alleviate their guilt, and blame the Nazis for having decimated their Jewish population ... The Anne Frank lore says to the world: Look, we Dutch hid her; the terrible Germans killed her. They were evil and we were virtuous'.[76] Turning Anne Frank into something approaching a Dutch patron saint, downplays the fact that she was a German Jew who was probably betrayed by a Dutch collaborator. While the Anne Frank story does point to the Netherlands as the place of refuges, and Dutch sheltering of Jews, it also points to a more murky side of Dutch wartime collaboration with the German occupiers.

The question of Dutch collaboration was raised specifically by post-war speculation over who had betrayed the Frank family. Suspicion rested on Van Maaren, who had been hired as a warehouseman at 263 Prinsengracht in Spring 1943, but dismissed after the war for petty theft.[77] An investigation was carried out by the Political Investigation Branch of the Amsterdam police in 1948, and a report submitted to the Public Prosecutor on 1 April 1948 which stated that 'the accused denies the charge of betrayal, and the circumstantial evidence is vague. Accordingly, there is no case to answer'.[78] In November Van Maaren was given a conditional discharge which barred him from taking public office or serving in the armed forces. He appealed against this sentence, and in August 1949 was cleared. The case was closed.

However, in 1963 the case was reopened following the tracing of the SD officer Karl Josef Silberbauer – who had led the raid on 263 Prinsengracht – by Simon Wiesenthal. As Wiesenthal himself commented, the significance of Silberbauer was that he had arrested Anne Frank: 'Of course, he [Silberbauer] doesn't matter at all. Compared to other names on my list, he is a nobody, a zero. But the figure before the zero was Anne Frank'.[79] Unlike the context in 1948-9 when the question of who had betrayed the Franks was first considered, by 1963 the name of Anne Frank was known throughout the world. Thus the investigation undertaken in 1963-4 assumed a greater importance. Silberbauer claimed that the raid on the 'secret annexe' was the result of a telephone message to his superior which stated that eight Jews were hiding at 263 Prinsengracht. However, the investigation got no further in determining who had betrayed those in hiding. The case was closed in November 1964. Karl Silberbauer – back living in Austria – was investigated by the disciplinary committee of the Austrian Ministry of Internal Affairs, but permitted to continue his post-war career in the Vienna Police Force. Seven years later the man who had long been suspected – yet never proved – of betraying the Frank family, Van Maaren, died.

Further official investigation of the case of 'Anne Frank' by the Dutch authorities came in 1974. This time the focus was not on the question of who had betrayed the Frank family, but on the question of the diary's authenticity. A January 1974 letter from Eric Pedersen to the Mayor and Aldermen of Amsterdam claimed that the diary had been written, not by Anne Frank during the war, but by the American journalist Meyer Levin after the war. This claim that the diary was a post-war piece of fiction was not new. As Pedersen's claims had been made before, an investigation into the authenticity of *The Diary of Anne Frank* was launched by the Amsterdam authorities, and those witnesses still alive interviewed once more.

Disputing the authenticity of the diary has become a staple of revisionist writers. Given the central place of 'Anne Frank' and her diary within the myth of the 'Holocaust', she has emerged as a highly visible target for those attacking the Holocaust. As Simon Wiesenthal has written,

A person denying the existence of the Auschwitz gas chambers is invariably either an old Nazi or a neo-Nazi ... Yet there is another argument by which persons leaning towards Nazism can be instantly identified: the quarrel about the *Diary of Anne Frank* ... The neo-Nazis know why they are attacking that book with such vehemence: to my mind it has moved more people than the Nuremberg trials or even the Eichmann trial.[80]

Thus the leading member of the British far-right organisation the National Front, Richard Verall, wrote – under the pseudonym Richard Harwood – that the diary was a 'hoax' and 'just one more fraud in a whole series of frauds in support of the 'Holocaust' legend and the saga of the Six Million'.[81] Another Holocaust revisionist – the American Arthur Butz – dismissed the diary in his pamphlet 'The Hoax of the Twentieth Century'.[82] Verall and Butz are not alone in their dismissing of the diary as a 'hoax'. Rather it has become a more or less standard plank in the arguments put forward by writers such as David Irving and Robert Faurisson. However, Irving's claim that 'many forgeries are on record, as for instance that of the "Diary of Anne Frank" (in this case a civil lawsuit brought by a New York scriptwriter [Levin] has proved that he wrote it in collaboration with the girl's father)',[83] was omitted from later editions of his 1975 *Hitler und seine Feldherren (Hitler and his Generals)* after the intervention of Otto Frank.

The claim that the true author of the diary was Meyer Levin was much repeated following the 1958 jury decision – later overturned – to award Levin $50,000 because his ideas had been used by the Hacketts. This claim confused the original diary and the later stage-play, essentially seeing them as one and the same, and authored by Levin. In essence, the 'Anne Frank' created in the United States in the 1950s was taken to be the Anne Frank writing in wartime Amsterdam. In collapsing the two together, revisionists could dismiss 'Anne Frank'. There is a real need to distinguish clearly between the myth of the 'Holocaust' which emerged in the United States during the post-war era, and the murder of the European Jewry – the Holocaust – which was perpetrated in wartime Europe. When the divide between the two becomes blurred, criticism of the former – which is often justified – can become denial of the latter. Thus to dismiss the Broadway 'Anne' as inauthentic becomes the denial of the Anne who wrote a diary between 1942-44. To blur the two in this way fails to take into account the history of the popularisation and recre-ation of 'the myth of Anne Frank': a 'myth' that contains dangers.

Yehuda Bauer reflects on the irony that the canonical text of the 'Holocaust' – *The Diary of Anne Frank* – is one with a history of manipulation:

It was the distorted diary that became an important catalyst for the penetration of the Holocaust into the consciousness of many millions, being the most widely read book and one of the most effective plays and films about the subject. It created the backdrop for undistorted and authentic presentations. The awful question then is whether we need kitsch and distortions in order to arrive at authentic interpretations of the Holocaust or any other major turning points in human history.[84]

It is a question that can be asked again and again of the myth of the 'Holocaust' which has emerged as the lens through which the present looks back on the past.

This question is more than simply one of aesthetic sensibilities. It is more than simply the question whether 'kitsch' presentations are appropriate when the murder of six million Jews is being considered. As Bauer signals, it is also the question of whether 'distortions' are appropriate. After all, the sort of 'distortions' which have emerged in the post-war myth of the 'Holocaust' are often easy targets for Holocaust deniers to take pot-shots at. If, in the popular mindset, the myth of the 'Holocaust' and the Holocaust itself become blurred – and indeed the former assumes an importance far greater than the latter – then the danger is that the questioning of the 'Holocaust' amounts to a questioning of the reality of the Holocaust itself.

Anne Frank's 'distorted' diary stands at the end of the twentieth century as *the* 'Holocaust bible', and 'Anne Frank' stands as *the* 'Holocaust victim'. Stripped of her burgeoning sexuality – through her father's judicious editing – this 'Anne Frank' is the ideal symbol of the 'innocent victim' and the ideal symbol of potential snuffed out. In direct contrast, Adolf Eichmann emerged in the 1960s as *the* 'guilty defendant'. After Hitler himself, Eichmann assumed a key role in the iconography of 'Holocaust' perpetrators, which in many ways stood unchallenged until Spielberg's 'Holocaust' villain Amon Goeth graced our screens.

2

# Adolf Eichmann

When – at 9 o'clock on the morning of 11 April 1961 – Adolf Eichmann made his first appearance in a Jerusalem courthouse, one of the recurring comments of observers was how normal this Holocaust villain looked. After all, the man sitting in the bullet-proof glass encased dock looked more like a middle-aged accountant than a mass murderer. The surprise expressed by Nazi hunter Simon Wiesenthal was fairly typical:

> For nearly sixteen years I had thought of him practically every day and every night. In my mind I had built up the image of a demonic superman. Instead I saw a frail, nondescript, shabby fellow in a glass cell between two Israeli policemen; they looked more colourful and interesting than he did. Everything about Eichmann seemed drawn with charcoal: his greyish face, his balding head, his clothes. There was nothing demonic about him; he looked like a bookkeeper who is afraid to ask for a raise … Dressed in a cheap, dark suit, he seemed a cardboard figure, empty and two-dimensional[1]

Eichmann's seemingly banal 'normality' was something which the Israeli agents who were involved in tracking down and ultimately kidnapping this suspect also expressed. The initial tip-off that Eichmann was living in the suburbs of Buenos Aires was rejected by the agents who went to track down the address, in large part on the grounds that someone of Eichmann's stature would not be living in such humble surroundings. When he was finally kidnapped, one of the Mossad agents – Zvi Aharoni – reflected on his feelings: 'He was made to lie down on the bed and undressed. I can still recall exactly how I was touched, even a bit disgusted, when I saw his shabby clothing, particularly his underwear. I could not help it and asked myself spontaneously: is this really the great Eichmann, the man who decided the fate of millions of my people?'[2] Aharoni's sense of surprise that this mass murderer wore greying underwear was – as I have suggested – the sense of surprise that greeted Eichmann's appearance in court.

Historian Dick de Mildt draws a parallel with an earlier trial in Jerusalem:

> But as with the first Jerusalem trial, the court room's public met with a grave disappointment. For, as the carpenter's son from Nazareth had hardly appeared to most observers as the Son of God, neither did the factory worker from Buenos Aires seem to have much resemblance with the envoy of the Devil ... Instead of showing the particulars of a demon in disguise, the criminal inside the Jerusalem dock turned out to be of a breathtaking human mediocrity.[3]

Here was a man who looked pretty much like any other 'good family man, the kind you meet every day going home on the subway'.[4] Yet *this* ordinary looking, middle-aged man faced extraordinary charges. As Israeli Attorney General Gideon Hausner expressed it during his opening speech, 'human history knows no other example of a man against whom could be drawn up such a bill of indictment',[5] that of the murder of six million Jews. And this incongruity between the ordinariness of the man in the dock and the extraordinary charges that this man faced, led Wiesenthal to suggest – without success – that Eichmann should be dressed in an SS uniform for his courthouse appearances. That way he would look more like a murderer (and less like one of us).

Adolf Eichmann had been spoken of – from the Nuremberg trials onwards – as a main player in the implementation of the 'Final Solution of the Jewish Question'. Moshe Pearlman, a former Israeli civil servant who wrote about the trial, suggests that 'if the ghost of Hitler hovered over Nuremberg as the trial opened, it was now joined by another ghost – the ghost of Adolf Eichmann'.[6] At Nuremberg, Eichmann's name was mentioned by both defendants and witnesses and in particular by SS Captain Wisliceny who had served in Hungary with Eichmann during 1944. His claim that Eichmann had told his men shortly before the end of the war that 'he would jump into his grave laughing, because the feeling that he had five million people on his conscience, gave him extraordinary satisfaction' was oft cited, and became a central tenet of the developing Eichmann myth.

Moreover, the surviving Jewish leadership emigrating to Israel at the end of the war spoke of the central role played by Adolf

Eichmann, who had not been brought to justice with the first round of Nazi leaders. Eichmann had dealt directly with Jewish Council members, who knew of the precise nature of his demands during the war and testified to the scope of his jurisdiction over the 'Jewish Question'. This combination of references to Eichmann meant that in the immediate aftermath of the war, he was being spoken of in 1945 by the man who was to become the first Israeli Prime Minister – Ben-Gurion – as 'the man who must be brought to justice if he is still alive'.[7] Thus, there were a number of early attempts to determine whether Eichmann had survived the war and was in hiding some-place, by Asher Ben Natan and Tuvia Friedman – Jewish Underground Defence Force representatives in Austria – and the self-styled Nazi hunter Simon Wiesenthal, amongst others. The next decade and a half saw intermittent press rumours of Eichmann sight-ings, culminating in the report at the end of 1959, that Eichmann was alive and living in Kuwait.

It was in this context of occasional rumours that Israeli Prime Minister Ben-Gurion announced that Eichmann was under arrest in Israel to a surprised Knesset (the Israeli Parliament) and an equally surprised world. When he stood up at 4 pm on 23 May 1960, only his cabinet knew the nature of the statement he was about to give. Before a packed Knesset, he made the historic announcement that

> ... a short while ago the Israeli Security Services captured one of the greatest Nazi criminals, Adolf Eichmann, who together with the Nazi leaders was responsible for what was termed the 'final solution to the Jewish problem', that is the destruction of six million European Jews. Eichmann is already in detention in Israel, and will soon be put on trial here under the Nazi and Nazi Collaborators (Punishment) Law, 1950.[8]

The background to this announcement was a secret Mossad campaign which would only really come to light fifteen years later as the agents involved started to speak out. At first the Israeli govern-ment was cagey about saying how Eichmann had ended up in Israel, but their hand was forced by a *Time* exclusive claiming that he was arrested by Israeli agents in Buenos Aires. This news led to months of diplomatic wrangling between Argentina and Israel starting with the request that the Israeli ambassador issue a statement explaining the run of events. This statement confirmed that Eichmann had been brought from Argentina, but that he had been kidnapped by Jewish 'volunteers' rather than by members of the Israeli security service. It was this story which was to remain the official Israeli version of events until the mid 1970s, when the fifteen year 'gagging order' on the Mossad agents involved was lifted. Thus when a joint compromise statement was finally issued by Israel and Argentina on 3 August 1960, it amounted to a condemning of the actions by 'Israel nationals that infringed fundamental rights of the State of Argentina'.[9]

The very fact that the Mossad's role in the tracking down and kidnapping of Eichmann was silenced, meant that others could assume their heroic place. In particular, it was Simon Wiesenthal who took much of the credit for tracing Eichmann. On the day of Ben-Gurion's historic Knesset announcement of Eichmann's capture, Yad Vashem (the official Israeli Holocaust memorial foundation) sent a telegram to Wiesenthal warmly congratulating him on his 'brilliant success'.[10] They also invited him to Jerusalem to tell his story of searching for Eichmann. Wiesenthal was careful to acknowledge that others had played an important part in bringing Eichmann to Israel, but despite this he was – in the words of Hella Pick who wrote a biography of Wiesenthal – 'widely feted and, for the first time, he savoured fame'.[11] There is little doubt that Wiesenthal's reputation was built upon the Eichmann case, and yet it was a case in which he had only played a minor part early on in the search for Eichmann. Despite this relatively minor role, the best-selling status of his 1961 memoir *I Hunted Eichmann* ensured that his name was to be associated with Eichmann's in the public mind.

However, Wiesenthal's self-publicised early role in tracking down Eichmann came to be challenged when the Mossad agents involved in the kidnapping started to publish their own version of events. In particular, the former Mossad chief Isser Harel offered a very different version of events in his 1975 telling of 'Operation Eichmann', *The House on Garibaldi Street*. In that book, Harel omitted Wiesenthal altogether from the story, and effectively denied that he played even a small part in the locating of Eichmann in Buenos Aires. Not surprisingly, there has been a good deal of personal animosity between Harel and Wiesenthal.

This feuding over 'Operation Eichmann' between Wiesenthal and Harel in many ways reflects the feuding between Meyer Levin and Otto Frank over the stage-play based on Anne Frank's diary. 'Operation Eichmann' – like 'Anne Frank' – is the stuff of which reputations are made and destroyed, and both have been bitterly contested 'brandnames'. In the case of 'Operation Eichmann' that contestation has become rather complex, involving not only Wiesenthal and Harel, but also the Nazi-hunter Tuvia Friedman and, more recently, the New York based World Jewish Congress and a number of the Mossad agents involved in the kidnapping. The result has been the publishing of a number of versions of the tracing and capture of Eichmann which highlight the role of the author, and downplay or ignore the roles of others. Thus Harel completely dismisses the role of Wiesenthal, Wiesenthal dismisses the role of Friedman, the World Jewish Congress dismiss the role of Wiesenthal, and Mossad agent Zvi Aharoni criticises both Mossad chief Harel and fellow Mossad agent Zvika Malchin.

The more recent twists to the bitter feuding over 'Operation Eichmann' have seen the World Jewish Congress accuse Wiesenthal in 1991 of fabricating his claim that he wrote to World Jewish Congress president Nahum Goldmann in 1954 informing him of Eichmann's presence in Argentina. Such a letter would point to Wiesenthal providing early information about Eichmann's place of residence which the World Jewish Congress failed to act upon. However, the World Jewish Congress are adamant that no such letter exists in their archives, and therefore that it was never sent. Copies of the letter have been produced by both Wiesenthal and the Central Zionist Archives, yet the World Jewish Congress has stuck by its rejection of Wiesenthal's claims. In large part this criticism of Wiesenthal in the early 1990s took place – as Pick suggests – in the context of anger of the World Jewish Congress over Wiesenthal's failure to accuse unambiguously Austrian Presidential candidate Kurt Waldheim of being a war criminal.[12]

Wiesenthal has, however, been defended to some extent by Mossad agent Zvi Aharoni who has criticised Isser Harel and accused him of selective memory in his telling of 'Operation Eichmann'. In particular, he claims that the Mossad closed the Eichmann case in late 1958 and put the file into the archives, and thus questions Harel's version of events:

> In his subsequent statements, Harel naturally tried to sweep these unpleasant facts under the carpet. He never tired of recounting how, from its very inception, Mossad had meticulously pursued the trails of escaped Nazis throughout the world. However, too many former Mossad agents know the truth.[13]

Aharoni's criticism of Harel should be seen in the context of personal antagonism towards his former chief.[14] However, despite this tendency to attack Harel personally, Aharoni's account does point to the hollowness of Mossad claims that Eichmann was searched for continuously by Israel from 1945 onwards.

During the 1940s and 1950s, throughout Israeli society, there was an effective silence about the Holocaust. This meant in practice that hunting down Nazi war criminals was low on the priorities of Ben-Gurion's government. It was in this context of a lack of Israeli interest in Eichmann that Wiesenthal played an important role. In the early years, one of the very few people interested in tracing Eichmann was Wiesenthal. As he saw it:

> The Israelis no longer had any interest in Eichmann; they had to fight for their lives against Nasser. The Americans were no longer interested in Eichmann because of the Cold War against the Soviet Union. I feel that, along with a few other like-minded fools, I was quite alone.[15]

This lack of interest in Eichmann which Simon Wiesenthal perceived in the early 1950s reflected a more general lack of interest in the Holocaust in both American Jewish and Israeli circles. Israeli officialdom – despite all later pronouncements by Harel to the contrary – had little interest in Eichmann. The Mossad was more concerned with Arab threats closer to home, than with what had happened in the past to the Diaspora Jewry. Indeed, even in the late 1950s, Harel's successor as Mossad chief – Meir Amit – points to opposition to 'Operation Eichmann' within the Israeli secret service. He reflects back on the late 1950s and notes that

> ... some of the intelligence community heads (mainly from among the military intelligence, responsible for the national security evaluation in Israel) felt at the time that Mossad was not fulfilling its proper role: the true enemies of Israel were the Arab armed forces, and the ongoing struggle against hostile neighbours demanded a constant supply of information on the current situation and events. There was no doubt that for many months, largely as a result of Operation Eichmann, the main efforts of Mossad were diverted from its prime target, and this fact angered a section of the military intelligence.[16]

Despite this opposition in the late 1950s, 'Operation Eichmann' went ahead with the support of Prime Minister Ben-Gurion, and under the leadership of Mossad boss Isser Harel.

It was during this period of minimal interest in Eichmann in particular, and the 'Holocaust' in general, that Wiesenthal discovered that Eichmann was living in Argentina. He came about this information accidentally, while discussing stamps with a fellow-collector who had been in the German Army. The collector – Baron Mast – showed

Wiesenthal a letter from a former colleague of his who was now living in Argentina, who wrote that he had met 'that miserable swine Eichmann'[17] who was now living in Buenos Aires and working for a water company. This information confirmed Wiesenthal's hunch that Eichmann was still alive and living with his family somewhere outside of Europe.

As early as 1947, Wiesenthal had successfully defeated the attempt by Eichmann's wife – Veronika Liebl – to have her husband officially declared dead by a German court. He discovered that the witness to Eichmann's supposed death during fighting in Prague in April 1945 – Karl Lucas – was in fact Liebl's brother-in-law, and that Lucas's testimony was invalidated by that of Wilhelm Höttl and Rudolf Scheide, who both claimed to have seen Eichmann after April 1945. For Wiesenthal,

> ... this unspectacular move was probably my most important contribution to the Eichmann case. Where I might possibly have been a 'hunter' I had failed ... But the search for Eichmann resembled a hunt only at the very beginning and the very end. In between it was a laborious compilation of more or less significant pieces of information, upon which we acted with greater or lesser skill. I was a dogged pursuer, but I was no marksman.[18]

In 1952, Wiesenthal learnt that Liebl and her children had left Austria. He was convinced that they had left Europe, as the Eichmann boys' school records were not being forwarded to another Austrian or German school. However, tracking them down outside Europe was beyond his resources. From his words to Tuvia Friedman, at the end of 1952, and his subsequent actions, it is clear that Wiesenthal saw Israel as the one country which should pursue Eichmann. Before Friedman left Austria for Israel in 1952, Wiesenthal had urged his fellow-Nazi hunter to

> ... keep reminding the Israelis about Eichmann. Don't let them tell you to forget about him. Let the Israel Government do everything it wants to do: build houses for immigrants, teach everybody Hebrew, make a strong army. Fine! Very good! But they must also start looking for Eichmann.[19]

However, during the early to mid-1950s, the Israelis did next to nothing about Eichmann, and next to nothing about the information that Wiesenthal passed on to them. He wrote to the Israeli Consul-

General in Vienna – Arie Eshel – in March 1953 that he had every reason to believe that Eichmann was in Buenos Aires. Eshel asked Wiesenthal to prepare a report for World Jewish Congress president Nahum Goldmann, which he sent on 30 March 1954, offering his further services. It is this letter which in the World Jewish Congress claimed it had no evidence of receiving in 1991. However, according to Hella Pick's biography, Wiesenthal received a reply a couple of months later from a Rabbi Kalmanowitz who stated that Goldmann had passed his letter on to him. Kalmanowitz requested the precise address where Eichmann was staying. Wiesenthal replied that he would need $500 to try to find that out. A further exchange of letters saw Kalmanowitz repeating his request for the precise address and Wiesenthal repeating his request for funds. Wiesenthal wrote once more to Goldmann, but again received no reply. Without funds, he closed up his Documentation Centre in Linz, sent the vast majority of his files to Yad Vashem and became involved in providing vocational training to Jewish refugees in Austria.

Pick describes the clash between Wiesenthal and Goldmann as 'an irreconcilable clash of one ego with extensive resources behind him, and another ego with equally supreme self-confidence, but bereft of funds to back it'.[20] However, there was more to this inaction in the early to mid 1950s than simply a clash of personalities. The lack of interest in the Holocaust – in America and Israel – which characterised the period seems to have been more important. The myth of the 'Holocaust' does not emerge in anything like its contemporary form until the 1960s and 1970s. For both the World Jewish Congress and the newly established State of Israel, the 'Holocaust' (and hunting down Nazi war criminals like Eichmann) was of rather peripheral concern in the decade or so after the war. Although Israel did pass the Law against Genocide and the Nazi and Nazi Collaborators Law in 1950, the former was intended to prevent genocide in the future and the latter to be making a symbolic 'statement about the past'.[21] In practice the Nazi and Nazi Collaborators Law formed the legal basis to investigations against *Jews* accused of collaborating with the Nazis during the early 1950s, rather than Nazi war criminals. When the Israeli Secret Services were restructured in 1951, there was seen to be no need for creating a specific department to investigate Nazi war criminals. As the journalist Tom Segev suggests – in the late 1940s – 'the hunt for Nazi criminals was not really a high priority; the Israel-Arab conflict and the organisation of the mass immigration were both much more urgent ... It seems that Israel did not see hunting down Nazi criminals as an overriding national mission, just as the leaders of the state-to-be had not given vengeance high priority'.[22]

When the Mossad received further information about Eichmann in 1957, Aharoni suggests that they failed to follow it up fully. This time the source was not Wiesenthal, but the German-Jewish Chief Prosecutor for the State of Hessen, Fritz Bauer. Bauer passed on to Israel's representative in Bonn, Eliezer Shinar, information that he had received about Eichmann's whereabouts. His justification for passing the information on to Israel was a fear that pursuing an extradition order in Germany would lead to Eichmann going underground (this would happen with Mengele in 1959). A Mossad agent was sent to Buenos Aires to investigate Bauer's tip but concluded that Eichmann was not living there. However, Bauer was convinced that Eichmann was in Buenos Aires and called for a further investigation and revealed the name of his source – Lothar Hermann – who was living in Argentina. Two agents met with him and his daughter while in Argentina on other business, but again concluded that someone of Eichmann's standing would not be living in a relatively poor Buenos Aires suburb. Aharoni claims that at this point the Eichmann case was closed, explaining why, when he travelled to Argentina in March 1959, he was not asked to investigate the matter further. He suggests that it was not until Bauer came to Israel in person and met with Attorney General Haim Cohen that a real interest was shown in the case. Segev points to Cohen introducing Bauer to Prime Minister Ben-Gurion himself, who was informed that unless Israel acted, Bauer would recommend that Germany apply for Eichmann's extradition. Ben-Gurion's reaction – as recorded in his diary – was: 'I suggested asking him not to tell anyone and not to ask for his extradition, but to give us the address ... If it turns out that he is there, we will catch him and bring him here. Isser will take care of it'.[23] Ben-Gurion ordered the Mossad to locate Eichmann, and to bring him to Israel. Early in 1960, 'Operation Eichmann' commenced.

The persistence of Bauer had paid off, and yet it had taken over two years for his information to be fully investigated. As Aharoni – no doubt in part motivated by personal antagonism towards Harel – reflected in his version of events,

> ... when we finally caught Eichmann in 1960, the chorus of famous and less famous Nazi-hunters who claimed the credit for having found him became louder and louder. Authors wrote about 'the untiring search lasting fifteen years'. I have little respect for these people. The sad truth is that Eichmann was discovered by a blind man and that Mossad needed more than two years to believe that blind man's story.[24]

It seems fair to conclude that the Mossad needed not just two years, but also intervention from the top. In being willing to go as far as sanctioning the 'illegal' kidnapping of a foreign citizen, Ben-Gurion clearly saw the capture and trial of Eichmann to be of critical importance to the State of Israel. This points to a growing awareness on the part of Ben-Gurion of the importance of the Holocaust to the State of Israel.

As I have already suggested, the early years of the State of Israel were characterised by near silence over the Holocaust. And during the late 1940s and early 1950s, Ben-Gurion was no different to anyone else. As Liebman and Don-Yehiya note, 'according to Ben-Gurion, the four critical events in Jewish history were the exodus from Egypt, the assembly at Mount Sinai, the conquest of the land of Israel by Joshua, and the establishment of the State of Israel'.[25] In other words, during the 1940s and 1950s, the Holocaust was seen to be only of secondary importance in Israel. This was because it was a part of Diaspora history, which for Ben-Gurion was a couple of thousand years of history when little of importance had happened. He only looked back to the biblical past for his heroes and largely ignored the more recent Jewish past, particularly the Holocaust.

However, the decision to pursue Eichmann – with all of the ensuing diplomatic wrangling which his capture involved – points to a shift in Ben-Gurion's attitude towards the Holocaust past. The year before Eichmann's capture, legislation had been introduced to fix the public observance of 'Holocaust Day' (Holocaust and Ghetto Rebellion Memorial Day). This official day of memory had been decided upon as early as 1951, but it had been largely ignored by the majority of the population. As Rabbi Nurok complained in 1958, 'places of entertainment are wide open on this day ... the radio plays happy music, dances, and humour, and the display windows glow. Merriment and happiness instead of sorrow and mourning'.[26] In part in response to the complaints of those like Nurok, the government introduced the Holocaust and Heroism Memorial Day Law in 1959. In 1961 – just before the beginning of Eichmann's trial – the Memorial Day Law was amended to enforce the closing of all places of entertainment from sundown on the previous day onwards. It is this memorial legislation and the bringing to trial of Eichmann which Liebman and Don-Yehiya point to as evidence that by the end of the 1950s Ben-Gurion had 'reversed his attitude toward the Holocaust'.[27]

This reversal in attitudes can be seen in the justifications for sanctioning 'Operation Eichmann' offered by Ben-Gurion. Shortly after announcing his capture, Ben-Gurion stated that Eichmann was to be tried in Israel for two reasons:

One was that the Israel[i] youth brought up since the Holocaust had only a faint echo of the atrocious crime, and the facts must be made known to them. The other was that hundreds of German and Arab Nazis, who had played their part in the slaughter of Jews in the past, were in the service of 'dictators in neighbouring countries'. These people harboured designs to destroy Israel, and world opinion should be reminded whose disciples they were.[28]

This concern with using the trial to teach lessons to both a domestic and foreign audience was reiterated by Ben-Gurion in a *New York Times* interview in December 1960. There he justified the decision to bring Eichmann to trial in Jerusalem on the grounds of wanting 'the nations of the world to know that there was an intention to exterminate a people' and because it was 'necessary that our youth remember what happened to the Jewish people. We want them to know the most tragic facts in our history'. As he himself recognised, the trial was not primarily about punishing Eichmann: 'We are not out to punish Eichmann; there is no fit punishment. Indeed, it is ridiculous to see in this trial, as some do, any motive of revenge'.[29] Rather, the trial was about reawakening a concern with the Holocaust past both inside and outside the country.

Ben-Gurion's concern with exposing Israeli youth to the 'Holocaust' past of Diaspora Jewry was partly motivated by a concern over the divisions between the *sabra* [native-born Israeli] and survivor populations in Israel. This sense of division and even hostility was commented upon by many survivors who settled in Israel. Tom Segev tells the story of Miriam Weinfeld who arriving at *Kibbutz Degania Bet*, 'felt shunned by the young people ... she sensed arrogance, sometimes even mockery and hostility.'[30] Weinfeld's experience was one common to survivors who were constantly challenged by Israeli youth with the question, 'Why did you not revolt?' It was a question that survivor Yoel Palgi reflects 'was fired at me ... everywhere I turned'.[31] And it was a question purposefully asked of witnesses during the trial, by both the judges and Gideon Hausner.

The aim of the trial was to stimulate – in Israeli youth – identification with the Diaspora Jews killed in Second World War Europe, rather than rejection stemming from a sense of shame at perceived passivity. This need for greater identification with Diaspora Jews was heightened by the growth of 'Canaanism' amongst sections of Israeli youth during the 1950s. These 'Canaanites' rejected any links between contemporary Israel and the Diaspora Jews. Rather than identifying with the European Jews who had experienced the

Holocaust, 'Canaanism' identified with Israeli Arabs. 1948 acted as a sort of year zero, from which a new 'Canaanite' – rather than specifically Jewish – nation was being created. In response to this, the government was eager that the 'Jewish' history of the Holocaust become part and parcel of 'Israeli' history.

To Israeli youth the trial presented not simply the specific charges levelled against Eichmann but the whole Nazi perpetrated 'Holocaust' and a potted history of antisemitism. It was intended to result in – as Ben-Gurion wrote to World Jewish Congress president Nahum Goldmann – 'the full exposure of the Nazi regime's atrocious crimes against our people'.[32] That this was the intention, was made explicit in Attorney-General Hausner's opening address, when he confirmed that 'it is not an individual that is in the dock at his historic trial, and not the Nazi regime alone, but antisemitism throughout history'.[33] Thus, not only did Hausner touch upon aspects of the Holocaust which had very little to do with the man in the dock, but he started off the prosecution case with the biblical stories of Pharaoh and Haman's persecution of the Jews and positioned the Holocaust as the culmination of several thousand years of antisemitism. The Jerusalem trial was therefore about antisemitism in general, the 'Holocaust' in particular, and Eichmann himself only rather peripherally. The result was that 'the court vacillated between trying a man and trying history'.[34]

That the trial was about much more than simply the man in the dock became clear once the prosecution case got underway. For 23 of his 121 sessions, Hausner presented 'background evidence' which was so tangential to the case against Eichmann, that it invoked the occasional ire of the three trial judges. In their final judgment they acknowledged that while the 'natural tendency ... to widen the range of the trial, to present a precise, historical description of the Nazi holocaust' was of considerable 'educational value', the court 'cannot allow itself to be enticed into provinces which are outside its sphere' and 'everything which is extraneous' to the court's appraisal of Eichmann's guilt or innocence 'must be entirely eliminated'.[35] Yet despite the reservations of the judges, and despite the historicity of the Holocaust *not* being in doubt, witness after witness continued to rehearse the major events of the Nazi murder of the Jews throughout Europe. Relatively few mentioned Eichmann by name. As Hannah Arendt noted, 'the bulk of the [prosecution] witnesses, fifty-three, came from Poland and Lithuania, where Eichmann's competence and authority had been almost nil'.[36] They could offer little in the way of evidence linking Eichmann to the specific charges he faced. But they could – and did – testify in detail to the acts of brutality performed by the perpetrators and the acts of resistance performed by the victims.

It was this testimony of acts of resistance presented by Hausner which for Arendt pointed to the profoundly ideological nature of the trial. When Hausner questioned the Warsaw ghetto survivors Antek Zuckermann and Tzivia Lubetkin about the uprising, Arendt suggested that 'Mr Hausner (or Mr Ben-Gurion) probably wanted to demonstrate that whatever resistance there had been had come from Zionists, as though, of all Jews, only the Zionists knew that if you could not save your life it might still be worth while to save your honour ...'[37] What was supposed to be a trial of Eichmann had become – so Arendt suggested – a piece of Zionist propaganda.

In arguing this case in her reports for the *New Yorker*, Arendt pointed to the greater concern shown by the prosecution with the heroic actions of the 'victims' than questions of the complicity of the Jewish leadership. The court spent more time listening to the history of the Warsaw ghetto uprising than it did the history of the Jewish Councils. The result was – Arendt argued – a partial rather than a 'full exposure' of the 'Holocaust' past, motivated by fear on the part of the prosecution that raising the question of Jewish Council involvement in deportations, would jeopardise 'their general picture of a clear-cut division between persecutors and victims'.[38] In direct opposition to what she saw as a partial cover-up, Arendt made the controversial claim that 'the whole truth was that if the Jewish people had really been unorganised and leaderless, there would have been chaos and plenty of misery but the total number of victims would hardly have been between four and a half and six million people'.[39] These conclusions are ones which provoked – and continue to provoke – considerable debate.

While Arendt did portray a rather simplistic version of the role of the Jewish Councils, which subsequent historians have challenged, she was right in pointing to a profound discomfort on the part of the prosecution in touching upon this particular episode of the 'Holocaust'. Survivors were asked why they had not resisted, but the cooperation of the Jewish Councils was not mentioned. And the question of Jewish Council complicity was downplayed during the trial as whole, except for the intervention of someone in the public gallery who accused one of the witnesses – Budapest Jewish Council member Philip Freudiger – of complicity with the Germans: 'You duped us so you could save yourselves and your families. But our families were killed ... He gave us injections to numb our minds. But he took his own parents out of Nyiregyhaza, and left mine there to die'.[40] The survivor was silenced and removed from the court during this session.

The Zionist agenda of the government clearly played a part in this, as did fears of reawakening the criticisms levelled at the government in the midst of the Kasztner case a few years earlier. In 1954-55, and then again in 1957-58, the accusations made against the Hungarian Jew Rudolf Kasztner of cooperating with the Nazis had been considered by a Jerusalem court. Kasztner was at the time of the trial both a member of the ruling Mapai party in Israel, and a spokesperson for the Minister of Trade and Industry. Attacking Kasztner's wartime role amounted to an attack upon Mapai's role – and by extension Ben-Gurion's role – during the war. Thus, the trial was highly politicised, and 'reflected a feeling of crisis, conflict, division, and lack of consensus'[41] in the nation as a whole. In contrast, the Eichmann Trial was to be a consensus-building exercise around the Holocaust, and thus – as Arendt claimed – was a partial telling of this complex past, which avoided the politically sensitive issues raised by the Kasztner trial.

However, while the Eichmann trial certainly was a partial telling of the Holocaust, it was arguably the most complete telling thus far in Israel. Up until 1960, there had been a mixture of a self-imposed and socially imposed silence upon survivors. Now, however, this silence was broken as hundreds of Holocaust survivors volunteered themselves as witnesses. From these hundreds of volunteers, 56 were chosen to take the stand opposite Eichmann, and they made up just under half of the 121 prosecution witnesses whose testimony dominated the trial. This summoning to the witness stand of Holocaust survivors was intended by Hausner to 'concretise' the Holocaust as he asked 'each of them to tell a tiny fragment of what he [sic] had seen and experienced'.[12] Through their testimony – often in considerable detail – of the gruesome experiences which they had witnessed, Hausner effectively shifted the focus of the trial from the perpetrators to the victims. Thus, rather than being primarily about what Eichmann had done, the trial became much more about what the victims had experienced (and done or not done). And much of the testimony was largely unconnected directly to the man sitting in the bulletproof glass encased dock. Attorney General Gideon Hausner himself was the first to admit the peripherality of the majority of these witnesses, as far as the case itself went. He recognised that there was a wealth of documentary evidence – more than 1,500 documents, most of them collected at the time of the Nuremberg trial – which was sufficient in itself to convict Eichmann. Indeed he went so far as to claim that,

... in order merely to secure a conviction, it was obviously enough to let the archives speak; a fraction of them would have sufficed to get Eichmann sentenced ten times over. But I knew we needed more than a conviction; we needed a living record of a gigantic human and national disaster.[43]

There is a sense in which the conviction itself – and the sentence that was to be meted out – was never in any doubt. The day after Ben-Gurion announced to the Knesset that Eichmann had been captured and would stand trial, the newspaper *Maariv* proclaimed confidently that 'there is but one sentence for genocide – death!',[44] and other papers adopted the same line. In the weeks that followed, Segev points out that 'newspaper editors, as well as police stations, were flooded with proposals of methods for inflicting horrible tortures and cruel death on Eichmann'.[45] There was widespread popular support for both the arrest of Eichmann and his predicted eventual execution. All of this could have meant that the trial itself would have been something of a formality. Yet it is clear that for Hausner – and Ben-Gurion – the trial itself was not simply a means to an end, but an end in itself. Not only was the verdict to be historic, but also the trial itself.

Hausner wanted more than documents. He wanted flesh-and-blood testimony, the absence of which at Nuremberg had meant – he reflected – that 'the proceedings there failed to reach the hearts of men [sic]'.[46] The aim in this Jerusalem courtroom was to 'reach ... hearts', and not simply to secure a conviction, and it was an aim which was successfully achieved. As one of the Israeli journalists covering the trial commented: 'not one of us will leave here as he was before'.[47] Perhaps the most 'shocking' moment came when one of the witnesses spoke of visiting Treblinka after liberation, and seeing there

> ... a sight which I shall never forget: an area of several square kilometres covered with bones and skulls, and nearby tens upon tens of thousands of shoes, many of them children's shoes. I took one pair as a token of those terrible days – one pair among one million such children's shoes that are scattered over the fields of death.[48]

As he spoke these words, he carefully unwrapped a tiny pair of shoes and held them up for the whole courthouse to see. The combination of hearing those words and seeing those shoes had a powerful impact, leading one observer to write that,

... no one who attended the sessions that day will ever forget the sight of these two tiny tot's shoes, held aloft in the Jerusalem courtroom. For seemingly endless seconds, we were gripped by the spell cast by this symbol of all that was left of a million children. Time stood still, while each in his own way tried to fit flesh to the shoes, multiply by a million, and spin the reel back from death, terror and tears to the music and gay laughter and the animated joy of youngsters in European city and village before the Nazis marched in.[49]

This dramatic testimony had next to nothing to do with Eichmann, but it had plenty to do with the 'Eichmann trial'. It provided a potent image of the 'Holocaust', later to be incorporated into the Historical Museum at Yad Vashem where a lone child's shoe is displayed on a plinth bearing the number of child victims of the Holocaust. It also drew attention away from Eichmann, and refocused it on the victims in general and the Jewish children who had been murdered in wartime Europe in particular. Within Israel, the trial therefore became less an encounter with a perpetrator, and more an encounter with the victims of the Holocaust. It was their testimony which seized the imagination of both those inside and outside the Jerusalem court house.

Such was the popular interest in the testimony given at the courthouse, that 1961 became dubbed – as Prime Minister Ben-Gurion himself noted – 'the year of the Eichmann trial'. For four months in the summer of 1961, news of the trial dominated the Israeli media and the conversations of ordinary Israelis. The first sessions had been broadcast live by Israeli radio, with an estimated 60 percent of the population listening to either the morning or afternoon sessions and 38 percent listening to both. On subsequent evenings, large numbers tuned into the special summary of the day's proceedings broadcast on Israeli radio. As a study undertaken by three Israeli psychologists showed, the media interest in the trial served to create a 'climate of opinion' within Israel, and that

... it was the contact with this climate of opinion – and not just the content of a specific broadcast or report in a newspaper – that was the main source of ... influence. Questions relating back to the period of the holocaust were discussed intensely – often heatedly – as if they were questions not of yesteryear but of this day ... This climate of opinion heightened the salience of the holocaust in the minds of an already involved population.[50]

The trial created a climate of opinions in which the Holocaust – which had been relatively little discussed in Israeli society – became *the* central topic of conversation. After 1961 the Holocaust ceased to be a taboo, and instead assumed an increasingly central – if contested – position in Israeli society and politics. The trial therefore marked the breaking of the silence over the 'Holocaust' past which had characterised the late 1940s and early 1950s. During this period, the Israelis had simply paid no attention to the stories of survivors.

This refusal on the part of Israelis to listen to survivors' stories was expressed in a popular film (made in 1972) after the story told by survivor Michael Goldman – who had played a dramatic role at the trial eleven years earlier. Goldman recalled telling his uncle and aunt of the eighty lashes that he had been given in a Nazi forced labour camp. Yet 'during the night from behind the wall, I heard my uncle say: they suffered so much they are beginning to imagine things'. Yitzhak Zuckermann – leader of the Jewish resistance in the Warsaw ghetto – had commented that this was 'the eighty-first blow, which every one of us receives'.[51] The response to this threat had been to remain silent about the past. And this image of yet another blow to the survivors had struck a powerful chord, and gave its name to the film, the *Eighty-First Blow*, the first of a trilogy of films on the Holocaust made by Haim Gouri.

The Eichmann trial spelt the ending of that silence and the creation of a ready audience within Israel for the stories of the survivors. These stories were told day after day within the Jerusalem courtroom and were being listened to by people throughout the country. Hausner had purposefully chosen witnesses of different ages and backgrounds, because he wanted

> ... the story told by a broad cross-section of the people – professors, housewives, artisans, writers, farmers, merchants, doctors, officials and labourers. That is why we called such a mixed collection of individuals to the witness box. They came from all walks of life, just as the catastrophe struck the whole nation. I asked a plumber to give evidence on the events in Bialystok, and important Jewish centre. After his statement was recorded, a well-known writer, a leader of the underground in the same place, volunteered to give evidence on the same events. By many standards the latter witness might have been preferable. But I wanted to have the plumber tell his story in his own simple words; so, finally, I kept him on the list and summoned him to court.[52]

By having a cross-section of Israeli society speak out in the witness box, Hausner intended that some of these voices would resonate with those listening. And resonate they did.

The speaking out of these survivors in the Jerusalem courthouse became the signal for a more general speaking out of survivors throughout the country. The silence was broken both within and outside of the courthouse. As the novelist and poet Haim Gouri reflects, with the opening of the trial 'Holocaust survivors were finally given the chance to speak. Overnight, they became the focus of national attention'.[53] The result was that the early 1960s became a time in Israel when 'in many families the true identity of the parents was now unveiled and their life story unearthed ... the Eichmann trial heightened an awareness of the "staircase mystery" – the mystery of who your neighbour was, and where he or she came from. The trial legitimised the disclosure of one's past. What had been silenced and suppressed gushed out and became common knowledge'.[54]

It was this private testimony being expressed throughout Israel which was perhaps ultimately more important than the public testimony being given in the Jerusalem courthouse. In the courthouse itself, those who queued for admission to the public gallery tended to be – as Arendt pointed out – 'middle-aged and elderly people, immigrants from Europe, like myself, who knew by heart all there was to know, and who were in no mood to learn any lessons and certainly did not need this trial to draw their own conclusions'.[55] They were primarily Jews rather than 'Israelis', and primarily the old, rather than the young whom Ben-Gurion wished to influence through the trial. Yet outside the courthouse 'young Israelis' were both listening to Holocaust testimony and discussing that period.

The result of this discussion of the Holocaust past was 'a greater sense of identification by Israelis, young people in particular, with Diaspora Jewry'.[56] Thus the trial did more than simply bring about a new concern with the 'Holocaust'. Through arousing interest in the 'Holocaust' history of Diaspora Jewry, the trial led to an identifying with that history on the part of native born Israelis. And perhaps more particularly, through the shift in attention from Eichmann to the victims, it led to identification with the survivors. The result was something of a reconciliation of Israeli and Jewish identities. The trial – Gouri suggests – 'compelled an entire nation to undergo a process of self-reckoning and overwhelmed it with a painful search for its identity'. He goes on to raise the dilemma of identity faced up to during the trial:

Who are we? On the one hand Israelis, free in our homeland, speaking our national tongue, served [sic] in an army that had not known defeat. On the other hand we belong to the slaughtered Jewish people ... It was the trial, with all its dark implications, that unveiled the duality of our existence – the Jews as a murdered people and the story of Israel as a nation sitting in judgment.[57]

The very trial itself was a symbol of the bringing together of the separate histories and geographies of Europe during the war, and 'Israel' after the war. Here being tried in a Jerusalem courtroom by the Israeli state was the man who a little over fifteen years earlier had been giving orders to the Jewish Council. The tables had been turned. And that sense of the tables being turned was not simply at an abstract level of national identities, but at the level of individual life stories. Gouri tells of the testimony of a doctor at the trial who saw

> ... 'how the ghetto commandant Schwemberger gave a Jewish youth eighty lashes.' The witness then testified that 'a child's body cannot withstand more than fifty lashes. And the boy remained alive.' 'Is this boy here in the hall?' asked the attorney-general. 'Yes', the witness said in Polish, 'Where is he?' 'This is he' – and the witness pointed to Captain Mickey Goldman, a member of the 06 Bureau of the Israel Police, charged with the preparation of documentation for the trial, and sitting a few steps from Eichmann's glass cage.[58]

That duality of roles of Goldman then, and Goldman now was the experience of a whole nation seeking to reconcile the past and the present.

The trial itself pointed to a continuity and connection between the Jews of Second World War Europe and the contemporary Israel where Eichmann was to be tried. This sense of continuity was stressed by Ben-Gurion when justifying the holding of the trial in Israel. Trying Eichmann in Jerusalem was for Ben-Gurion fitting and appropriate given that 'Israel is the only inheritor of these Jews for two reasons. First it is the only Jewish state. Second, if these Jews were alive, they would be here because most if not all of them wanted to come to live in a Jewish state'.[59] He used similar language of Israel as the true inheritor of Europe's Jews when writing to World Jewish Congress president Nahum Goldmann. Ben-Gurion told Goldmann that trying Eichmann for 'atrocities against hundreds of thousands of its sons and daughters' was 'the duty of the State of Israel, the only sovereign authority in Jewry'.[60] Thus the Holocaust's victims were effectively made into a part of the Israeli family. And this came on the back of the decision made a few years before to make them symbolic citizens of Israel.

That Israel was the true inheritor of the 'Holocaust' was stressed by Hausner, who claimed to be speaking on behalf of all the victims of the 'Holocaust'. He told the bench during his opening speech,

> ... when I stand before you, O Judges of Israel, to lead the prosecution of Adolf Eichmann, I do not stand alone. With me here are six million accusers. But they cannot rise to their feet and point their finger at the man in the dock with the cry 'J'accuse' on their lips. For they are now only ashes – ashes piled high on the hills of Auschwitz and the fields of Treblinka and strewn in the forests of Poland. Their graves are scattered throughout Europe. Their blood cries out, but their voice is stilled. Therefore will I be their spokesman. In their name will I unfold this terrible indictment.[61]

Hausner claimed, in effect, that the Israeli state had the right to speak for European Jews killed by the Nazis. In claiming this right, Israel also claimed the right to try the perpetrator.

However, the decision to try Eichmann in Israel was contested by, amongst others, American Jewish organisations. Nahum Goldmann's suggestion that Eichmann should be tried by an international court given that his victims were not just Jews was countered by Ben-Gurion. He stressed that it was Israel – not the World Jewish Congress – which was 'the Jewish people's only sovereign entity' and that 'antisemitism is caused by the existence of the Jews in the Exile', and that included Jews such as Goldmann living in America.[62] Responding to the request of American Jewish Committee president Joseph Proskauer that Eichmann be tried outside of Israel, Ben-Gurion made it perfectly clear to the American Jewry that Israel – and not New York Jews – had the sole right to speak on behalf of Europe's murdered Jews. As it had already done with the founding of Yad Vashem and would do so again, Israel was claiming a monopoly over the 'Holocaust'. Ben-Gurion argued that while 'at Nuremberg it was American, British or French prosecutors who submitted the indictment and the representatives of the Jewish people were no more than bystanders',[63] things would be very different for the trial of Eichmann in Jerusalem. This would be an Israeli trial.

That – as I've already suggested – was not the only difference between the Nuremberg trial and that of Eichmann. At Nuremberg the 'final solution of the Jewish question' had received scant attention in a trial more concerned with crimes against peace, war crimes and crimes against humanity. But in Jerusalem the 'final solution of the Jewish question' was to dominate. Never before had the nature of the 'Holocaust' been outlined in such detail. And the result of such a comprehensive telling of the 'Holocaust' was a profound shift in the way that the Holocaust past was perceived in Israel. As Gouri reflects, 'we do not have a geiger counter to gauge the intensity of the trial's radiation on the nation's soul. But one can safely generalise that by the time it ended Israelis knew more, much more, about what had happened to their fellow Jews during the Third Reich.[64]

This process of learning about the 'Holocaust' past was not restricted solely to Israel. In Israel this breaking of silence by the survivors was the most profound, but the same process of survivors being given a hearing was taking place throughout Europe and America in the wake of the Eichmann trial. As Geoffrey Hartman reflects upon American survivors,

> ... there have been three periods when survivors of the Holocaust recovered their voice and an audience materialised for them. The first was immediately after the war, when the camps were disclosed. That period did not last: a devastated Europe had to be rebuilt, and the disbelief or guilt that cruel memories aroused isolated rather than integrated the survivor ... A second opening was created by the Eichmann trial in 1960, and a third came after the release of the TV series *Holocaust* in 1978.[65]

In some ways, it could be said that a fourth came with the release of *Schindler's List*.

With the world's media reporting the arrest and then the trial, the 'Holocaust' received a world-wide audience. On the first day of the trial, a total of 376 journalists from 50 countries crammed into the public gallery along with 166 Israeli journalists, official observers and assorted invited guests. The trial was filmed in its entirety by the US film and TV company Capital Cities, and at the end of each day an edited selection of clips from the day's proceedings was made available to TV networks. Through this combination of newspaper reporting and TV footage, Eichmann – and Hausner's 'parade of Holocaust witnesses' – was brought directly into sitting rooms throughout the world, creating an impact that reached far beyond Israel.

Yet, arguably the trial meant something rather different outside of Israel. As the writer on Jewish literature Sidra Ezrahi suggests

n America the Eichmann trial, through the mediation of Hannah
endt, focused attention on Eichmann himself and on the psychic
components of evil ...

Whereas

> ... in Israel the appearance of a plethora of witnesses, the
> impassioned speech and physical collapse of survivor-writer
> 'Katzetnik' and the reams of recorded testimony directed
> attention to the survivors and contributed to a process of indi-
> viduation and an appreciation of the ambiguity of issues that
> had hitherto been parcelled into ideologically cogent and
> facile categories.[66]

In Israel the trial had primarily been about the victims, and in
particular Hausner's 'parade of Holocaust testimony', but in America – and Western Europe – the trial was primarily about the perpetrators and in particular Arendt's coining of the phrase 'the
banality of evil'. Despite her book, *Eichmann in Jerusalem*, being in
many ways a seminal work, it was not translated and published
in Hebrew, and aside from a few translated reports in *Haaretz*,
Arendt's work made little impact in Israel. However, her thesis did
have a considerable impact in Europe and America.

Arendt introduced the world to the 'banality of evil' through
Eichmann, who offered as his defence the plea that he was simply
carrying out orders: 'I sat at my desk and did my work'.[67] In introducing the world to the 'desk-killer', the trial played a role in shaping
the emerging myth of the 'Holocaust'. The 'Holocaust' perpetrator
was not some crazed axeman, but a pen pusher who sent train loads
of people to a large camp where they were sorted, gassed and cre-
mated with brutal efficiency. There was something terrifying, about
this 'perpetrator' being portrayed, not as a madman, but as a man
like us. Gone was the immediate post-war hyperbole which had
talked of 'the beast of Belsen' and 'the bitch of Belsen'. As Arendt commented: 'despite all the efforts of the prosecution, everybody could see
that this man was not a "monster".'[68] It was the normality and banality of the perpetrator that emerged from this trial. As the trial judges
themselves concluded in their judgment: 'We do not mean that the
viciousness of the accused was unusual within the regime he served.
He was a loyal disciple of a regime ... which was wholly evil ...'[69]

Described by the psychiatrists who had examined him as 'normal'
and 'not only normal but most desirable',[70] – the psychiatrist who
had examined Eichmann concluded: 'This man is entirely normal ...

more normal than I feel myself after this examination'[71] – Eichmann came to stand for the 'Holocaust perpetrator'. And it was not
just that such a 'normal' man would do such abnormal things which
was shocking. It was above all the realisation that being a 'desk
killer' means carrying out some seemingly normal tasks. Bruno
Bettelheim reflects upon 'the incongruity ... between all the horrors
recounted, and this man in the dock, when essentially all he did was
talk to people, write memoranda, receive and give orders from
behind a desk'.[72] What was remarkable about the Eichmann trial
was that it pointed to the reality of death by memoranda.

Hausner clearly pointed to this in his opening speech, but he also
sought to point to Eichmann being a face-to-face killer, with blood –
not just ink – on his hands. In both his opening speech, and in the
course of the prosecution case, he sought to prove that Eichmann
himself had killed a Jewish boy who had been stealing fruit from a
tree in the garden of his Budapest home. When he first stood up to
outline the prosecution's case, he told the court,

> In this trial we shall ... encounter a new kind of killer, the
> kind that exercises his bloody craft behind a desk and only
> occasionally does the deed with his own hands. Indeed, we
> know of only one incident in which Adolf Eichmann actually
> beat to death a Jewish boy who had dared to steal fruit from a
> ... tree in the yard of his Budapest home. But it was his word
> that put the gas chambers into action. He lifted the telephone,
> and railway trains left for the extermination centres. His sig-
> nature it was that sealed the doom of thousands and tens of
> thousands.[73]

This incident was deemed important enough for Hausner to
make reference to right at the beginning of the proceedings because
he saw it pointing to 'the writing-desk killer's personal participa-
tion in the murder of an individual Jew'. He continued

> We did not make it the subject of a specific charge – it would
> not do to single out this one Jewish boy from the six million
> victims – but the incident was certainly indicative of Eich-
> mann's attitude and so we introduced evidence on it.[74]

It is almost as if Hausner was determined to prove that rather than
simply writing memoranda, Eichmann had physically killed this Jew.
If this allegation could be proved, then Eichmann could be portrayed
as a more 'normal' murderer, and not simply as a 'desk killer'.

Yet – as Hausner himself phrased it in his post-trial account –

> … in its judgment the court, though expressing its 'positive appreciation' of … evidence, refrained from arriving at a finding on the cherry orchard murder in the absence of corroboration as to the details.[75]

With the accusation that Eichmann had killed with his own hands left unproven, Eichmann was convicted and executed solely for being a 'desk killer'. This had a profound impact on how the typical Holocaust perpetrator was viewed. He – or she – could be a thousand miles away from the scene of death. And from the publication of Hilberg's thorough investigation of the bureaucratic details of the murder of Europe's Jews and Arendt's articles in the *New Yorker*, the Holocaust perpetrator acted as a result of their position within a larger organisation, rather than because of their murderous personality. An ordinary individual such as Eichmann had done the most extraordinary things because of his position within a murderous bureaucracy, rather than because of something about his personality.

Rather than being the devil incarnate, Eichmann seemed to be one of 'us'. This was a frightening discovery. Pearlman speaks of Eichmann's entry into the Jerusalem courthouse in similar terms to those used by Wiesenthal

> … after the first gasp of surprise, the audience began to feel that his very ordinariness was somehow the more terrifying. If he had had horns in his head, knifelike eyes, and a gash of cruelty for a mouth, he would have been true to form. But he had none of these. He was everyone's next-door neighbour, the grocer in his Sunday clothes, the clerk at the accountant's office, the would-be executive in a commercial firm, the fellow strap-hanger on whose toes you tread. And one was suddenly struck by the fearsome thought that the men who had bullied and raped and tortured and shot and burned and gassed millions of innocent people were ordinary folk – just like any of us – who had gone wrong somewhere along the line and had been led into a strange world, a world without principle, without scruple and without compassion.'[76]

The trial raised the possibility that all the Nazis were as ordinary as Eichmann appeared to be. And this made a considerable impression. There is an almost voyeuristic fascination with the perpetrators of the Holocaust, motivated by a desire to see who would do these things. In part, perhaps, we come wanting to comfort ourselves that they look nothing like us and that their motives are far removed from ours. Yet face-to-face with Eichmann, the Holocaust perpetrator appeared uncomfortably similar to us, with ordinary foibles and delusions.

It is almost as if we really want these 'perpetrators' to be psychotic. I've often found that a number of my students assume this to be the case. When they argue in the initial seminars 'Well the majority of them were mad, weren't they', they are almost longing for that to be the truth. However, they later find the truth is much more disturbing. I'm reminded of the words of Raul Hilberg, who reflected after decades of researching and teaching on the Holocaust, 'wouldn't you be happier if I had been able to show you that all the perpetrators were crazy?'[77] Of course we would have been much happier if he had been able to show us that. There is a sense in which we feel that such an outrageous notion as the systematic murder of people because of their Jewishness must have been the product of crazy minds. What is disturbing is when we come to the dawning realisation that such a degenerate scheme was thought up and carried out by men and women who were 'normal' (people like Eichmann).

That almost makes it worse. As I am confronted by the Holocaust, I want to turn back the clock and undo what has been done. Visiting empty synagogues in Hungary forces me to try to imagine what these places were like in the inter-war years or even as late as early 1944 when there was still a large, vibrant Jewish community in Hungary. But I can't really visualise such life because I'm overwhelmed by images of the deaths brought upon Hungary's Jews during a few months in the hot summer of 1944. And I so want to believe that the mindless activity of those few months was simply an aberration. Some psychotic pogrom perhaps, carried out by crazy men and women for the craziest of reasons. But I know that crazed murderers don't collect hundreds of thousands of people into ghettos, then take them to transit camps, place them on slow trains north, select those fit for labour and gas and burn the rest. These Jews who I've been studying weren't killed by psychopaths, but by civil servants. They were killed by banal individuals for banal reasons, and that somehow makes their deaths seem all the more meaningless. There is something terrifyingly nihilistic about the idea of banal murder and banal murderers.

So I don't blame my students for wanting to discover that the perpetrators of this thing which we call the 'Holocaust' were mad. Indeed, I almost feel guilty when they reach the opposite conclusion. Perhaps I should sit them down and show them *Schindler's List* and tell them that all of the perpetrators were like Goeth. That Eichmann never killed with his own hands. That he was the exception proving the rule. The rest were sadists who delighted in their murders. However, I know that – because of his mediocrity – Eichmann makes a terrible screen villain, but that he is – because of his mediocrity – a fairly typical Holocaust perpetrator. And that Goeth – because of his sadistic psychosis – makes a great screen 'villain', but that he is – because of his sadistic psychosis – a fairly atypical Holocaust perpetrator. Yet despite this, perhaps the success of *Schindler's List*, and the remarkable portrayal of Goeth's character in that movie, means that it will be Amon Goeth – rather than Adolf Eichmann – who will stand – if he doesn't stand already – as *the* 'Holocaust killer' in contemporary iconography. A similar process of re-demonising the 'perpetrators' can be seen in Daniel Goldhagen's controversial riposte to historian Christopher Browning's portrayal of perpetrators as *Ordinary Men*. In his best-selling popular history of the Holocaust *Ordinary Germans*, Goldhagen's 'perpetrators' – who take sadistic pleasure in their killing – are clearly closer to Goeth than Eichmann.

# 3

# Oskar Schindler

Thomas Keneally – author of *Schindler's List* – wrote in 1994 that, 'Schindler is out there now, in the minds of millions, celebrated at the National Holocaust Museum in Washington, DC, honoured in Hollywood, a household name ...'[1] While Keneally himself had first brought the story of Oskar Schindler to the public's attention in his 1982 novel, he was among the first to acknowledge that it was not until the release of Spielberg's filmic telling of the story that Schindler became 'a household name'. Named 'Movie of the Year' by *Newsweek* (and just about everyone else), and awarded seven Oscars at the Academy Awards ceremony in March 1994, *Schindler's List* was quickly being spoken of as something more than simply a movie. US President Bill Clinton urged people to watch *Schindler's List*, as did TV chat show host Oprah Winfrey who told viewers that watching the movie had made her 'a better person'.[2] Walt Disney studio boss Jeffrey Katzenberg went even further in his support, and claimed that it was a movie which 'will affect how people on this planet think and act ... I don't want to burden the movie too much, but I think it will bring peace on earth, good will to men. Enough of the right people will see it that it will actually set the course of world affairs'.[3]

It was clearly not seen to be simply another movie, nor indeed simply another 'Holocaust' movie. After all it is not that often that the US President recommends weekend movie viewing. Perhaps more remarkable than the endorsement of the US President, and Oprah and Katzenberg's redemptive claims, was the decision to screen the movie without the normal array of advertisements and trailers in movie theatres, and then to show it free of the usual commercials on American television, when it premiered on NBC on 23 February 1997. Ford Motor Company bought the advertisement rights for the film but chose to allow the film to be screened without commercials, apart from short intermissions (for trips to the toilet and kitchen) which featured the Ford logo. When it premiered on British television seven months later, it was shown without any commercial breaks on the publicly funded BBC.

No doubt the decision to screen the movie without commercial breaks was in part a response to the criticism which had accompanied the US screening of the television mini-series *Holocaust* two decades earlier. In a particularly unfortunate juxtaposition of one of the 130 commercials (noted by *New York Times* television critic John O'Connor)'a story that includes victims being told that the gas chambers are only disinfecting areas is interrupted by a message about Lysol and its usefulness in "killing germs".'[4] However, this decision was more than simply a response to the criticism that had surrounded *Holocaust*. It reflected the sense of reverence accorded to this movie. Going to see *Schindler's List* was about more than simply movie-going.

Watched by approximately 25 million Americans at the movie theatre, and 65 million Americans when it was first shown on TV, *Schindler's List* has become 'for the present generation the most important source of historical information affecting popular perceptions of the Holocaust'.[5] It is a movie which has made a considerable impact, being responsible for what one writer describes as the emergence of a '*Schindler's List* Effect'.[6]

In part, the impact of *Schindler's List* reflects the contemporary fascination with the 'Holocaust'. However, the movie does not simply reflect that fascination. It also contributes to it. The myth of the 'Holocaust' has emerged over the course of the last thirty years as a defining moment in modern history. Spielberg's movie both points to that mythical status, and has been critical in reshaping the myth of the 'Holocaust'. Spielberg has drawn on historical, literary and filmic representations of the 'Holocaust' from the last thirty years in making *Schindler's List*. For example he takes the girl in the red dress not from Keneally's novel, but from testimony given at the Eichmann trial. Her inclusion by Spielberg, points to the way in which this movie relies not only on Keneally's book, but also on the many strands of the myth of the 'Holocaust'. Similarly, when Spielberg shows a German soldier sitting at a piano playing Mozart while the ghetto is being liquidated, he is drawing not on Keneally, but on George Steiner's reflections on Nazism.[7] But Spielberg has not simply recycled a number of existing images in making *Schindler's List*. He has also created new images of the 'Holocaust' which are now seared on the public consciousness, and which will have a lasting impact. After *Schindler's List*, the 'Holocaust' can never be the same again, because this movie 'is already beginning to affect the way our culture understands, historically orders, and teaches how the Holocaust should be remembered ...'[8]

Indeed for some, *Schindler's List* has almost the status of a primary source. It is not seen as simply representation, but as the 'real thing'. And in many ways one can't be blamed for thinking this way. Spielberg has spoken of *Schindler's List* as being a document rather than a film, and his role as being that of witness rather than film director.[9] Thus he shot on location using hand-held shots and black and white film, which gives large parts of the movie the feel of being an authentic newsreel film of the ghettoisation and deportation of Polish Jews. As a result, the film 'particularly because of its style' is – it has been suggested – in danger of 'displacing the evidence and documentation on which it is based' and therefore 'acting in people's minds as a metatext of historical evidence'.[10]

That this film has attained the status of reality in its own right, can be seen in the current popularity of '*Schindler's List* tours' of the site of the Kraków ghetto and nearby Plaszow labour camp. On these, '*Schindler's List* tourists' do not so much see sites of 'Holocaust' history, as sites of *Schindler's List* history. They are shown the sites where the movie was filmed – for example the street along which Schindler sees the girl in the red coat walking during the liquidation of the ghetto – rather than sites where the Holocaust was enacted.[11] For these tourists, Kraków is being visited because that is where Spielberg filmed his movie. And while Spielberg filmed his movie there because that is where the ghetto was, for the '*Schindler List* tourists' it is the film location – rather than the ghetto – that is being visited, because the virtual reality of Spielberg's 'Holocaust' is more real than the 'Holocaust' of history.

It is that blurring of image and reality that has led to an outpouring of critical comments on Spielberg's movie and the subsequent '*Schindler's List* Effect'. But it is important to remember that it is not simply *Schindler's List* which can be criticised for blurring image and reality and presenting a virtual 'Holocaust' which threatens to usurp the Holocaust of history. The emergence of the myth of the 'Holocaust' from the 1960s onwards is in effect the emergence of a virtual 'Holocaust'. A virtual 'Holocaust' can be experienced by walking through the permanent exhibition at Washington, DC, Auschwitz, Anne Frank House or Yad Vashem. *Schindler's List* is not unique in being open to the criticism of 'posing as the "real thing"' or being a film which 'usurps the place of the actual event'.[12] The same criticism can be levelled against the last thirty or forty years worth of 'Holocaust' representations. Since the emergence of the myth of the 'Holocaust', the constant danger has been that the 'myth' becomes more 'real' than the historical 'reality'. And at the end of the twentieth century it seems to me that there can be no doubt that the myths have become more real than historical reality.

The criticism of *Schindler's List* – by academics and journalists primarily – is therefore more than simply the criticism of this one film in particular. As film historian Frank Manchel remarks, the divided reactions to the film 'make it clear that *Schindler's List* is not just a movie. It has become part of an ongoing worldwide cultural war that for decades has been debating both the nature and causes of the Holocaust and the advisability of having artists interpret the events surrounding the Nazi genocide'.[13] Spielberg's film has become the focus for a growing sense of disquiet, on the part of some, at the cultural products of '*Shoah* business'. That it was this particular movie which got it in the neck, was largely a result of the massive impact that *Schindler's List* had, rather than because this was a particularly poor movie. It quite blatantly was not. Spielberg has produced a memorable movie, just as the United States Holocaust Memorial Museum has created a memorable exhibition. Yet both have been heavily criticised by those who question how beneficial the contemporary American fascination with the 'Holocaust' really is.

In large part, those criticisms point out how these particular mythical tellings of the 'Holocaust' are ideologically laden and thus, by definition, partial representations of historical reality. Both Spielberg's movie and the Washington, DC, museum are ultimately 'Americanised' tellings of the 'Holocaust', which 'foster particular national values and celebrate certain fundamental values associated with "the American way" in reference to the Holocaust'.[14] But *Schindler's List* is more than simply another example of the 'Americanisation' of the 'Holocaust'. Spielberg hasn't given us a documentary film in *Schindler's List*, but *the* contemporary example of the Hollywood 'Holocaust'. In the same way that the 'Americanisation' of the 'Holocaust' is to be expected in a museum located a few hundred feet from the Washington Monument, and the 'Israelisation' of the 'Holocaust' is to be expected in a museum on the hills surrounding Jerusalem, the 'Hollywoodisation' of the 'Holocaust' is to be expected in a movie made in Hollywood by one of its most successful directors of all time. The man who gave us *ET* has also given us the 'Hollywood Holocaust' hero Oskar Schindler, and the man who gave us *Jaws* has also given us the 'Hollywood Holocaust' villain Amon Goeth. As Manchel reflects, 'in classical Hollywood style, the story of the millions is demonstrated by the fortunes of the few' in a film which 'besides its scenes of nudity, terrifying violence, outstanding performances by the film's three major actors, and spectacular

cinematography – all ingredients that appeal to mass audiences – ...
contains a macabre sense of humour'.[15]

In following Hollywood conventions, Spielberg did not necessarily
do anything different in *Schindler's List* from what George Stevens
did in the movie *The Diary of Anne Frank* in 1959. Writing in 1983 –
a decade before the release of *Schindler's List* – Langer reflected that
over the course of the last three decades of 'Holocaust' movies

> ... visually we have progressed in thirty years from the
> moderate misery of a little room in Amsterdam to execution
> pits and peepholes into the gas chambers of Auschwitz in
> *Holocaust*; but imaginatively, most of these works still cling
> valiantly to the illusion that the Nazi genocide of nearly eleven
> million human beings has not substantially altered our vision
> of human dignity.[16]

His words remain just as relevant after *Schindler's List*, which is
a movie which takes us further – visually – than ever before. We don't
simply peep into the gas chambers, but accompany Schindler's female
Jews into what they – and we – assume to be a gas chamber, only to
join them in their relief as water flows from the shower heads rather
than Zyklon B.

However, while we are taken further visually by Spielberg, we are
not taken that much further imaginatively, because *Schindler's List*
gives us a Hollywood 'Holocaust' with a happy ending. As I have
already noted, the 1959 filmic 'Anne Frank' closes with the reassurance that 'in spite of everything ... people are really good at heart'. It
is these words of Anne that we take with us as a symbol of hope
rather than despair. And so the 'Hollywood Anne' comforts us that
people are still basically pretty decent, thus silencing any challenge
that the Holocaust might make to our naive optimism in human
potential. *Schindler's List* is in many ways little different to the filmic
'Anne Frank' in that it also offers us a happy ending, where the 1,100
Schindler Jews survive, rather than one where the 6 million Jews not
on the list are killed. In choosing to tell Schindler's story one critic
has noted somewhat cynically, 'good old Spielberg has succeeded in
acquiring from amongst all the Holocaust stories the one which has
a happy end'.[17]

While in the 1959 movie *Diary of Anne Frank* only Otto Frank
survives and in the 1978 television mini-series *Holocaust* only one of
the family's children survive, in *Schindler's List* 'virtually every character in whom the audience has emotionally invested lives!'[18] This is
a 'Holocaust' where the people who matter to us as an audience live,

rather than die. As one journalist has noted, Spielberg has made 'a movie about World War II in which all the Jews live. The selection is "life", the Nazi turns out to be a good guy, and human nature is revealed to be sunny and bright.' Thus, Spielberg has made a movie which amounts to 'a total reversal' because he has given us a 'Holocaust' which leaves us with a sense of 'triumph'.[19] It is triumph we feel as Schindler's Jews emerge unscathed from the factory at Brinnlitz, and walk over the hill and into the technicolour sunlight of contemporary Jerusalem. They have survived.

Why have they survived? Because of Oskar Schindler. *Schindler's List* – despite becoming the Holocaust movie of the 1990s, if not of all time – is first and foremost a movie about a man called Oskar Schindler. It is Schindler who we encounter right at the beginning of the movie, as we watch him dress before going out for an evening of drinking with attractive women and powerful men. And it is Schindler who remains the central character to the end. Spielberg himself has acknowledged that this is not a representative Holocaust movie, but a telling of 'one story from the Holocaust'.[20] And that story – as the movie's distributors make clear – is 'the indelible true story of the enigmatic Oskar Schindler, a member of the Nazi party, womaniser, and war profiteer who saved the lives of more than 1,100 Jews during the Holocaust. It is the triumph of one man who made a difference, and the drama of those who survived one of the darkest chapters in human history because of what he did'.[21]

As this description makes clear, *Schindler's List* tells of a 'Holocaust' where one 'good' man makes a difference, rather than a 'Holocaust' characterised by the banality of evil and the indifference of many. By focusing primarily on Schindler and 'his Jews' – rather than the masses of Jews herded into the ghetto and then on to the deportation trains – Spielberg made a movie about power rather than powerlessness. It is a celebration of the freedom of the individual to act, rather than a reflection on the fate of powerless individuals in the face of a regime which decided that Jews should die. Watching *Schindler's List* reaffirms our belief in the power of the individual to change the course of events. It is a film which is strong on human responsibility, and therefore 'qualifies the widespread view of the Holocaust as an inherently inevitable, fateful, unstoppable event, one over which human agency had no control'.[22]

We are given a typically Hollywood action hero who himself survives the movie and in the process ensures the survival of the world. Schindler is, after all, told by Stern, 'Whoever saves one life, Saves the world entire'. Schindler is in essence little different to the heroes in a countless number of Hollywood action movies – from

*Superman* to *Independence Day* – who by the time that the credits start to roll have managed to save the planet. He is a character we are used to encountering at the movie theatre. After all, 'it is very American, at least in the movies, to see a single person, usually male, singularly conquer events'.[23] And so *Schindler's List* is in some ways little different from most Hollywood movies, and most movies previously made by Spielberg. As Manchel reflects, Spielberg's 'entire career had been devoted to making sentimental movies with optimistic endings, always reassuring his audiences that they can triumph over their fears if they have the courage and the will to do so'.[24] In making *Schindler's List*, Spielberg has gone and done that all over again.

This 'Hollywood Holocaust' is one where the individual can make a difference, and where Schindler does. Therefore 'Spielberg's [Holocaust] is an evil we can live with, made in Hollywood, that can be defeated by skill and perseverance, willpower and determination'.[25] It is 'a palatable version of the Holocaust in which individual talents allegedly could have helped victims survive'.[26] And thus it is a 'Holocaust' that leaves us with an essentially optimistic belief – in many ways like that of the Hollywood 'Anne Frank' – in human potential. Rather than facing the pointless, industrialised murder of six million which causes us to wonder at what human potential can lead to, we see Oskar Schindler and the 1,100 Schindler Jews and are comforted at the thought that flawed people like Schindler – and us – are after all basically good.

In part this stress upon the actions of one heroic individual is the byproduct of *Schindler's List* being a typical Hollywood movie. Spielberg, in 'following the Hollywood model of the historical epic, chose an individual to function as the protagonist of history'.[27] However, it is also a result of Spielberg's own beliefs. As one writer suggests, 'Spielberg ... is a humanist, and that is his starting point in the film. He talks about mercy and sanity in a mad, chaotic, and cruel universe'.[28] And in many ways he can't be blamed for doing that. Spielberg has – through *Schindler's List* – reached back into the chaos of the Holocaust, and found the story of one individual who *did* make a difference.

And by doing this, Spielberg not only affirms our belief in human potentiality, but he reassures us that even the most evil of circumstances can bring out the good in us. After all, the Schindler that Spielberg presents is one who achieves some sort of redemption by the end of the movie. Schindler is presented throughout as a flawed hero, but it is clear that Spielberg wants us to believe that by the end of the movie he has changed. Just before the close of the movie,

Spielberg's Schindler pledges faithfulness to his wife, reveals to Stern the extent of his sabotage of the war effort, tells the rabbi that he should celebrate the Sabbath, is shown – again through Stern – to have spent everything on 'his Jews', tells the German guards to return to their families 'as men instead of murderers', leads 'his Jews' in three minutes silence for those murdered and crosses himself. And then this newly redeemed Schindler breaks down just before leaving the factory for the last time with his wife.

This final scene – where the playboy and manipulator Schindler weeps over the realisation that he could have done more, and then flees westwards with the wife whom he has pledged faithfulness to – doesn't fit with the Schindler shown to us during the course of the movie. Nor does it fit with the Schindler of history. As a number of Schindler Jews have noted, the Schindler of history simply made a speedy getaway just prior to liberation, with his wife *and* mistress.[29] This Schindler of history obviously did not achieve the same sort of redemption through his actions that Spielberg's Schindler does. Spielberg had to re-write history, to stress not only that one 'good' man can – and should – make a difference, but also to suggests that redemption can – and should – be achieved through virtuous actions. In re-writing the past, Spielberg has created a Schindler who is not simply a liberal icon, but also a humanist icon.

The effect of this screen redemption is to transform Schindler into not just a hero, but something of a saint, whose tomb on Mount Zion is shown to be a site of pilgrimage. Indeed it may not be going too far to suggest that Spielberg transforms Schindler into a Christ-like figure. The final scene in which he breaks down is after all a Gethsemane of sorts. One writer has pointed to 'Schindler's virtual apotheosis as a modern Christ figure in his sermon to the awestruck Jews looking up at him from the Brinnlitz factory floor' which he sees as a 'direct crib from every Hollywood sand-and-sandals epic, from *The Ten Commandments* and *Ben-Hur* to *Jesus Christ Superstar*'.[30]

If the 'Holocaust' has gained such an iconic status that it can be seen as acquiring almost a religious aura, then surely Oscar Schindler has emerged in the aftermath of *Schindler's List* as a contemporary Holocaust saint (if not a new Holocaust 'Christ'). In some ways he has eclipsed Raoul Wallenberg. Wallenberg – a Swedish diplomat who saved the lives of Hungarian Jews in Budapest in the autumn and winter of 1944 through the issuing of safe passes and diplomatic papers – was featured in a number of movies and television mini-series during the 1970s and 1980s. For example, in 1985 the television mini-series *Wallenberg: A Hero's Story* was aired. During this period, Wallenberg was an attractive hero because his post-war capture by the Soviet Union ensured that he could be seen as both Cold War martyr and 'Holocaust' hero. It is clear that his heroic status persists, as he features both in the permanent exhibition at the United States Holocaust Memorial Museum, and the museum itself is located on the newly renamed Raoul Wallenberg Place. However, the recent supplanting of Wallenberg's primacy as *the* 'righteous gentile' reflects wider shifts in the contemporary world. While Wallenberg spoke both of the Cold War and the 'Holocaust', Schindler speaks both of capitalism and the 'Holocaust'. And in post-Cold War capitalist America it is the lessons of St Oskar that are deemed the more important.

Schindler offers – as the 'Holocaust' cartoonist Art Spiegelman claims – 'the benign aspects of capitalism – Capitalism With a Human Face'.[31] He is the philanthropist who uses his money to save lives, which – as Israeli film critic Uri Kleine suggests – raises some obvious parallels with Spielberg himself. As Kleine notes, 'both Spielberg and Schindler gravitate proudly to the centre of capitalism and both attempt to redeem the easy money they have made through the performance of "a good deed". As Schindler was trying to save life through his capital, so Spielberg is trying to resurrect destroyed life through his capital'.[32] Spielberg himself can be seen as seeking a redemption of sorts through his funding of the *Survivors of the Shoah Visual History Foundation* which is involved in a massive project of videoing interviews with Holocaust survivors. There is an uncanny parallel with Schindler here. Schindler used his profits to rescue 1,100 Jewish lives, and now Spielberg uses his profits from *Schindler's List* to rescue the testimony of Holocaust survivors. Whether that parallel be coincidental or intended, there is no doubt that Spielberg's Schindler can be seen to represent capitalism tempered by humanism. He is a suitable hero for modern America.

This heroisation of Schindler has angered Hilberg, who claims that 'there is nothing to be taken from the Holocaust that imbues anyone with hope or any thought of redemption, but the need for heroes is so strong that we'll manufacture them'.[33] Yet regardless of Hilberg's claim that the Holocaust is not the place to look for heroes, Spielberg has successfully mined the depths of the Holocaust and come up with the hero Schindler. In seeking for heroes in this past, Spielberg has not done anything new. As the example of Yad Vashem (further down) shows, Israel engaged in a process of looking for 'Holocaust heroes' in the 1950s and 1960s. Yet Israel found her Holocaust heroes from amongst the Jews – primarily those who fought in the Warsaw ghetto uprising – whereas Spielberg has found his hero from amongst the Germans.

For it is Germans – rather than Jews – who dominate in Spielberg's movie. Throughout *Schindler's List*, 'the fundamental dramatic confrontation in the film is not one between Jews and Germans but one between an evil German and a German who comes to exemplify righteous behaviour'.[34] The result is that 'we find Schindler and Goeth towering both physically and personally over a mass of weak, featureless Jews. The potential victims thus largely serve as a mere background to the epic struggle between the good guy and the bad guy'.[35] That epic struggle over helpless Jews is seen most clearly when Schindler and Goeth play a game of cards to determine the fate of Helen Hirsch.

In stressing Schindler's heroism and Jewish passivity, Spielberg adopts – as the historian Judith Doneson has pointed out – a gendered approach. Heroism is given a masculine face and victimhood a feminine face, as Spielberg suggests that for the weak feminine Jew to be saved, there needs to be a strong, Gentile male. And that saviour is Schindler, who is the very epitome of masculinity. We are, after all, left in no doubt about his sexual prowess. In contrast, Itzhak Stern – the one Jew whose character is developed most fully during the course of the movie – is portrayed as a slightly effeminate and bookish character who needs the protection of Schindler. Quite early on in the movie, Stern has to be rescued from a deportation train by him. He – like the other Jews portrayed – is dependent upon the actions of Schindler for his survival.

We are left in no doubt by Spielberg that it is the 'Righteous Gentile' Oskar Schindler who was the hero, rather than any of the Jews who did – or didn't – make it on to the list. Indeed the Jews in *Schindler's List* are not simply shown as passive rather than resisting, but to some extent as complicit with the perpetrators. For example, both Stern and Goldberg are shown working for Goeth rather than resisting him. This focus on Jewish passivity and complicity rather than resistance, contrasts quite markedly with the Israeli telling of the 'Holocaust' in which Jews are the heroes. In American tellings of the 'Holocaust' it is either the liberating American Army who are the heroes – the portrayal favoured at the United States Holocaust Memorial Museum – or Righteous Gentiles – the portrayal favoured by Spielberg. Hollywood did not look for a story of Jewish heroism – the Warsaw ghetto uprising is an obvious example – but for a story of Gentile heroism.

As mentioned above, by focusing on this single 'heroic' individual, Spielberg 'reaffirmed classical Hollywood narrative's psychohistorical approach to history in which the private story is accorded more weight than public history'.[36] *Schindler's List* is a movie which provides a narrative of the past in terms of 'great men in history'. But more than simply reducing the complexity of the past to biography, Spielberg reduced the complexity of the Holocaust to a clear-cut moral tale.[37] His 'Holocaust' is one in which good is pitted against evil, for example, when Schindler and Goeth – living apparently parallel lives, yet lives which increasingly diverge – are portrayed playing a game of cards for the soul of Helen Hirsch. His 'Holocaust' has been simplified to a story of 'good versus evil'. We aren't told why the Nazis have decided to kill Kraków's Jews, apart from a suggestion that it is a byproduct of the psychosis of Nazis like Goeth. We aren't told why Schindler decides to save 'his Jews', apart from a suggestion that this is part of his increasing goodness.

The result is that *Schindler's List* ignores any consideration of the structural context to the mass murder of Europe's Jews. By situating this murder within the classic categories of hero and villain, Spielberg effectively takes the Holocaust out of history. It is, for example, a radically different telling of the 'Holocaust' to that of sociologist Zygmunt Bauman who sets the industrialised murder of six million Jews in the context of modernity. Bauman's 'Holocaust' thus raises questions about the very nature of modernity which Spielberg's 'Holocaust' sidesteps. Spielberg's 'Holocaust' ends with the hanging of Amon Goeth and the arrival of Schindler's Jews in a filmic Jerusalem. The hanging of Goeth effectively brings the murders to an end because it spells the end of the protagonist of evil. The equation is simple: No people like Goeth, no murders. Yet Bauman's 'Holocaust' continues to haunt us long after the summary execution of the perpetrators. His 'Holocaust' is there latent within modernity and raises questions about the present where Goeth limits the implications of Spielberg's 'Holocaust' to the past.

In Goeth, Spielberg chose a stereotypical villain. This filmic Nazi acts and looks much more like a villain than the Eichmann who sat in the dock of the Jerusalem courthouse. Unlike Eichmann, this Nazi shoots Jews from his balcony before breakfast. While at the Jerusalem trial Hausner failed to prove that Eichmann had killed anyone with his own hands, we are left in no doubt that Goeth is a killer who murders his victims face-to-face and not simply a desk killer. He is 'a psychopath who appears to murder indiscriminately',[38] rather than an example of mediocrity such as Eichmann. He is a 'tyrant'[39] rather than simply a man who represents the banality of evil. He is not at all like us. He is not simply inhuman. He is unhuman.

The result of this psychotic portrayal is – as the historian Alvin Rosenfeld reflects – that 'identification with such a character as

Amon Goeth, who is the incarnation of the murderous passions of limitless evil, is out of the question for most filmgoers, who are far more likely to align themselves sympathetically with the "good" German Oskar Schindler, the "rescuer" of the Jews, rather than with Goeth, the ostensibly mad and vicious killer'.[40] Spielberg does not encourage us to identify with this Nazi, in the same way that the United States Holocaust Memorial Museum does not give out the identity cards of perpetrators. He encourages us to identify with the 'Righteous Gentile', in the same way that the United States Holocaust Memorial Museum encourages us to identify with the liberators and the victims. We leave the movie theatre – and the United States Holocaust Memorial Museum – comforted that we are nothing like the perpetrators. We are left 'outside the film, admiring one man, condemning the other' and therefore we are 'never implicated in the moral economy of the film' nor forced to examine our 'own social and political ethics'.[41]

Watching Spielberg's perpetrator is a very different experience from encountering the perpetrators described by Browning in his book *Ordinary Men*. Browning's group of murderers are men motivated by peer pressure and a concern to advance in their careers. They do not kill Jews – Browning suggests – because they are devils incarnate, but because they are human. They are perpetrators whose petty concerns it is all too easy to identify with. And thus we find ourselves implicated and forced to reconsider our own motives. These murderers are after all – in Browning's memorable phrase – simply 'ordinary men'. And yet in *Schindler's List* it is Schindler who is the 'ordinary man', not Goeth. And thus it is Schindler with whom we identify rather than Goeth. He encompasses that mixture of good and evil that we see in ourselves. He is a hero, but a flawed hero. He is not portrayed – at least initially – as an angel, but as a manipulator, playboy and concerned above all else with making money.

Spielberg draws very different conclusions from his 'Holocaust' than Browning does from his. Browning finds himself concluding

> There are many societies afflicted by traditions of racism and caught in the siege mentality of war or threat of war. Everywhere society conditions people to respect and defer to authority ... Everywhere people seek career advancement. In every modern society, the complexity of life and the resulting bureaucratisation and specialisation attenuate the sense of personal responsibility of those implementing official policy. Within virtually every social collective, the peer group exerts

tremendous pressures on behaviour and sets moral norms. If the men of Reserve Police Battalion 101 [the perpetrators who form the basis for Browning's study] could become killers under such circumstances, what group of men cannot?[42]

But Spielberg raises a different set of questions. Rather than forcing us to consider that we might have been part of the problem, Spielberg assures us that we would have been part of the solution. His Oskar Schindler would seem to prove that the Holocaust brings out our better natures, rather than our dark side. As Spielberg himself has suggested, *Schindler's List* is a movie 'about tolerance and remembrance, and it is for everyone'.[43]

In reality of course the Holocaust of history was rather different to the Hollywood 'Holocaust'. Yet Spielberg is giving us the latter rather than the former, so we finish with Hollywood's optimism rather than historical pessimism. We witness the execution of Goeth and are comforted that justice has been done and that the bad guy is no more. And then we see the survivors who walk past Schindler's tomb, and are comforted that those whose lives have been threatened so many times have been saved by this one man. When Helen Hirsch walks past with the actress who played her in the movie, we know that ultimately Schindler won out over Goeth and good triumphed over evil.

However, it is surely questionable whether a 'happy ending' – be it George Stevens's ending to the film of Anne Frank's diary or Steven Spielberg's – is an appropriate way to conclude any telling of the 'Holocaust'. As the historian Yehuda Bauer reflects, the acclaimed director Claude Lanzmann who made the 'Holocaust' documentary film *Shoah*, 'knew that … he could not have a happy ending to a film on the Holocaust'.[44] Thus he closes not with a note of triumph but one of despair. The final words in the movie are spoken by Simchah Rotem – a participant in the Warsaw ghetto uprising – who says to himself, 'I'm the last Jew. I'll wait for the morning, and for the Germans'.[45] In many ways it is brilliant ending to the story, characterised as it is by total despair. Yet – as Loshitzky points out – even Lanzmann hints at redemption. Not only is Rotem still alive and therefore able to reflect back on his feelings, but Rotem is filmed by Lanzmann at the Ghetto Fighters Kibbutz in Israel, where those words of despair are given a new meaning. In essence, therefore, Lanzmann offers us a Zionist closure on the Holocaust which is similar to that offered at Yad Vashem and which Jacob Neusner sees as characterising the American Judaism of 'destruction and rebirth'.

Neusner suggests that this contemporary Judaism of 'Holocaust and Redemption' engages in an imaginary journey from wartime Europe –

and specifically Poland – to contemporary Israel. This journey is physically made by thousands of American Jewish teenagers each year as they follow the increasingly well-trodden route of 'Holocaust' pilgrims-cum-tourists who visit the sites of destruction in Europe (above all Auschwitz) and then end up at the sites of redemption in Israel. And that journey is the one which Spielberg takes us on imaginatively in *Schindler's List*. Like Lanzmann, he chooses to begin his movie in Poland but end it in Israel. And through taking us on this journey, both stories give us the message that the Jew is not really safe until they discover the safety offered by the Israeli state.

In *Schindler's List*, this Zionist ending is made more explicit than in *Shoah*. When at liberation Schindler's Jews ask 'Where should we go?', they are told by the Red Army soldier 'Don't go east that's for sure. They hate you there. I wouldn't go West either if I were you'. The lesson is clear – there is no safety for the Jew in Europe. And this is made all the more clear when in the next scene we see the Schindler Jews climbing over the hills of Jerusalem to the sound of the song 'Jerusalem of Gold', a song made popular during the 1967 Six-Day-War. They leave a black and white Second World War Eastern Europe to emerge, blinking, in the full technicolour sunshine of contemporary Jerusalem. And they leave the suffering of the European past, to enter the victorious Israel of the present.

Yet when the movie was previewed in Israel the closing soundtrack was changed after being heavily criticised. When the film went on general release in Israel, Schindler's Jews no longer walked over the hill top to the song 'Jerusalem Gold', but to the tune 'Eli, Eli'. By changing the ending in this way, Israeli audiences were not only spared – in historian Omer Bartov's view – 'such a crass and yet disconcertingly ambiguous connection between the destruction of the Diaspora and the triumph of the Israeli Defence Forces',[46] but given in its place a song with connotations of Jewish heroism. The song 'Eli, Eli' is a musical version of Hannah Senesh's 1941 poem 'To Caesarea' and by using it at the end of the movie, it was not so much memories of 1967 which were being awakened as memories of Hannah Senesh. She was one of the volunteer commandos who were parachuted into occupied Hungary in 1944 in order to set up Jewish underground groups to fight the Nazis. Senesh was captured and executed, and became a symbol of wartime heroic martyrdom in the early years of the Israeli state. Her remains were eventually brought back from Hungary and reburied on Mount Herzl.

The choice of 'Eli, Eli' for the Israeli ending points, therefore, to an Israelisation of *Schindler's List*. It amounted – as Bartov notes – to the shifting of 'the politics of the film's ending from the Arab-Israeli conflict to the Israeli sponsored "heroic" aspect of the Holocaust, stressing not only resistance to the Nazis but also the reinvented, "normalised" Jews "made in Palestine", as the proper answer to gentile hatred and persecution'.[47] Despite this being an American 'Holocaust' in which the hero is a 'Righteous Gentile' rather than Jew, in the Israeli ending there is an attempt to point beyond the 'Righteous Gentile' to the heroic 'Israeli Jew'.

The movie closes in the Israeli present as the – by now elderly – survivors file past Oskar Schindler's tomb in the Catholic graveyard on Mount Zion, accompanied by the actors who played them on the screen. Myth and reality merge as the survivors and those who have represented them walk together. As they lay a stone on Schindler's grave they are engaged in both an act of remembrance of and gratitude to their rescuer. Their very presence points to Schindler's success in protecting 'his Jews' and affirms his status as a 'Righteous Gentile'. They are saying if you like – 'I'm here today because of Oskar Schindler'. And in saying that they celebrate both rescue and survival.

*Schindler's List* is a movie less about perpetrators and victims than it is about rescuers and survivors. It is a movie which through 'narrating the story of 1,100 Jews rescued from what doubtless would have been a gruesome death for most, is a film that 'celebrates "survivors".'[48] And in celebrating the survivor, this movie both reflects and contributes to what Alvin Rosenfeld sees as 'a paradigm shift of significant proportions'.[49] By focusing on Schindler – the rescuer – and the Schindler Jews – the survivors – 'Spielberg has in effect repositioned the terms of the Holocaust "story" away from those favoured by Hilberg and others – the Holocaust encompassing essentially "perpetrators", "victims", and "bystanders" – and has placed the emphasis squarely on "rescuers" and "survivors".'[50]

This shift in emphasis away from 'victims' to 'survivors' is one which can be seen to have taken place over the last couple of decades in the United States in particular. From being simply 'displaced persons' or 'war refugees', 'Holocaust survivors' have emerged as a distinct and honoured category in the United States, with Elie Wiesel as their principal spokesman. Indeed 'Holocaust survivors' in general – and Schindler Jews in particular – have something of a celebrity status within the United States. As the journalist Elinor Brecher reflected from her own experience of interviewing Schindler Jews after the release of the movie, they are very much a group of people in demand. As she discovered,

> ... some *Schindlerjuden* are booked for speaking engagements a year in advance. There is no question that the list has

conferred a certain mystique on the listees. In fact, by the time I got to them, some had been used, abused and burned out by the media. Over and over I heard about the invasion of the television crews. Holocaust survivors as celebrities *du jour*?[51]

In large part, Schindler Jews are 'celebrities *du* jour' because of the success of Spielberg's movie, but it is not simply Schindler Jews who are contemporary celebrities, but Holocaust survivors more generally. At the end of the twentieth century, 'surviving itself ... has ... a new quality'.[52] While 'in *Shoah* for example nobody speaks about the way they survived' and many survivors suffered from a psychological complex dubbed 'survivor's guilt', things have changed to the extent that 'surviving itself became a very prominent idea'.[53] And this suggestion of a change in attitudes towards survival is echoed by Keneally. In contrast to 'the early 1980s' when

... there was a considerable reluctance among most of them to speak of their lives as prisoners of that frightful system. Many of the survivors had become successful people in their own communities, and by the early 1980s they were at the height of their powers. Omens of mortality that strike people in their sixties and seventies had not yet presented ... [themselves]

Keneally found that ten or so years later – 'the survivors are older now, and they are faced with deniers of their experience. While they still have voices, they want to relate the atrocities and barbarities that were practised on them'.[54]

For a host of reasons – and the desire to counter the claims of Holocaust revisionists appears to be one of them – Holocaust survivors have become increasingly active and increasingly vocal. Indeed, Alvin Rosenfeld is surely right to suggest that 'without the extraordinary commitment of these people there would be no United States Holocaust Memorial Museum, no video archives for Holocaust testimony, no endowed chairs at American colleges and universities for the teaching of the Holocaust – and no *Schindler's* List'.[55] It was, significantly, the survivor Leopold Pfefferberg who first interested Keneally in the story of the man who would – a decade and a half later – become a household name through the release of a film based upon the survivors' stories.

In some ways survivors' stories are problematic. As survivors such as Primo Levi and Paul Celan themselves have recognised, there is a danger – 'that the stories told by the saved distort the past, not because they are not authentic, but because they exclude the stories of the majority, who drowned ...'[56] By reason of their survival, their stories are the exception rather than the norm. And that stands for both those who survived because of the intervention of 'Righteous Gentiles' such as Schindler and Wallenberg, and those who survived simply by a stroke of luck or the nature of circumstances they found themselves in. After all, the Holocaust is about mass killing and not survival.

Yet in stressing rescue rather than unhindered mass murder, *Schindler's List* is 'the culmination of a development in Holocaust narrative that has been building momentum for a number of years now'.[57] Spielberg's story does not stand alone. It is merely the most successful of the 'at least 40 films and 35 books that relate stories of Christian rescue of Jews' which have appeared in the last decade.[58] It is not just Schindler who has been celebrated as the rescuer of 1,100 Kraków Jews, but Wallenberg as the rescuer of thousands of Budapest Jews and Miep Gies as the – ultimately unsuccessful – rescuer of Anne Frank.

The celebrating of 'Righteous Gentiles' came – the psychotherapist Eva Fogelman suggests – as a reaction to 'the brutal testimony of the Eichmann trial' which

> ... set off an urgent quest for evidence of human kindness during the war. People around the world needed to feel that the heart of man was not unrelievably black. Rescuers were discovered. Oskar Schindler, who was visiting Israel at the time of the trial, was greeted at the airport by hundreds of his survivors and their families.[59]

If Fogelman is right to see the search for happy stories as a result of the disclosures of the Eichmann trial, then surely the telling of the story of rescue can be seen as a byproduct of the telling of the story of destruction. It is the Eichmann trial which is a critical event in leading to the emergence of the myth of the 'Holocaust' – in Israel in particular – and it is also this trial which Fogelman sees as critical in leading to the emergence of the 'myth of rescue'. She argues that 'by facing past evil' through this trial, 'the world was finally in a position also to acknowledge the heretofore invisible heroism and decency of rescuers'.[60]

However, I think that the telling of stories of rescue was something other than simply the acknowledging of 'the heretofore invisible heroism and decency of rescuers'. Heroism was not simply acknowledged, but actively sought out. And this – I think – is because the emergence of the 'Holocaust' from the 1960s onwards made necessary a search for stories of rescue to temper the horror of this event. It is almost as if the 'Holocaust' is too horrific an event to confront without the solace offered by stories of rescue offered by individuals such as Oskar Schindler. It is perhaps the case that evil can only be confronted when good can also be discerned to act as a comfort of sorts in the midst of despair. And contemporary representations of the 'Holocaust' in particular shy away from the prospect of having to face total despair without hope of salvation. The emergence of the myth of the 'Holocaust' from the 1960s onwards is characterised by the representation of acts of heroism and redemption alongside the representation of 'the anus of European civilisation'.[61] Thus in Jerusalem, Yad Vashem celebrates both Jewish heroism and rebirth in Israel as the devastation of the 'Holocaust' is revealed. In Washington, DC, the United States Holocaust Memorial Museum celebrates both liberation and survival as the destruction of the 'Holocaust' is revealed.

And in *Schindler's List*, Spielberg has given us the acts of Oskar Schindler and the final triumph of the State of Israel to temper scenes of harrowing brutality. These scenes of horror – surely some of the most memorable 'Holocaust' images ever produced – are given to us within a context which provides such seemingly random acts of brutality a sense of meaning. Thus the horrific scene of 10,000 corpses being exhumed and burnt is given purpose within *Schindler's List* as a part of the process whereby Schindler becomes a rescuer. The same can be said for the earlier scene of the liquidation of the ghetto. In both, the girl in the red coat – the only use of colour by Spielberg in the main body of the film itself – is somehow 'saved' because it is through seeing her that Schindler's eyes are opened. Her corpse acts as the trigger to Schindler's conscience and thus her brutal (off-screen) murder is linked to the scenes of final redemption. She does not die in vain, as in some ways we are led to believe by Spielberg that it is through her death that 1,100 Jews are ultimately saved. She dies so that others might live.

In *Schindler's List* we are given a Hollywood 'Holocaust' in which scenes of graphic violence are spread throughout what is ultimately a 'feel-good' movie. Not only are these scenes made more palatable by an ending in which the hero triumphs and the villain gets his just desserts, but they also show acts of violence committed in the main against nameless individuals rather than characters whom we have in some way invested in emotionally. Most of those murdered in this filmic 'Holocaust' are mere faces who we view from the perpetrators perspective – sometimes literally, as for example when we see through the sights of Goeth's rifle as he takes pot shots from his balcony. On the whole we aren't put through the trauma of seeing 'our Jews' murdered, but sit as outsiders watching the murder of anonymous Jews.

However, Spielberg does give us one scene in which 'our Jews' appear to be in real danger. Taken to Auschwitz rather than Schindler's factory in Brinnlitz, the female *Schindlerjuden* are made to undress and then herded into what appears to be a shower room. The doors are closed by the SS guards, the lights go out, the women begin to scream. It is a harrowing scene because we know what happened in the 'showers' at Auschwitz-Birkeneau, and we know that these women also know what we know. Spielberg has given us an unforgettable cliffhanger. We sit terrified that he is actually going to show us this room of women being gassed, and we get ready to turn away from the horror.

But of course he doesn't. This is Hollywood. The showers produce hot water, not Zyklon B. We feel the immense sense of relief that these women felt. In reality it is perhaps we – rather than they – who are the more relieved. We are relieved for them, but we are primarily relieved for ourselves. We didn't want to see women with whom we identified being gassed. Who would want to see that? We feel grateful to Spielberg that he didn't take us all the way and show us that. We feel immense relief that we weren't forced to become witnesses to the gassings, which are at the end of the scene hinted at by the shots of lines of people descending into what we know to be gas chambers (although we hope these also are simply showers). But we see all of this from this side of the wire, and we can hardly make out the faces of this long line of humans. We see from a safe distance. And we feel immensely grateful that in our 'Holocaust' we didn't have to follow 'our Jews' into the gas chambers and then on to the crematoria. As Rabbi Schulweis acknowledges, if Schindler's List 'has become the defining symbol of the Holocaust, it is ... not because of its artistry alone, but because it enables the viewer to enter the dark cavern without feeling that there is no exit ...'[62]

Spielberg has given us an exit from the gas chambers in Oskar Schindler. He comes and rescues the women and girls on the list of life, and brings them to the safety of Brinnlitz where they are reunited with their husbands and sons. And from then on we know that we are in for a happy ending. We have a sense that we have been through the final cliffhanger, and experienced the final last-minute rescue. We know now that Schindler has finally been triumphant. And even when Schindler tells the guards in Brinnlitz that they can choose to be 'murderers' or 'men', we know that they are going to choose the latter and we won't be left with a massacre. We have been spared the gas chambers and we are spared a final scene of mass shootings. We have – perhaps – been spared the 'Holocaust'.

But who would want to show the 'Holocaust' on film anyway? I was relieved that

> ... there were no hangings in *Schindler's List*. No Jews dangled from iron rings in Amon Goeth's office. The dogs wore muzzles; audiences didn't see them gnawing men's genitals and women's breasts like so much hamburger. Spielberg's storm troopers refrained from swinging infants by their feet into brick walls, smashing their skulls like melons. He spared audiences Goeth's theoretically nonlethal punishment of choice. Every one of the *Schindlerjuden* to whom I spoke had either undergone it or witnessed it at sickeningly close range: twenty-five strokes of a lead-tipped leather whip on the bare buttocks, with the victim – laid over a slatted table – counting the blows in German for his or her tormentor. Miss a count and the series began all over again.[63]

I agree with journalist Elinor Brecher that 'Spielberg can be forgiven a certain amount of cinematic license with the story'.[64] After all we don't even want to read about this, let alone watch it.

And yet I knew that everything the *Schindlerjuden* had told Brecher was true. There were hangings at Plaszow, the dogs weren't muzzled, children were swung against walls and Goeth did use a lead-tip leather whip. And from quite a number of years of reading about the Holocaust, and reading survivors' memoirs I knew all sorts of things that in many ways I wished I didn't know. So I wanted to stand up in the cinema as the credits were rolling and say to all these people: 'It was much worse'. But of course I didn't. It had been bad enough for many of these people who now sat in silence or wept quietly.

Surely Bartov is right to reflect that 'no film can recreate an unhuman reality' and so

> ... we cannot blame *Schindler's List* for not showing people actually being gassed, but only for showing them not being gassed; we cannot blame it for not showing the emaciated bodies of concentration camp inmates, but only for showing us the attractive, healthy naked bodies of young actresses, whose shorn hair strangely resembles current fashions. It is precisely because of the inability of cinematic representation to authentically recreate a distorted reality that the claim of

authenticity – and the sense of the viewers that they are seeing things as they 'actually were' – is so troubling.[65]

We aren't seeing things as they 'actually were'. We are simply seeing things as Hollywood has made them to be. Hollywood from 'Anne Frank' to 'Oskar Schindler' offers a 'Holocaust' which 'still believes that humans are good at heart'. It constructs an 'Auschwitz' and a 'Holocaust' which it can come to terms with. In *Schindler's List*, it turns to the small group of Jews who discovered that the showers at Auschwitz-Birkeneau contained warm water, and that the chimneys weren't the only way that you could escape that place, and it pleads with them to tell their story with the happy ending. And as those who died in Auschwitz-Birkeneau are nothing more than ashes now, contemporary Hollywood can ignore them.

This is perhaps a generational thing: 'the kids of survivors [or in Spielberg's case the grandchildren of survivors] have different memories; they start restating these memories in which the Holocaust has a kind of happy end, because at least one of the parents survived'.[66] The second and third generation see the 'Holocaust' rather differently to those who witnessed it first hand, and it is they who have both made and watching *Schindler's List*. Spielberg's film is, 'a film generated by an American post-Cold War generational sensibility distanced from the Holocaust both temporally and spatially'.[67] The result of this is that, 'for a director like Spielberg (as for the American Jewish community at large), what matters is survival. The mourning over the six million Jews who perished in Europe is symbolically transformed into a celebration of the approximately five million Jews living in America today'.[68] We have perhaps, in reality, forgotten the dead and now remember only the living. It is stories of survival which we tell. And so when Hoberman asks – rhetorically – whether it is 'possible to make a feel-good entertainment about the ultimate feel-bad experience of the twentieth century?',[69] we have to answer, of course it is. The last half century of Hollywood 'Holocaust' movies proves that not only is it possible, but also an immensely popular and profitable thing to do.

Spielberg has taken us right into 'the holy of holies' in his pursuit of the ultimate of Hollywood suspense. We accompany 'Schindler's Jews' into the very bowels of Auschwitz-Birkeneau, and are in some ways trespassers. What is 'the most horrible, terrifying, and sacred space of Holocaust memory and a locus of denial for the assassins of memory'[70] has become for Spielberg simply a movie set. His original intention had been to shoot scenes in Auschwitz-Birkeneau itself, however, his plans to build a 'fake gas chamber' within the perimeter

re challenged by the World Jewish Congress which saw this
to 'disturb the dignity of a site that ... requires solemnity'.[71]
ielberg constructed his 'gas chamber' – where the showers
spurt water, not Zyklon B – just outside the perimeter fence of
Auschwitz-Birkeneau. In recreating the 'gas chambers' – on Polish
soil – and then filming inside them, Spielberg has demonstrated – it
has been suggested – 'the complete absence from this film of any
humility before its subject'.[72] From America, he went with camera in
hand, into the place where it isn't just angels who fear to tread.

Part II

# PLACES

# 4

# Auschwitz

The drivers of the regular bus service from Kraków to Oswiecim are used to the 'Holocaust' tourists who clamber aboard the bus in Kraków, and then step down when the driver pulls over and shouts 'Museum'. We shuffled down the aisle of the bus, past locals who make this journey to Oswiecim often. All of them knew where we were going, as did each of us who stepped from the bus in turn and walked quietly down the track towards 'Auschwitz'. We were tourists of guilt and righteousness: guilt at an almost pornographic sense of expectancy of the voyeurism ahead. And yet guilt tempered by a sense of righteousness at choosing to come to this place. Those who talked did so in hushed tones. Most just looked around, trying to work out what was the former concentration camp 'Auschwitz', and what was simply the Southern Polish town of Oswiecim. We weren't interested in Oswiecim, we were on our way to 'Auschwitz', a place visited by an estimated 700,000 'Holocaust' tourists-cum-pilgrims each year.

By the end of that day, I had visited two 'Auschwitzs'. The first 'Auschwitz' was the one which the tourists come to: the 'Auschwitz' with tourist facilities. This 'Auschwitz' has a movie theatre, a book shop, a cafeteria, exhibition halls in old barrack buildings and glass display cases filled with piles of suitcases, shoes, glasses and women's hair. And it was quite crowded on the April morning that I visited. But in the afternoon, when I walked the mile and half to the other 'Auschwitz' – the 'Auschwitz' without tourist facilities – I found that I was alone. Here, there weren't any display cases or visitor's toilets, but simply a large fenced-off site with a railway line running through the middle, empty barracks and the shells of barracks on either side, and woods at the far end. I didn't know quite what to expect when I made this journey to Oswiecim, but I certainly wasn't expecting to find two 'Auschwitzs' in this town.

More than any other place, 'Auschwitz' has come to symbolise everything about the 'Holocaust'. 'Auschwitz' is to the 'Holocaust' what 'Graceland' is to 'Elvis'. It has become a staple of the 'Holocaust myth'. It is the place of 'the angel of death', Joseph Mengele. It forms the backdrop to such filmic 'Holocausts' as *Sophie's Choice* and *Schindler's List*. And it is a prime site of 'Holocaust' tourism. Not only is the word 'Auschwitz' virtually synonymous with 'Holocaust', but the word has become virtually synonymous with generic 'evil'.

And yet the name Auschwitz, was – as the historian Tony Kushner has pointed out – little known in the West until the 1960s. 'At the end of the Second World War', he argues, 'Auschwitz simply had no popular resonance in liberal culture'.[1] Prior to the emergence of the myth of the 'Holocaust', Bergen-Belsen and Buchenwald were to 'Nazi atrocity', what 'Auschwitz' now is to the 'Holocaust'. As Kushner notes, Bergen-Belsen was the first German concentration camp liberated by British troops, and through the reporting of Richard Dimbleby became known in Britain as a symbol of Nazi brutality. The harrowing film footage of piles of corpses was shown in British cinemas shortly after liberation on 15 April 1945, and ensured that 'Belsen' became a synonym for Hitlerian atrocities. A parallel process was taking place after the liberation of Buchenwald by American troops, as Ed Murrow represented Nazi brutality to the American public. The haunting images of corpses were appropriated as evidence of the justness of the Allied cause, and thus at this point, 'Belsen' did not serve as a symbol of the 'Holocaust' specifically, but of Nazi atrocities on the one hand, and Allied 'liberation' on the other.

The iconic status of 'Belsen' – rather than 'Auschwitz' – in the post-war West, can be seen in use of the nicknames 'the bitch of Belsen' and 'the beast of Belsen' to refer to the infamous SS guard Irma Grese and her colleague Josef Kramer. While both had served at Auschwitz as well as at Bergen-Belsen, it was 'Belsen' which – at this stage – was the more familiar place. Similarly, while Anne Frank had been an inmate in both Auschwitz and Belsen, it was 'Belsen' which became associated with her during the 1950s. After the success of the play in Germany, 2,000 young Germans made a pilgrimage of sorts to Belsen. In part, this linking of 'Anne Frank' and 'Belsen' – rather than 'Anne Frank' and 'Auschwitz' – was a result of Bergen-Belsen being the place of her death. However, it was also a result of the historical context to the publication and popularisation of Anne Frank's diary. That context was one of 'Belsen' as the site of Nazi atrocity.

Because Auschwitz was liberated – at the end of January 1945 – by the Red Army, not the Western Allies, Auschwitz remained effectively unknown in the West. Within a divided Europe, a divided geography of remembering the Nazi atrocity emerged. 'Belsen' was remembered by the West, and 'Auschwitz' by the 'East'. Both sides of the iron-curtain had their own symbolic places of the Nazi past. 'Belsen' was appropriated by the Western liberators as a place which provided ultimate justification for the war, and 'Auschwitz' was similarly appropriated by the Eastern liberators.

In 1947, the newly formed Polish government decided that 'on the site of the former Nazi concentration camp a Monument of the Martyrdom of the Polish Nation and of Other Nations is to be erected for all times to come'.[2] Andrew Charlesworth, a geographer, has pointed out that 'by emphasising its international character and ignoring the fact [that] the victims were Jewish, the Communists linked Poland through the memorialisation of Auschwitz to the other Warsaw Pact countries'.[3] This 'Auschwitz' was not about the 'Holocaust', but was a symbol of fascist aggression in the past, a warning of the potential threat still posed by West Germany and a comforting reminder of the 'liberating' presence of the Soviet Union. This link between West Germany as the enemy in the past, and the enemy in the present was made explicit in the Fifth Edition of the Museum guidebook published in 1974, which warned visitors that:

> ... in spite of the fact that, according to the Potsdam Agreement, Germany was to be entirely demilitarised ... a new army ... has been organised and is continually increasing in numbers. All peace loving nations are protesting against the violation of the Agreement, fearing the possibility of a new war scourge, which could prove to be even more disastrous in its results than the last war. We should keep this in mind when [walking] along the streets of the former concentration camp in Auschwitz-Birkeneau, where, not so many years ago, lorries had passed, loaded with the corpses of prisoners, both of those who had died in the camp and of those who had been shot in the yard of Block 11; their blood had soaked into the road leading to the crematorium.[4]

Visits to the State Museum at 'Auschwitz' were made compulsory for Polish schoolchildren, who were shown the 'Auschwitz' with tourist facilities (Auschwitz-I) which had housed Polish political prisoners and Soviet POWs – a group of 600 of whom had been gassed experimentally – during the war. The Jewishness of the victims of the other 'Auschwitz' (Auschwitz-II) was downplayed not only in the monument finally unveiled there in 1967 – which remembered the 'four million [sic] people [who] suffered and died here at the hands of the Nazi murderers between the years 1940 and 1945' – but also in the setting up of national pavilions at the State Museum. At the 'Auschwitz' for tourists, the 'Pavilion of Martyrology of Jews' – closed between 1967 and 1978 – was only one pavilion amongst many. In the others – the pavilions of 'the Hungarian People's Republic', 'the Federation of the Yugoslav People's Republics', 'the Czechoslovak Socialist Republic', 'the Union Soviet Socialist Republics', 'the German Democratic Republic' [but not the Federal Republic of West-Germany], Belgium and Denmark – victims were remembered as citizens of largely socialist republics first and foremost, and as Jews only secondarily.

And thus, 'Auschwitz' can be seen as emerging very much as the Eastern parallel to the 'Belsen' of the West. In the West in the 1940s and 1950s, the camps of 'Belsen' and 'Buchenwald' became 'part of western Allied war history rather than being connected to any specific Jewish disaster'.[5] And in the East in the same period, the camp of 'Auschwitz' became part of eastern Allied war history rather than being connected to any specific Jewish disaster. These concentration and death camps were about things other than the 'Holocaust', which is hardly surprising given that the 'Holocaust' as a distinct – Jewish – event had not yet entered Western – or Eastern European – consciousness.

However, with the emergence of the myth of the 'Holocaust', 'Auschwitz' came into its own as not simply the Warsaw Bloc symbol of fascist aggression, but as *the* symbol of the 'Holocaust'. 'Auschwitz' came to replace 'Belsen' in Western consciousness, as the 'Holocaust' came to replace more vague notions of Nazi atrocity and the imaginary geography of the 'Holocaust' shifted eastwards. As early as 1955, it was the name 'Auschwitz' – not 'Belsen' – which Theodor Adorno chose to use in his well known statement that 'to write poetry after Auschwitz is barbaric'.[6] And by 1965, Sylvia Plath was putting 'Auschwitz' alongside 'Belsen' in her poem 'Daddy', which Kushner sees as 'an important cultural guide in which Belsen and Auschwitz are accorded equal weight'.[7] In the present of course, Belsen and Auschwitz are no longer 'accorded equal weight'. The last three decades have seen the emergence of 'Auschwitz' as *the* symbol of the 'Holocaust'.

In part, the emergence of 'Auschwitz' – rather than Bergen-Belsen – as the symbol of the 'Holocaust' is a reflection of the fact that 'Auschwitz' fitted with the emerging sense of what the 'Holocaust' was perceived to be about. From the Eichmann Trial and the pioneering historical writing of Raul Hilberg onwards, the 'Holocaust' came to be seen as systematic industrialised murder of Jews by gas, rather than isolated, individually perpetrated atrocities. Whereas

'Belsen' had been about individual evil – operating within traditional judicial categories of 'guilt' and 'innocence' – perpetrated by 'bitches' and 'beasts', 'Auschwitz' came to represent mass, bureaucratic, industrialised evil perpetrated by those who – like Eichmann – exemplified the 'banality of evil'. Unlike the camps in the West, Auschwitz had been the site of mass killings by gas, and thus its gas chambers became the centre of the 'Holocaust' world. The 'Holocaust' was seen to be of 'Auschwitz' rather than 'Belsen'.

But Auschwitz was only one of six other sites of mass gassing of Jews in Poland. The others – Chelmno, Belzec, Sobibor, Treblinka and Majdanek – had been the place of death of approximately two and a half million Polish Jews. These camps never gained the kind of reputation that 'Auschwitz' did. This was not simply – as Charlesworth notes – a result of both the infrastructure and relatively large numbers of forced labourer inmates surviving at Auschwitz. Chelmno, Belzec, Sobibor and Treblinka were razed to the ground by the departing Germans, but both Auschwitz and Majdanek were liberated largely intact. At both Auschwitz and Majdanek, there were not simply remains to look at but also testimonies to listen to because the complex of camps included both death and labour camps. In many ways, Majdanek would seem to have as much of a claim on memory as Auschwitz.

Yet it was Auschwitz and not Majdanek which was chosen by the Polish government as the site for a state museum. And this, Charlesworth suggests, was determined not simply by the fact that the number of victims at Auschwitz outnumbered the number of victims at Majdanek, or that the victims at Auschwitz were more international in make-up. It reflected also the geographical location of the two. Auschwitz looked westwards and pointed to German aggression, but Majdanek faced eastwards and while pointing to Soviet liberation, also pointed to a darker side of Polish-Soviet relations. Majdanek was liberated and then promptly made into a concentration camp for the Soviet secret police. Therefore, it was Auschwitz, not Majdanek, which became the symbol of fascist atrocity in post-war Poland.

Of all the death camps within Poland, it was 'Auschwitz' which had already been constructed as *the* Nazi concentration camp, and thus it was 'Auschwitz' which became *the* 'Holocaust' death camp. From the 1960s onwards, the original meaning given to 'Auschwitz' became overlaid with a new set of 'meanings'. From being a site of Warsaw bloc memory of fascist atrocity, 'Auschwitz' became recognised not simply as a site of the mass gassing of Jews, but *the* site of Jewish memory of the 'Holocaust'.

Yet alongside this 'Jewish Holocaustisation' of Auschwitz, a process of 'Catholicising' Auschwitz started to take place,[8] in particular centred on the Polish-Catholic martyr Father Maximilian Kolbe. Kolbe was an inmate in Auschwitz-I, who chose to die in place of a man who was due to be executed. His martyr's death was recognised when he was beatified in 1971, and then canonised in 1982. In this context, his cell in Block 11 of Auschwitz-I became a site of Catholic pilgrimage, complete with wall plaque, candles and wreaths of flowers. Thus 'Auschwitz' has not merely come to represent the 'Holocaust', but from the 1970s onwards, it has become a site of Catholic pilgrimage.

The prime site of Catholic pilgrimage is Kolbe's cell in the 'tourist Auschwitz' (Auschwitz-I). But the process of 'Catholicising' 'Auschwitz' has extended also to the other 'Auschwitz' (Auschwitz-II). As Charlesworth points out, in 1979, Pope John Paul II celebrated mass at Auschwitz-II on the ramp where Jewish selections had taken place in 1944. A cross with a barbed-wire crown of thorns stood above the altar. Hanging from the cross was a striped cloth representing the camp uniform, upon which was a red triangle – the symbol of political prisoners – and the number 16 670 – the number given to prisoner Father Maximilian Kolbe. Kolbe was effectively taken the mile and half down the road to the other 'Auschwitz' and the Jewish specificity of the suffering there subsumed and universalised into the individual sacrifice of Maximilian Kolbe, and ultimately Jesus. However, unlike Kolbe – and Jesus – the Jews taken to Auschwitz-II did not have the option to choose a path of self-sacrifice. When they were packed into trains in provincial Hungary in May 1944, their fate was already decided. Principled self-sacrifice was not an option for those designated to die. And yet taking Kolbe's example to Auschwitz-II represents an attempt in some way to provide a spiritual meaning to what was nothing more than mass, racially motivated killing. In essence, the Church was attempting to make sense of death at Auschwitz through the symbol of Kolbe – and Christ – and yet it is an analogy that simply doesn't work. The Pope spoke of Kolbe's 'victory through faith and love',[9] however, the same lofty sentiments don't apply to the hundreds of thousands of Jews condemned to death at Auschwitz-II.

After the 1979 mass at Birkeneau, the Catholicising of 'Auschwitz' shifted back to Auschwitz-I. The cross that was used in the 1979 celebration of mass was moved from Auschwitz-II to Auschwitz-I, and erected in the garden of the Carmelite convent established in 1984 just outside of the perimeter fence. And it was this convent which was to provoke international dispute over the ownership of 'Auschwitz' in the late 1980s. This dispute can be seen in some ways as surprising. Christian buildings had been located at former Nazi concentration camps before without causing international Jewish-Christian conflict. The lack of response to the building of a Carmelite Convent at Dachau in 1964 can be explained in part as a result of the site being Dachau, and not Auschwitz, and the time being the 1960s not the 1980s. A similarly mild reaction had greeted the establishing of the Church of the Blessed Virgin Mary Queen of Poland in a former administrative building at Auschwitz in 1983.

Conflict over the Carmelite convent during the mid to late 1980s revolved in part around the original plan that the convent be dedicated to the memory of Maximilian Kolbe and Edith Stein, who would be two named victims through whom the Church 'pays homage to each and every victim'.[10] As has already been noted, the attempt by the Church to make Kolbe representative of the 'Auschwitz' victim does not fit with the reality of those who were not given any option over whether they chose to live or die. Moreover, Jewish groups pointed to Kolbe's pre-war editorship of an antisemitic paper, and membership of an organisation committed to seeking conversions amongst the Jews. In the case of Edith Stein, Jewish groups pointed to the fact that she was taken to Auschwitz-II and murdered as a Jew, and yet was posthumously being held up as a Catholic martyr. This smacked of a Christian failure to come to terms with the patchy record of the Church vis-à-vis the Jews before and during the Holocaust.

However, the focus of the conflict was less about what was being done with the memory of Kolbe and Stein and more about the specific location of the convent which developed into 'a debate about the symbolic ownership of Auschwitz'.[11] In 1984, a group of Carmelite nuns moved into a vacant building just outside of the perimeter fence of Auschwitz-I. When the camp had been barracks for the Polish Army, this building had been a théatre. The Nazis had later transformed it into a store house – reputedly where Zyklon B canisters were kept. With the entry of the nuns, the former store house became a place of prayer a matter of yards from the symbolically significant Block 11, where Kolbe had been shot. The location of the convent aroused little interest until a Belgian Catholic charitable organisation – *Aide à l'Église en Détresse* – began a fundraising campaign for the sisters in 1985. Not only did they publicise the little-known convent, but they did so in triumphant language which sparked Jewish protest. In speaking of the convent as 'a spiritual fortress and a guarantee of the conversion of strayed brothers from our countries as well as proof of our desire to erase the outrages so often done to the Vicar of Christ',[12] the siting and the purpose of the convent came under attack from the Belgian Jewish Community, and eventually Jews and non-Jews worldwide. It was seen as an attempt to rehabilitate the questionable wartime record of Pope Pius XII, convert the Jews and de-Judaise the 'Holocaust' by 'Catholicising' 'Auschwitz'.

The location of the convent was discussed at a series of high level meetings culminating in the issuing of a joint agreement by Jewish and Catholic representatives at the Geneva meeting on 22 February 1987. The Polish victims of Auschwitz-I were acknowledged, while the Jewish specificity of 'Auschwitz' was spelled out explicitly with recognition that 'Auschwitz remains eternally *the* symbolic place of the *Shoah* which arose from the Nazi aim of destroying the Jewish people in a unique, unthinkable and unspeakable enterprise'.[13] This amounted not simply to an acceptance that 'Auschwitz' was a symbol of the almost one million Jews who died at Auschwitz-II, but an acceptance that 'Auschwitz' was *the* symbol of the 'Holocaust' – the murder of six million Jews. In effect it amounted to official recognition of Jewish ownership of 'Auschwitz' as the 'Holocaust' brand name. This was seen by Jews as little more than the acknowledging of what was already – in practice – the case. As the Jewish spokesman Ady Steg commented, 'if Auschwitz has become the symbol of the Holocaust it is not we who have decided this: a symbol does not decree itself. It is the universal conscience which has seen in Auschwitz, and not in Birkeneau, Treblinka or Sobibor, the place of the Jewish catastrophe'.[14] Ironically, Steg failed to recognise that 'Auschwitz's' reputation owed far more to the actions of the post-war Polish government than it did to notions of 'universal conscience'.

Under the terms of the agreement hammered out at Geneva, the Convent was to be moved to a centre outside of the symbolic area of 'Auschwitz' within two years. However, when the deadline passed on 22 February 1989, a site had still not been decided upon for the new centre and the nuns remained in the convent. The deadline was extended to 22 July 1989, yet in June it was announced that the building of the new centre would not commence until 1990 and Jewish demands that the building be vacated by 22 July were ignored. In Poland there was increasing opposition to what was seen to be unreasonable demands being made on the sisters, and an increasing opinion – especially in Oswiecim – that they should stay put. In this context, the American Orthodox Rabbi, Avraham Weiss, led a group of seven dressed in prison uniforms on 14 July 1989 into the walled grounds of the convent and demanded that the nuns leave immediately. The protesters were ejected by workmen at the site – violently claimed Weiss. Two days later Weiss returned. His direct action provoked strong responses from both Catholic and Jewish organisations, as well as the world press.

The extended deadline for relocation – of 22 July – passed in the midst of the controversy over Weiss's actions, with the sisters staying put. In early August, one of the signatories of the original Geneva Agreement, Cardinal Macharski, issued a statement which stated that the relocation to the new centre would no longer be taking place. His words prompted new protest, as it appeared that the Catholic side was reneging on their 1987 agreement. Jewish groups called on the Pope to intervene over the heads of the local Church authorities. During August and September 1989 the temperature of the whole debate rose quite considerably – on the back of the provocative Weiss action – with Cardinal Glemp accusing Jews of anti-Polonism, and Israeli Prime Minister Itshak Shamir claiming that 'Poles imbibe anti-Semitism with their mothers' milk'[15]. In this atmosphere of accusation and counter-accusation, the Pope intervened and announced on 19 September 1989 that the Convent would be relocated to a centre to be financed by the Vatican. In 1993, the relocation of the sisters finally took place.

What the long-running Carmelite controversy pointed to, was just how important 'Auschwitz' had become. In particular, the controversy pointed to the fact that 'Auschwitz' has come to mean a lot more than simply the physical remains of the camp complex. What was being contested during the controversy was less ownership and use of the physical fabric of the camp, and more ownership and use of the 'brandname' 'Auschwitz'. As the discussions at Geneva revealed, this 'brandname' 'Auschwitz' had become – and was accepted as becoming – the symbol of the murder of all six million Jews and not simply the 900,000 or so who had died in the place of Auschwitz-II.

This mythical 'Auschwitz' – which stands as *the* symbol of the Holocaust – does draw upon the historical camps in Oswiecim, but pays scant regard to the historical complexity of the wartime group of camps called Auschwitz. While the wartime Auschwitz was a network of around forty satellite camps and three main camps – Auschwitz-I, Auschwitz-II (Auschwitz-Birkeneau) and Auschwitz-III (Auschwitz-Monowitz) – which differed in both size and function, the mythical 'Auschwitz' is a single entity which draws upon elements from all of these camps. In particular, it draws from two of them – Auschwitz-I and Auschwitz-II – in creating an imaginary 'Auschwitz' divorced from geographical realities. Auschwitz-I – the 'tourist Auschwitz' today – was both a prison camp and the administrative headquarters for the whole Auschwitz network of camps. Here, the prisoners were predominantly Polish intellectuals and political prisoners and Soviet POWs. The larger labour and death camp of Auschwitz-II – the 'other Auschwitz' today – was a place where predominantly Jews were taken. Those deemed 'unfit' for labour were gassed on arrival and the remainder kept at Auschwitz-II or taken to Auschwitz-III. This third camp – the 'forgotten Auschwitz' today – was a labour camp for the IG Farben works. The mythical 'Auschwitz' tends to obliterate or downplay these different geographies and collapse the distinct elements of the wartime complex of camps called Auschwitz into one imaginary 'Auschwitz'. As Isabel Wollaston notes, 'historically, Auschwitz may have consisted of a number of camps fulfilling a variety of functions. Symbolically, it stands as one undifferentiated mass. Such symbolism seeks to explain the significance of the history'.[16] At the end of the twentieth century, 'Auschwitz' has become so much more than simply a place, it is 'a place of the mind, an abstraction, a haunted idea'.[17]

It is that 'Auschwitz' – as 'a place of the mind' rather than a place of history – which has emerged as virtually synonymous with the 'Holocaust'. The filmic 'Auschwitz' shown to us in *Sophie's Choice*, for example, is a single mythical 'Auschwitz' constructed from its constituent elements. 'Sophie's Auschwitz' is not only an amalgam of different places, but also an amalgam of the different chronological periods of Auschwitz. It combines the landscape of Auschwitz-II as it would have been at the time of the story, plus the later landscape of Auschwitz-II once the rail tracks went directly into the camp, as well as combining the landscape of both Auschwitz-I and Auschwitz-II. 'Sophie's Auschwitz' is an imaginary 'Auschwitz' where it is possible to walk past Block 25 (in Auschwitz-II) on the way to the Commandant's House (in Auschwitz-I).

And that eclectic mix of Auschwitz-I and Auschwitz-II is recreated also at the United States Holocaust Memorial Museum. Here, we are taken through a virtual 'Auschwitz', which combines a casting of the *Arbeit macht frei* gateway from Auschwitz-I with a barrack from Auschwitz-II, which houses a model of the gas chambers and crematoria of Auschwitz-II. It is essentially a repeating of the amalgam of Auschwitz-I and Auschwitz-II on offer at the 'tourist Auschwitz'. There I was taken on a tour which commenced with the *Arbeit macht frei* gateway, and ended at a gas chamber and crematoria complete with tell-tale chimney. And I felt a sense of *déja vu* as I repeated that imaginary journey in Washington, DC, four years later. 'From *Arbeit macht frei* to the gas chambers' sums up what this mythical 'Holocaust' 'Auschwitz' is about, but it confuses the complex history and geography of the physical network of camps called Auschwitz.

It might seem pedantic to point out this blurring of the distinct places of Auschwitz-I and Auschwitz-II within the imaginary 'Auschwitz', but the result of the blurring of the distinct camps is that the distinct camp populations, too, become blurred. The creation of a single imaginary 'Auschwitz' which results in the homogenisation of the 'Auschwitz prisoner' tends to downplay the particularity of those imprisoned and murdered in the individual camps. For the Auschwitz complex as a whole, it is estimated that 960,000 Jews, 70-75,000 Poles, 21,000 Gypsies, 15,000 Soviet POWs and 10-15,000 other nationals died. The majority of Poles were killed at Auschwitz-I, and the majority of Jews and Gypsies at Auschwitz-II. And yet a single symbolic 'Auschwitz' can be – and has been – constructed as a symbol which denies either the Jewishness or the Polishness of the victims of Auschwitz. This can be seen in the holding of separate Jewish and Polish ceremonies at the fiftieth anniversary celebrations of the liberation of the camp, after Polish refusals to acknowledge the Jewishness of the victims of Auschwitz. While Polish President Lech Walesa spoke at commemorations held in Kraków on 26 January without mentioning Jews, the survivor and writer Elie Wiesel spoke of the Jewish victims at a counter-ceremony held at Auschwitz-II. After discussions that evening, both Walesa and Wiesel did visit Auschwitz-I and II together the next day, when Walesa did speak of the particular suffering of Jews. However, the separate ceremonies the day before, pointed to continuing disagreement over what 'Auschwitz' should represent.

While a symbol such as 'Auschwitz' can sustain multiple and competing meanings, the competition between 'Polish-Catholic' and Jewish claims can be seen to have been pushed to breaking point in the last two decades. The Carmelite Convent controversy was clearly the climax of this history of contestation. And thus it is perhaps not surprising that in the midst of that incident, an exasperated Rabbi Weiss even went so far as to call for 'Auschwitz' to be given over to the Israelis. His argument – in August 1989 – was that, 'if Israel does not administer and supervise Auschwitz it will be impossible to preserve the unique message of this place where the Nazis attempted to liquidate the Jews'.[18] For Weiss, Israel was perceived to own the 'Holocaust', and this meant that Israel should also own the supreme symbol of the 'Holocaust' – 'Auschwitz'. In arguing this, he went even further than his earlier justification of breaking into the grounds of the convent on the grounds that it was an international site belonging to all and his invasion could not amount to trespassing. In saying this, he was no doubt drawing on the 1979 transformation of the site from a Polish state museum to the status of a UNESCO World Heritage Site. The physical site is in a Southern Polish town called Oswiecim. While there has been, since 1990, an International Council of the Auschwitz-Birkeneau State Museum, the question of competing Jewish and Polish ownership of 'Auschwitz' remains far from being resolved.

A solution to the impasse between Jewish and 'Polish' claims upon this site, was suggested by Cardinal Glemp in the context of the Carmelite convent controversy. His suggestion was to differentiate between the two 'Auschwitzs': 'Oswiecim-Auschwitz, where mostly Poles and other nations perished' and 'Brzezinka-Birkeneau a few kilometres distant, where mostly Jews perished'.[19] This proposal is dismissed by Isabel Wollaston on the grounds that 'while such a distinction can be drawn historically, it plays no part in the symbolic meaning of Auschwitz. If Auschwitz is viewed symbolically as one undifferentiated mass, then such historical distinctions are – in one sense – irrelevant'.[20] Wollaston seems to assume that the symbol 'Auschwitz' is like a genie which has been loosed from its lamp, and will now never return. However, as I have suggested, there was nothing inevitable about the emergence of 'Auschwitz' as symbol of the 'Holocaust'. Moreover, that symbol (like all symbols) is not necessarily fixed, but rather open to reworking.

In the light of that, Glemp's solution does seem to be in many ways attractive. His separation of Auschwitz-I and II is something advocated by the historians Robert Van Pelt and Deborah Dwork, who assert that 'Auschwitz-I needs to be recognised as a central site for Poles in particular and Christians in general' and Auschwitz-Birkeneau as the place of memory of the 'Holocaust'. To this end, they have proposed plans for 'a permanent exhibition to present the history of the *Shoah*' on the site of the Canada – the storerooms used to house the belongings of prisoners – at Auschwitz-II.[21]

Nonetheless, the danger of the binary division of 'Auschwitz' into a 'Polish Auschwitz' and a 'Jewish Auschwitz' is that it excludes the other 'victims' such as gypsies and Soviet POWs. What is needed is – despite Wollaston's dismissal as 'irrelevant' – a new concern with the historical Auschwitz in all its complexity. Van Pelt and Dwork point in the right direction when they suggest that in a new Auschwitz-I 'the didactic labels and informational plaques cannot collapse the history of Auschwitz-I and II'.[22] This is to retreat from the mythical 'Auschwitz' and reconsider the historical and geographical complexities of the camps called Auschwitz. Such a return to the historical Auschwitz is not only a way of dealing with present conflict, but also of engaging with the claims of revisionists.

Given that the generic 'Holocaust' and 'Auschwitz' have become almost synonymous, when Holocaust deniers attack the reality of the Holocaust they attack 'Auschwitz' as one of their first marks. 'Auschwitz' is so central to the myth of the 'Holocaust', as to be – along with Anne Frank's diary – a prime target. In particular, it is the gas chambers and crematoria of Auschwitz-II which have come under the scrutiny of a host of self-styled 'chemical experts'. One of the dubious methods adopted by revisionists has been to read back into the past of Auschwitz from the present 'Auschwitz'. They dismiss the Auschwitz of the past. Thus for example, the writer David Cole points to the questionable post-war reconstruction of the gas chamber and crematorium in 'tourist Auschwitz' (which is mostly Auschwitz-I), and notes quite

> ... accurately, that the crematorium chimney is a freestanding structure, in no way connected to the ovens. One entrance to the gas chamber does not have a door, or even any evidence of hinges. Inside the chamber, a tight rectangular space with a low ceiling, there are marks where walls have obviously been removed. To one side, there are pipes where a bathroom once stood. In the centre of the room is a manhole with an iron cover.[23]

This becomes – for Cole – proof that the mass gassing of Jews did not take place at this site.

Such a shoddy reconstruction can hardly be taken as proof that people were never gassed at Auschwitz, but such an embarrassingly problematic reconstruction doesn't help when countering revisionist claims that 'Auschwitz' is little more than a post-war Polish creation. This gas chamber and crematoria at the 'tourist Auschwitz' – which Cole points to as inauthentic – has a twisted history. Created as an experimental gas chamber in September 1941, it was converted by the Germans into an air-raid shelter in 1943. After liberation, it was destroyed by the Soviet Army, and then reconstructed as a gas chamber and crematoria – rather badly – by the Polish authorities in 1948. In what was clearly a merging of the separate histories of Auschwitz-I and Auschwitz-II at the single site of 'tourist Auschwitz', the experimental gas chamber and

> ... crematorium-I was reconstructed to speak for the history of the incinerators at Birkeneau ... A chimney, the ultimate symbol of Birkeneau, was re-created; four hatched openings in the roof, as if for pouring Zyklon B into the gas chambers

below, were installed, and two of the three furnaces were rebuilt using original parts.[24]

In many ways then, the 'tourist Auschwitz' is little more than a post-war Polish creation. However, the historical Auschwitz was not. But the danger is that in constructing a mythical 'Auschwitz', we distort the horrific reality of Auschwitz, and in its place create an 'Auschwitz' which is open to the attack of those who would deny that the Holocaust ever took place. Representing the complexities of the past in a ghoulish theme park for the present has consequences. The 'tourist Auschwitz' threatens to trivialise the past, domesticate the past, and ultimately jettison the past altogether.

As the 'heritage industry' does elsewhere, the 'Holocaust heritage industry' does not recover the original Auschwitz, but produces an 'Auschwitz-land' for the present from the Auschwitz of the past. All claims to authenticity of the mythical 'Auschwitz' are therefore open to question. As Dwork and Van Pelt point out, the museum does not include all of the physical territory that was Auschwitz-I, while making claims to authenticity. A large part of the wartime camp of Auschwitz-I was used after liberation as housing to alleviate the post-war shortage. When the museum was established, these sections of Auschwitz-I were excluded from 'Auschwitz-land'. Moreover, the landscape at tourist 'Auschwitz' is ambiguous as soon as you walk into the visitor centre. This building combines all of those tourist essentials – cafeteria, toilets, souvenir shop, cinema – and as Dwork and Van Pelt note, is assumed by visitors to have been built after the decision to turn the camp into a museum. In reality, it was constructed between 1942-1944 as the place where prisoners were 'registered, tattooed, robbed, disinfected, shaved'.[25] Auschwitz-I's place of prisoner initiation has silently become the place of 'Auschwitz-land's' tourist initiation. In a very real sense, the contemporary tourist enters Auschwitz unawares before he or she enters tourist 'Auschwitz': the two are far from synonymous.

The tourist's experience of 'Auschwitz-land' starts at the gate proclaiming *Arbeit macht frei*, and ends at the reconstructed Crematorium. It is a manipulated tour which makes claims to authenticity, and yet owes much more to the constructed symbol 'Auschwitz'. As I have suggested, that symbolic 'Auschwitz' is about an amalgam of the pre-1942 gateway of Auschwitz-I and the post-1942 gas chambers and crematoria of Auschwitz-II. At 'Auschwitz-land' the two are collapsed together in an attempt to present an authentic tourist experience. We are taken from the gate which was no longer the entry-way to the camp after 1942, past 'artificially aged' barbed wire replacing that which has long since perished,[26] to the crematoria which was reconstructed after the war to represent the crematoria at Auschwitz-II. Along the way, we are shown authentic relics – piles of shoes, cutlery, suitcases, glasses, prayer shawls, human hair and Zyklon B gas containers. These have been taken from Auschwitz-II, and placed behind glass in an Auschwitz-I barrack.

Walking through 'Auschwitz-land' we do not see an authentic past preserved carefully for the present. We don't experience the past as it really was, but experience a mediated past which has been carefully created for our viewing. And the end result is that 'the greater the intervention at historic places, the greater the manipulation. And the greater the manipulation, the greater the contrivance. As we stray from strict preservation, we come nearer to pure entertainment, and ultimately, the land of the imaginary'.[27] At 'Auschwitz-land' we perhaps unwittingly enter a 'Holocaust theme-park' rather than a 'Holocaust concentration camp'.

We visit a contrived tourist attraction, which offers that which a culture saturated with the myth of the 'Holocaust' expects to see. 'Auschwitz-land' both plays a part in creating and perpetuating that myth, and depends upon the myth for its continued popularity. A tour round 'Auschwitz-land' is about the consumption of a familiar landscape, where the tourist passes

> ... from glass case to glass case [in 'Auschwitz-land' full of shoes and eyeglasses] or ... in the streets, from famous square to historic fountain [in 'Auschwitz-land', from famous gateway to historic crematoria], they may scarcely look at the exhibit or the monument: their essential function is to read the guide-books, the explanatory cards or commemorative plaques, or to listen to hired cassettes [in 'Auschwitz-land', our tour guide]. What matters is what they are told they are seeing. The fame of the object becomes its meaning.[28]

At 'Auschwitz-land', it is the fame of the 'Holocaust' that becomes its meaning. And that is why we stop and stare at the display cases piled high with the possessions of the dead. Here the crowds of visitors are the greatest, and one jostles for a position to get as good a look as possible at these shoes, suitcases and piles of hair. These battered leather suitcases, with their hotel and railway labels from pre-war trips to the South of France, speak of the vibrancy of life before Auschwitz. And I can't help seeing them being packed for a trip to Nice a few summers before the trip to the Polish town of Oswiecim in the summer of 1944.

But the suitcases are empty now, and so are the shoes which are piled in a high mound in this room which speaks of absence. Looking around I begin to ask myself what those who are also visiting 'Auschwitz-land' make of these piles of suitcases, shoes and hair which we file past in silence. As the historian Paul Levine reflected back on his own visit to these cases,

> ... these are not easy things for someone to see, yet everyone there chose to look at these grotesque artefacts. I had seen much of this before – were they shocked? Upset? I wondered what they were thinking?[29]

It is a question also asked by Young:

> ... what has the viewer learned about a group of artefacts, about the history they represent? On exiting the museum, how do visitors grasp their own lives and surroundings anew in the light of a memoralised past? ... What precisely does the sight of concentration-camp artefacts awaken in viewers? Historical knowledge? A sense of evidence? Revulsion, grief, pity, fear? That visitors respond more directly to objects than to verbalised concepts is clear. But beyond affect, what does our knowledge of these objects – a bent spoon, childrens' shoes, crusty old striped uniforms – have to do with our knowledge of historical events?[30]

Do these authentic relics in and of themselves help us to interpret and understand the past? What are we thinking when we see these piles of shoes? Does the very physicality of them allow us to stop thinking, and simply get caught up in the voyeurism of the 'Auschwitz-land' equivalent of a 'chamber of horrors'? This 'chamber of horrors' can become divorced from its history and geography and simply exist to titillate. Or do these relics act – as the guidebook claims – as 'material evidence of crimes'?[31] Young notes that 'we must continue to remind ourselves that the historical meanings we find in museums may not be proven by artefacts, so much as generated by their organisation'.[32] As we see our own reflection in the glass case and the relics beyond, do we see 'evidence' of the 'Holocaust' or simply a collection of 'grotesque artefacts' of the 'Holocaust'? If we rely upon piles of shoes before us as proof that the 'Holocaust' happened, then what do we do when the last shred of leather has rotted away?

The 'relics' on display at 'Auschwitz-land' (and the United States Holocaust Memorial Museum) are perhaps particularly problematic.

As Young suggests, there is a danger of 'fetishisation' of artefacts and ruins which leads to the risk of 'mistaking the piece for the whole, the implied whole for unmediated history'.[33] The danger is that the shoes, the hair, the suitcases, the Zyklon B containers do our remembering for us. As long as the piles of shoes, hair, suitcases and Zyklon B containers lie in glass cases in 'Auschwitz-land', we remember the 'Holocaust'. We can say that the 'Holocaust' really happened: Here is the proof.

And yet the relics are decaying, as is the infrastructure of the camp itself. The human hair displayed at 'Auschwitz-land' has been washed and treated with naphthalene to keep moths from it. It is now so brittle that nothing has been done with it for the last twenty years. Hair tested by the Institute of Forensic Medicine in Kraków after the war was found to contain 'traces of cyanide, particularly the poisonous compound bearing the name Zyklon'.[34] But when the hair was retested in 1991, it was found that the traces of cyanide had been removed by the washing and treatment necessary to preserve this relic.

And that is where the danger lies if authentic relics are required to do our remembering for us. Indeed it could be that the existence of authentic relics allows us to forget and to distance ourselves from a past that lies heaped in glass cases. But those authentic relics perish, and demand preservation which removes something of their authenticity. If proof of the existence of gas chambers is to be verified by testing relics, then we are fast approaching a time when those relics will cease to be held to be certain evidence. In 1991 chemical traces of gas were still found in wall fragments from the gas chambers, but surely the natural process of weathering will erode those traces. Like the survivors, the relics and ruins of the past will fade away, and then all we are left with is the memory of the 'Holocaust' that was created for us, rather than one formed by ourselves. All we are left with is a 'Holocaust' created for tourist consumption and the end product of 'Holocaust tourism'.

'Auschwitz-land' is only one of a growing number of sites of 'Holocaust tourism'. With an estimated 700,000 visitors each year, 'Auschwitz-land' is one of Poland's most important tourist attractions. Other sites of Holocaust tourism attract similarly large numbers of visitors. Each year around 6 million visitors go to the six major 'Holocaust' museums in Amsterdam, Dachau, Jerusalem, Los Angeles, Oswiecim and Washington, DC. Ironically perhaps, the number of visitors to these top 'Holocaust tourist' sites each year equals the number of Jews murdered in Europe in the early 1940s. Each visitor no doubt has a variety of reasons for making their trip, and those reasons vary from one visitor to another. For some there is a personal connection to the Holocaust, and the visit is made as a pilgrimage of sorts. For others, 'Holocaust tourism' is simply one facet of a broader genre of modern tourism: the tourism of 'black spots'.[35] These new tourist attractions are the sites of mass killings or the death of celebrities. The 'black spot' tourist visits 'Auschwitz-land' with its crematoria and gory collection of relics, along with visits to other 'black spots': the Bridge over the River Kwai, Graceland, the Junction of Highways 466 and 41 near Cholame, California where James Dean died in a car crash, the Texas Book Depository in Dallas from where Lee Harvey Oswald (supposedly) shot JFK, the site of John Lennon's assassination in New York, and the site of the car crash in a Paris underpass which killed Diana Princess of Wales. At the end of the twentieth century death tourism is big business. Graceland is the number one tourist attraction in Memphis with an estimated 700,000 visitors a year. The Texas Book Depository has become almost obligatory on any tourist's trip to Dallas. There is a fascination with the sites of 'significant' deaths.

While it might seem rather banal – if not sacrilegious – to suggest that part of the popularity of 'Auschwitz-land' lies in its being a site of 'significant' mass death, there can be little doubt that an element of voyeurism is central to 'Holocaust tourism'. It is the ultimate rubbernecker's experience of passing by and gazing at someone else's tragedy. In visiting the sites of death we are afforded a degree of titillation, albeit titillation camouflaged by more 'worthy' reasons for visiting. That sense of titillation found in encountering the 'Holocaust', is commented on by Israel Charny in his book on genocide. He recalls reading Simon Wiesenthal's book *The Murderers Among Us* and noting down:

> All of us must know how depraved men [sic.] can be so that we can fight the madness around us ... and in us ... The reading becomes exciting ... One murderous incident follows another ... My excitement mounts ... It is almost a sexual feeling ... I flow into the next account of a killing and become one with the murderer ... Part of me still says this could never be me ... But I am increasingly excited, and it is almost as if I am experiencing myself as one of the killers whom I swore I could never be.[36]

There are surely mixed motives in visiting 'Auschwitz' just as much as there are in encountering the 'Holocaust' in a book or film.

I like to think that I went to 'Auschwitz' with the loftier intentions of the 'pilgrim'. Visiting the museum centred on the former camp of Auschwitz-I – the place I dub 'Auschwitz-land' – was for me like visiting any other museum, albeit one with horrific exhibits. However, at Auschwitz-II, I was a 'pilgrim' walking along the ramp where 437,000 Hungarian Jews arrived during the late spring and early summer of 1944.

Back in my hotel, I reflected on Jonathan Webber's reflections on 'The Future of Auschwitz'. As my own jarring experience of visiting what felt to me like two rather different 'Auschwitzs' confirmed, Auschwitz is a place which

> ... means many different things at the same time. Auschwitz is ... a museum, a place that tourists come to, on their own or in guided tours. But Auschwitz is also one vast cemetery, a place of pilgrimage, where people come to lay flowers, light candles, say their prayers, observe their silences – at the ruins of the gas chambers, at the fields where human ashes were dumped, at the wall of executions, at the large international monument that has been erected.[37]

And that problematic duality of roles has meant, and continues to mean, that 'Auschwitz' is not simply a symbol contested by 'Poles' and Jews, but a site contested by 'pilgrims' and 'tourists'.

That contestation between 'pilgrim' and 'tourist' is not unique to 'Auschwitz-land'. It is a more general feature of death sites. The distinction between 'pilgrims' and 'tourists' is recognised both by visitors to the war graves from the First and Second World Wars, and by the tour operators who take them there. One writer has estimated that around one quarter of those who went from Britain on battlefield tours in 1991 were self-defined 'pilgrims' rather than simply 'tourists'.[38] And at Graceland, the thousands of 'pilgrims' who take part in a candlelit vigil on 16 August, the anniversary of Elvis Presley's death, are clearly distinguishable from the casual 'tourist'. They leave 'votive offerings' at the grave of Elvis Presley, which 'run the gamut from hand-scribbled notes and lone flowers to elaborate posterboard collages and box dioramas depicting key scenes in Elvis's life or explaining to the world how much Elvis meant to the pilgrim in question'.[39] At 'Auschwitz-land', 'pilgrims' light candles throughout the camp on All Saints Day (1 November), and especially at the Wall of Death and the cell of Maximilian Kolbe at Block 11 in Auschwitz-I. Visiting dignitaries leave wreaths here or at the monument in Auschwitz-II. Jewish survivors and relatives of victims return to Auschwitz-II to say *kaddish*.

These 'pilgrims' to 'Auschwitz-land' share the site with 'tourists' who come with differing expectations. Jon Ronson notes that on his visit to the museum at Auschwitz he saw a tourist wearing a *Megadeath* T-shirt: 'A man who should have thought more carefully, I think, when he got dressed that morning' he ruefully comments.[40] As Ronson observed, the dress and behaviour of the 'tourist' can come into conflict with that of the 'pilgrim'. This conflict emerged during the course of the May 1990 Yarnton meeting of Jewish intellectuals to reflect on the future of Auschwitz. Young reported back that

> ... at one point, after viewing slides of boisterous tourists, teenagers munching on ice cream and candy among the barracks at Auschwitz-I, one of the British participants demanded a dress and behaviour code. 'No way, ' shot back an incredulous American. 'How are we going to force stuffy Western modes of dress on seven hundred thousand tourists a year, from all over the world? How are these tourists supposed to dress?'[41]

Everyone comes to 'Auschwitz' with differing expectations, yet walks through the exhibits at 'Auschwitz-land' together. Reflecting back on his visit to this ambiguous place, historian Paul Levine describes

> ... walking alongside a grandfatherly type, I heard him ask his fellow tour members if they thought the day's schedule permitted shopping that afternoon. His companions seemed equally concerned about the time – and my mind reeled. Is that what most concerns the average visitor at the end of their visit? How, why, do normal people contemplate the importance of buying souvenirs for their grandchildren back home while still in the shadow of Auschwitz?[42]

At the end of the twentieth century, 'Auschwitz' is both a site of mass tourism and a site of pilgrimage. Indeed, as the site has assumed an international significance – fuelled by the emergence of the myth of the 'Holocaust' – these tourists-cum-pilgrims come from further afield. The number of Polish visitors has declined, while the number of visitors from overseas – particularly from Germany, the United States and Israel – has increased. In part this is a result of the changes in the former Warsaw Pact countries. In 1989, the coaches of teenagers from East Germany stopped coming to 'Auschwitz' and in the early 1990s trips to 'Auschwitz' ceased to be a compulsory part of a Polish child's schooling. In their place, came Western 'Holocaust' tourists and pilgrims.

That 'Auschwitz' has assumed a primary role as a site of 'Holocaust' pilgrimage became clear in 1996 when there was uproar following the revelation that Queen Elizabeth II would be making a state visit to Poland without visiting 'Auschwitz'. The Board of Jewish Deputies chief executive Neville Nagler expressed surprise at what he saw to be 'an omission ... When heads of state come to England, they lay wreaths at the tomb of the Unknown Soldier in Westminster Abbey; and in Poland they lay wreaths at Auschwitz'.[43] And the historian David Cesarani spoke in similar terms of his astonishment that, 'the Queen is not making the 40-minute drive from Kraków to Auschwitz. It has been an obligatory place of pilgrimage for all visiting heads of state in memory of the Polish victims of the Holocaust as much as the Jewish'.[44] In the end, the Queen laid a wreath at the *Umschlagplatz* in Warsaw, which was the site of Jewish deportations from the city. However, the *Umschlagplatz* was not 'Auschwitz'.

The shock expressed at the time of the Queen's visit to Poland was countered by the comments of the late Rabbi Hugo Gryn, himself a Hungarian Jew deported to Auschwitz in 1944. He expressed no surprise whatsoever that the Queen did not want to go to such a 'very unpleasant place'.[45] But that 'very unpleasant place' has become an increasingly popular site of pilgrimage for American Jews in particular, who engage in ' "negative sightseeing" tours of the sites of destruction of European Jewry'.[46] Indeed, one writer has suggested that 'for Jews, visiting the death camps of Poland [and Auschwitz in particular] has become obligatory, as if there were no other way to really know the recent past'.[47] Such trips have become a secular rite of passage for the secular Jewish teenager. Thousands have taken part in the 'March of the Living' pilgrimages to Europe's death camps, and thousands more in school and youth group organised tours. In the manner of ancient pilgrimage, in which sites were to be seen in a certain order with accompanying rituals, the 'Holocaust' pilgrims from the contemporary United States follow almost identical pilgrimages, in an almost identical order. First comes 'Auschwitz', then comes 'Israel'. First comes 'defeat', then comes 'victory'. This is a pilgrimage of the 'Judaism of Holocaust and Redemption' which Neusner suggests is the dominant 'Judaism' in modern America, and which Spielberg takes us on in *Schindler's List*. It is pilgrimage that makes sense of the past, and offers a happy ending in the state of Israel. And yet Israel remains – for the American Jew – a place to visit, rather than a place to live.

The pilgrimage to 'Auschwitz' and then on to Israel is one which is powerful in its symbolism. The historian Jack Kugelmass cites the reflections of one such pilgrim:

> Tonight we are going to Israel. Before I came here I had thought I was going on this trip to see Poland. I was happy about going to Israel, but I honestly felt that the time we would spend there wouldn't be very meaningful to me since I have been there several times before. But as everyone was running around the hotel, dragging suitcases and completely hyper, the thought of going to Israel began to lift my spirits, and pretty soon I was jumping out of my skin with excitement like everybody else.
>
> Every other time I've gone to Israel, I have simply visited as a tourist. But after being in Poland all week, I really wanted to go to Israel – because of a feeling I'd experienced the entire time we were there. Have you ever felt so unwelcome somewhere you could taste it in your mouth? Have you ever felt as though there was nothing left for you in a certain place, so much that everywhere you looked you could see only desolation? Have you ever walked through a graveyard and known there would never be anything else? I was excited to go to Israel because I needed to look around without seeing only death, to pull myself out of the ashes and out of my own despair. On other trips to Israel, I have always been only a tourist. This time, I was going as a survivor.[48]

That kind of reaction can be seen over and over again, and is consciously looked for in the very ordering of the pilgrimage.

'Auschwitz' has become the sacred space of a secular religion, and pilgrimage there has become 'a secular ritual, one that confirms who they are as Jews, and perhaps, even more so, as North American Jews'.[49] For an American Jew, the 'Holocaust' and 'Auschwitz' are powerful ethnic markers, which many have pointed to as taking the place of traditional Judaism for an increasingly secular generation. Lopate reflects how he

> ... first began to notice the usurpation of the traditional Passover service by Holocaust worship at a large communal seder in Houston, about 1982 ... For many of the people at that seder in Texas, the Holocaust was the heart of their faith; it was what touched them most deeply about being Jewish ... The table conversation turned to accounts of pilgrimages to Buchenwald and Bergen-Belsen and Auschwitz, package tours

organised by United Jewish Appeal. The ancient Jewish religion was all but forgotten beside the lure of the concentration camp universe.[50]

It is surely ironic – as Kugelmass suggests – if American Jews feel their most Jewish when walking through 'Auschwitz'. How ironic that this place where hundreds of thousands of assimilated European Jews were taken because they had been defined as Jews in the Nuremberg Laws, has now become the place where hundreds of thousands of assimilated American Jews go to rediscover their Jewishness.

But perhaps more ironic still is that for a number of survivors, 'Auschwitz' is seen as a potential burial site. As the Deputy Director of the Auschwitz museum told Timothy Ryback in 1993

> ... recently a number of Holocaust survivors have contacted us and asked that their remains be buried at Birkeneau ... Many of these people lost their entire families here – mothers, fathers, grandparents, siblings. We understand their desire to have their remains interred here. Birkeneau is a cemetery, but not a cemetery where you can conduct funerals.[51]

A symbolic funeral of sorts was held there in 1988, when the Israeli government minister Avraham Scharir made a visit to Auschwitz, to lay 'a little sack of earth from the Holy Land' as 'a symbolic gesture in honour of the ashes of the millions who could have no grave, whose ashes and bones were strewn among foreign fields.[52] In taking the a symbolic handful of earth from Israel to this place, Scharir reasserted the connection between Auschwitz and Israel which both Steven Spielberg and the organisers of the March of the Living articulate. It is a connection which is made in the other direction through the burial of ashes from Auschwitz at Israel's shrine to the 'Holocaust': Yad Vashem. And it is a connection which is highly politicised within contemporary Israel as Avraham Scharir self-consciously reflected on his return. His visit had reminded him of the significance of this place which represents the 'Holocaust' to contemporary Israel and therefore he urged that, 'every boy and every girl must visit Auschwitz'. And why? Because after visiting this field in Southern Poland, Scharir's assumption was that they would draw the same kind of conclusions as he did:

> They will return permeated with the feeling of the necessity of a homeland. We must be a strong people in our homeland. We

must build up the state and increase its power. We need a strong army and a high national morale. We are obligated to stop all internal strife and superfluous parties. We are Jews, we have a common fate which offers an answer to all our problems in the present and in the future.[53]

But not everyone in contemporary Israel draws the same kind of lessons from 'Auschwitz' and the 'Holocaust' that Scharir did at the end of the 1980s.

5

# Yad Vashem

We weren't really that hungry, so we settled for cheese *borekas* and
cups of sweet black tea from mass catering cups. The cafeteria was
crowded, but we found a place amidst tables of Israeli soldiers on
national service. The 'no smoking' signs on the cafeteria walls didn't
stop them smoking, and their recently completed tour of the
Holocaust exhibition and Children's Memorial didn't stop them
talking excitedly and laughing loudly. After a while they moved on, to
be replaced by a bus load of Pentecostal pastors from Florida and a
name-badge-wearing 'Christian tour' from the mid-West. This being
Sunday lunchtime, I suppose they had come from a church service in
the morning, and were going to be spending the afternoon here.

Yad Vashem is after all a compulsory place to visit, whether you
are a member of the Israeli Defence Force, an Israeli schoolchild or a
foreign tourist. Our guidebook had recommended visiting Yad
Vashem on a par with seeing the Western Wall, the Dome on the Rock
and the Church of the Holy Sepulchre. So we had left our guesthouse
in the Old City that morning in the pouring rain, waited at the bus
stop just outside of the Jaffa Gate, and taken the number 20 through
West Jerusalem and up past Mount Herzl to Yad Vashem. The woman
at the Information desk suggested that we buy a map of the museum
and memorial park, and then sent us off walking up the 'Avenue of
the Righteous Gentiles' to the museum. Making our way through this
grove of carob trees, we started our journey back to the 'Holocaust' as
we were meant to: in heroism. We walked between trees planted by
'righteous gentiles', past a boat in which Danish fishermen rowed
Jews to safety in neutral Sweden, and up to a square which celebrates the heroics of the Warsaw ghetto uprising in bronze. It is 'a
memory path' which – in the words of James Young – takes us 'from
Gentile to Jewish heroism, into the Warsaw Ghetto Square, bordered
by a reproduction of Rapoport's Ghetto Monument'.[1]

In his book *The Seventh Million*, the journalist Tom Segev sees the fact that we meet 'the righteous gentiles and the ghetto rebels, two exceptions in the history of the Holocaust, before learning anything of the extermination of the Jews' to be little more than the unintended consequence of 'improvisations and financial compromises'.[2] But, in fact, our initial encounter with heroism at Yad Vashem is clearly quite deliberate. Museums are not places for wandering aimlessly, but 'for "organized walking" in which an intended message is communicated in the form of a (more or less) directed itinerary'.[3] At Washington our 'directed itinerary' was to take us through the experience of liberation before starting us out on our 'Holocaust' journey. Here in Yad Vashem this 'directed itinerary' is one which starts with heroism. Far from 'righteous gentiles' and 'ghetto rebels' being exceptions in Yad Vashem's 'Holocaust', they are absolutely central to the plot. Starting as we mean to go on, we walk around this windswept hilltop site seeing through the eyes of 'Holocaust' heroes.

From its inception, Yad Vashem – 'The Memorial Authority for the Holocaust and Heroism' – was to be as much about 'heroism' as it was to be about 'martyrdom'. The 1953 founding legislation – passed unanimously by the Israeli Knesset – spoke first of the responsibility of the memorial authority to remember the dead and their destroyed communities, but it spoke in greater length of the need to remember Jewish heroism. Of its nine memorial objectives, three were concerned with remembering Jewish destruction, five with remembering Jewish 'heroism', 'fortitude' and 'struggle', and one with remembering the actions of 'high-minded Gentiles'.[4] 'Heroism' outnumbered 'destruction' two to one.

In placing such emphasis upon 'heroism', Yad Vashem reflected the common approach to the 'Holocaust' in the early years of the Israeli State. This emphasis upon heroism was one aspect of what Segev terms 'a kind of ideological-emotional compact' which 'arose spontaneously' in the early years of the State between native-born Israelis and the around 350,000 Holocaust survivors who had settled in Israel by the end of 1949. This compact operated on the assumption that 'the Holocaust has proven once again that the only solution to the Jewish problem was an independent state in Israel', that 'the rest of the world was hostile and had done nothing to save the Jews during the Holocaust', that Jewish heroism had been a central aspect of the Holocaust and that 'the less everybody talked about the Holocaust, the better'.[5]

What one sees in the early years of the Israeli state – as mentioned earlier – is a profoundly ambivalent relationship with the Holocaust.

On the one hand there was a recognition that the new state owed a considerable debt to the Holocaust, and yet on the other hand there was a sense in which the Holocaust was seen as the inevitable result of a shameful diasporic community which had turned its back on Zionism, and thus left itself vulnerable to persecution. There were therefore pressures within the newly founded state to forget the Holocaust, as much as to remember it. This pressure to forget may today appear somewhat surprising given the immense contemporary importance of the 'Holocaust' in Israel. It is difficult to escape the 'Holocaust' in modern Israel.

At the elite level, the Zionist leadership made little of the Holocaust past in their justification of the newly emerging Israeli State. After studying the positions held by the Zionist leadership in the late 1940s, the historians Jehuda Reinharz and Evyatar Friesel conclude that

> ... it is difficult to point to a direct influence of the Holocaust on the shaping of Zionist policy or the political behaviour of the Zionist leadership. The decision to change the strategic course of Zionist policy – to direct it to Jewish statehood, to build a strong American connection – was taken as a result of the 1939 White Paper.[6]

Thus the 'Holocaust' played a peripheral – rather than a central – role within political discourse in these early years of the State. While the 1948 Declaration of Independence did mention the 'Holocaust', it did not justify the new state solely – or even largely – in terms of the 'Holocaust'.

At the popular level, the 'Holocaust' was similarly peripheral – as mentioned earlier. Indeed, when the Second World War featured in Israeli popular culture during the late 1940s and early 1950s it was in terms of images of the glory of war, rather than images of the 'Holocaust'. For 'compared with the heroics of the war, the ordeal of the Holocaust seemed miserable, even repulsive. One could talk endlessly about the war, tell stories, wax enthusiastic about acts of bravery. But it was very difficult to talk about the Holocaust. People did not know how to handle the horror stories and did their best to avoid hearing them.'[7]

The only exceptions to this tendency to retreat into silence on the subject of the 'Holocaust', were the tales of heroism associated with the Warsaw ghetto uprising and the Jewish partisans. These tales were 'easier to understand, closer to the associational frameworks of a member of a youth movement in Palestine, and therefore more easily accepted as an object of identification' than the 'incomprehensible' and 'alien' world of the Holocaust'.[8]

This early ambivalence with regard to the 'Holocaust', reflects the wider ambivalence that Zionism felt in relationship to the Jewish past. This is something highlighted by Charles Liebman and Eliezer Don-Yehiya who reflect on the profound dilemma facing Zionism when confronted with the legacy of Jewish tradition:

> If Zionism is the heir to the Jewish tradition then by that definition it inherits a history and culture of passivity, self abnegation, humility, and a host of traits which Zionism seeks to negate. But if Zionism constitutes a revolt against the tradition, what is the basis of its legitimate right to speak on behalf of all Jews, to affirm the claims of Jewish history to the land of Israel?[9]

With regard to the specific dilemma that Zionism faced when considering the Holocaust past, a solution was found in the stressing of heroism in that past. Thus Zionist values could be read back into a past which was therefore transformed from 'passivity, self-abnegation' and 'humiliation' into a more suitably appropriate 'Zionist' past of heroism and resistance. This transformation enabled the new state to speak on behalf of all 'Holocaust' Jews, and thus to acknowledge the legacy owed to the European catastrophe. In practice this solution was achieved through the twinning of 'Holocaust' and 'heroism', which became 'the ideological basis for the memorial culture that developed over the years'.[10]

The Holocaust was to be remembered by the Israeli state – rather than forgotten – but it was to be remembered as *Shoah Vegurah* (destruction and heroism) rather than simply as 'Holocaust'. As Sidra Ezrahi reflects in a study of the use of the Holocaust in Hebrew literature, 'in order to incorporate the events of the holocaust into prevailing historical codes, emphasis was placed on instances of bravery and revolt'.[11] And it is this which explains our initial encounter with heroism at Yad Vashem. The site reflects the official telling of the Holocaust past. Walking into the Warsaw Ghetto Square on the start of our tour, we stand before 'the wall of remembrance' where a copy of Nathan Rapoport's sculpture 'The Ghetto Uprising' is placed a short way to the left of his relief 'The Last March'. Our eyes scan from right to left; from the relief set into the wall of red brick to the more dominant sculpture; from the deportations to the scene of ghetto resistance. In this square, where each year the televised annual ceremony which signals the beginning of the national

'Martyrs' and Heroes' Remembrance Day' takes place, the 'Holocaust' is remembered through the trope of the Warsaw ghetto.

In many ways, the geographical complexity of the Holocaust has been microscoped at the end of the twentieth century into two places which have assumed mythical proportions: 'Warsaw' and 'Auschwitz'. These two Polish towns have come – in the popular imagination – to represent the 'Holocaust'. One represents the ghetto experience characterised by the heroics of the uprising, while the other represents the concentration camps characterised by gas chambers and smoking crematoria chimneys. 'Warsaw' is about resistance and 'Auschwitz' is about destruction.

Both representations have been taken visually and physically to Jerusalem. 'Warsaw' is there in the red bricks along the far side of Warsaw Ghetto Square which 'symbolise the Ghetto walls',[12] in the copy of Rapoport's statue of the 'Warsaw Ghetto Uprising' and in Boris Saktsier's statue of 'Korczak and the Children of the [Warsaw] Ghetto'. Inside the historical museum that symbolism is made concrete through 'authentic' artefacts: we looked at three bricks from the Warsaw ghetto wall and walked on a floor covered in cobblestones from the Warsaw ghetto. 'Auschwitz' has also been taken to the hills of West Jerusalem: symbolically in Elsa Pollak's smoke-stack shaped pillar 'Auschwitz', and physically in the ashes from Auschwitz (and other camps) buried in the Hall of Remembrance. Here the words 'Auschwitz – Oswiecim' take the central place amongst the twenty-two principal concentration camps whose names are spelt out in tiles on floor.

While both feature in Yad Vashem as 'Holocaust' symbols, it is clearly 'Warsaw' – and heroic resistance – that rises physically and metaphorically above the destruction of 'Auschwitz'. In the memorial landscape of Yad Vashem, symbols of resistance tend to tower above destruction. And this privileging of Warsaw over Auschwitz at Yad Vashem reflects the wider privileging of heroism over destruction in Israeli society in the period prior to the Eichmann trial. It can be seen, for example, in the story Tom Segev tells of a young child survivor arriving at a kibbutz after the war, who was teased by the other kids. Segev relates how 'Yosika, as they called him maliciously, did not admit to his tormentors that his father had been killed at Auschwitz. His father died in the Warsaw ghetto uprising, he lied to them, and tried hard to be accepted'.[13] In the early years of Israel, a heroic death in the Warsaw ghetto uprising was preferred to being 'led like a lamb to the slaughter' to the gas chambers of Auschwitz. And that preference was clearly articulated at Yad Vashem. As James Young points out, Yad Vashem is a place 'where the memory of the heroes is concretised in presence, in thrusting vertical figures, an uprising of form', while 'the martyrs are generally recalled in their absence'.[14]

In talking of heroic 'thrusting vertical figures', Young hints at a gendering of memory at Yad Vashem. On the hills of Jerusalem, heroism is remembered as masculine and martyrdom as feminine, with the hard 'thrusting vertical' memory of heroism being contrasted with the soft, dark, hidden memory of martyrdom. Thus Buki Schwartz's 'The Pillar of Heroism' – dedicated to 'those who rebelled in the camps and ghettos, fought in the woods, the underground and with the Allied Forces, who braved their way *to Eretz Yisrael* and those who died sanctifying the name of God' – is a 21-metre-high polished steel pillar which dominates the surrounding landscape. Similarly, polished steel 'thrusting' upwards is used in Bernie Fink's 'Soldiers', Partisans' and Ghetto Fighters' Monument'. Here a steel blade bisects a six pointed star formed by six hexagonal granite blocks. The steel sword – which 'symbolises the fighting opposition to Nazis' – cuts through the six stone blocks which stand for the six million Jews murdered by the Nazis,[15] in a monument which is inscribed 'Glory be to the Jewish Soldiers and Partisans who fought against Nazi Germany'. It is self-consciously a monument in which resistance triumphs over destruction, and is described in the Yad Vashem guidebook in just such terms:

> Commemoration of the Holocaust – in our own generation as well as in those to come – involves recalling and mourning not only the six million Jews who perished, but also those Jewish soldiers, fighters of the Ghettos and the resistance movements who gave their lives to help smash the Nazi regime. It is, both of profound historical as well as educational importance, that the Jewish people in particular, and the world at large, fully understand the extent of Jewish participation in the final victory over the Nazis and that it be known and comprehended, that the Jews were not only victims, they were also among the victors.[16]

While resistance is celebrated in the open through the phallus, destruction tends to be hidden and remembered through the womb. This feminising and hiding of the memory of the martyr can be seen most clearly at the Children's Memorial, where a winding path leads to a dark chamber which forms the dramatic heart of the memorial with its reflected candle light. It is also present in the dark-cave like Hall of Remembrance and the recently completed sunken, maze-like

'Valley of the Communities' which was quarried out of the bedrock. Remembering the 'Holocaust Jew' at Yad Vashem is thus a remembering in gendered terms, which draws upon the 'common stereotype that depicted the Exile as weak, feminine, and passive, and the *yishuv* [Jewish settlement in Palestine prior to 1948] as strong, masculine, and active'.[17] Thus the 'martyrs' are portrayed as members of the 'feminine' Exile community, whereas the 'heroes' are included within the 'masculine' community of Israel.

This use of gendered architectural forms within Israel is not limited to Yad Vashem. It is something which Amos Elon points to in the 'Shrine of the Book'. For him 'no building in Israel is as clearly based upon the exploitation of anatomical shapes and erotic symbols',[18] as this structure which was built in the late 1960s to house the Dead Sea Scrolls. Here, Elon suggests,

> ... within the dome, the upward phallic thrust of an enormous, clublike structure is said to represent the national will to persist. This, the heart of the shrine, is reached through a dramatically unbalanced, off-centre arched tunnel, narrowed by tilted walls of rough stone. At the end of this passageway, which is dark and cavernous and can only remind one of the fallopian tubes leading to the womb, is the domed rotunda in which the scrolls are displayed behind plated glass.[19]

Reading this description of reaching the heart of the 'Shrine of the Book', is to be reminded of the dark journey to the 'womb' of the 'Children's Memorial' at Yad Vashem, where we hear the names of the child victims of the Holocaust being read out. These children, because of 'their innocence, their unrealised potential, and as symbols of the next, never-to-be-born generation ... continue to represent the victim-ideal'.[20] At this central shrine in Yad Vashem, the concept of 'victim' is not only construed in gendered terms, but also in terms of age.

Although not completed until June 1987, the plans for the 'Children's Memorial' had been drawn up a decade earlier by the Israeli architect Moshe Safdie. However, it was only when the American Holocaust survivors Abraham and Edita Spiegel stepped in with the close to $2 million dollars required to construct the memorial, that building work could start. At Yad Vashem, there is considerable reliance upon the money of private donors for the funding of the plethora of new memorial structures. However, this reliance on private donations presents a number of problems at what is essentially a state museum and memorial park. Thus, for example, in the case of the 'Children's Memorial, the Spiegels' desire was that the whole structure would be named after their son Uziel who was killed at Auschwitz. Yet this was seen as giving the memory of one child – with wealthy parents – a place of special importance, rather than remembering the one and a half million child victims equally. In the end a form of compromise was reached whereby the name of the memorial was to be inclusive and yet Uziel Spiegel was to be given a position of prominence in an inscription and stone relief at the entrance. In effect, what we have is a memorial to all the child-victims of the 'Holocaust', but especially to Uziel Spiegel.

This sense of dual memory – the general and the specific – is reflected elsewhere at Yad Vashem as the compromise solution to the overly specific requests of private donors. Thus, the newly constructed 'Memorial to the Deportees' is a memorial to all the victims of the 'Holocaust', but it is particularly a memorial to the parents, brothers and sister of the donors. In effect what you see at Yad Vashem is a privatisation of 'Holocaust' memory, whereby the few are remembered by surviving relatives at this site to the many. And this is hardly surprising. It is perfectly understandable that Mr and Mrs Spiegel wish to remember their son Uziel rather than the more abstract 'one and a half million'. And it is perfectly understandable that the Merczynski brothers wish to remember their parents Szyja and Etla, their brothers Jidel and David and their sister Chaja rather than the more abstract 'six million'. They are seeking to remember family members, rather than a historical event – 'the Holocaust'. And yet they are seeking to do that at a site which is more than a collection of memorials to individuals and families. And this is where the sense of conflict between the specific requests of donors and the more general mission of Yad Vashem results.

Walking through Yad Vashem it is striking how this memorial site has evolved over the course of the last four decades. And over the last two decades in particular, private money has determined that evolution. Initially, the funding for Yad Vashem was provided by the state, and came in large part from the reparations paid by the West German government. This money paid for the earliest structures on the site – the administrative, library and archival buildings which were completed in 1957. These were followed by the Hall of Remembrance in 1961, the first plantings of the Avenue of the Righteous in 1962, the Historical Museum and the Warsaw Ghetto Square in 1973, Schwartz's Pillar of Heroism in 1974, the Art Museum in 1981, the ground-breaking for 'The Valley of the Destroyed Communities' in 1983 – completed in the 1990s – and Fink's Soldiers', Partisans' and Ghetto Fighters' Monument in 1985. More recently, single private donors have funded the Children's

Memorial – completed in 1987 – and the Memorial to the Deportees – completed a decade later. And it is private money which will fund the revamping of the Historical Museum and entrance to the museum in the planned Yad Vashem 2001 project.

Over the course of the forty or so years of development, another shift is discernible in the representation of the 'Holocaust' at Yad Vashem. As I have suggested, in the early days of state-building, 'the country wanted heroes' and 'stories of glory',[21] and thus the official telling of the 'Holocaust' made concrete at Yad Vashem offered an encounter with 'heroism' perhaps more than it did an encounter with 'martyrdom'. And yet more recently, the memorial architecture of Yad Vashem has laid less stress upon 'heroism' and more upon 'martyrdom'. The newer monuments – such as the Valley of the Communities and the Memorial to the Deportees (both constructed in the 1990s) – are concerned much more with 'destruction and rebirth', rather than with 'destruction and heroism'.

This shift away from a concern with heroism can be seen as taking place in Israel from the 1960s and 1970s onwards, and in particular in the aftermath of the 1973 Yom Kippur War. The war in 1973 had a profound impact upon Israeli national consciousness, with high losses – more than 2,500 dead in one month – leading to a questioning of traditional images of national heroism. The result was – Deputy Chief Education Officer in the Israeli Army, Ehud Praver argued – a rebellion against the myth of 'Holocaust heroism' and an increased identifying with 'those very people whom we had despised': the Holocaust Jews who had gone like lambs to the slaughter. He goes on to suggest that,

We rebelled against the Resistance ... We saw it as the great lie we had unmasked in the Yom Kippur War. Until then we believed in the pairing of the words Holocaust and heroism and identified ourselves with the heroism. The war made us realise the meaning of the Holocaust and the limitations of heroism'.[22]

After the reality of the 1973 war, myths of 'heroism' were harder to sustain. Thus

... for some Israelis, especially since the Yom Kippur War, it is Jewish suffering and the indifference of the world to that suffering which evokes an identification with the Holocaust, rather then the physical resistance or any other acts of courage by the Jews.[23]

That broader background of changing attitudes towards the Holocaust provides the context within which the physical environment of Yad Vashem has evolved. 'Heroism' is still present at Yad Vashem, and is perhaps the most surprising feature for the non-Israeli visitor. Yet, the importance of 'heroism' has been balanced with new concerns. That this is the case, can be seen from a conversation which Tom Segev had with Yad Vashem's director Yitzhak Arad, where 'Arad said something that a head of Yad Vashem would not have said in the past; as far as he was concerned, the term heroism could be done without; Holocaust is sufficient'.[24] Segev himself goes further and suggests that 'after five wars, Israelis no longer needed this heroic myth to cancel out the shame of the Holocaust'.[25]

Arad's words reflect the changing attitude towards the 'Holocaust' in Israeli society. Instead of a myth of heroism, a new myth has been developed 'to cancel out the shame of the Holocaust': the myth of 'rebirth'. In essence what you see at Yad Vashem today – being a conglomeration of official Israeli memory from the course of the last forty years – is the old myth of 'heroism' overlaid with the newer myth of 'rebirth'. It is thus not simply a place of *Shoah Vegurah* (destruction and heroism), but also a place of *Shoah Vetekumah* (destruction and rebirth) and *Shoah Vegeulah* (destruction and redemption). And in this it reflects other Israeli 'Holocaust' museums. As Young comments more generally on Holocaust museums in Israel, they deliver 'this era ... to us primarily through images of resistance and heroism, references to martyred children and the survivors' new lives in *Eretz* Israel'.[26]

What is perhaps surprising to the non-Israeli visitor, is that the message of 'destruction' alone is most noticeable by its absence. Even in the new Memorial to the Deportees which at first glance appears to be primarily about destruction, there is a tale of redemption. The architect Moshe Safdie (who also designed the Children's' Memorial) has placed an 'authentic' box car of the type used for transporting Jews (given to Yad Vashem by the Polish government in 1990 – they gave one to the United States Holocaust Memorial Museum the year before) onto rail tracks that stretch out from the hill-top of Yad Vashem. The tracks are severed, and the cattle car perches almost on the edge of the world. This is not a hidden memorial to destruction, but one which is right out in the open – a cattle car perched in the air. And that visibility is I think because of the sense in which this memorial sees beyond the destruction, to the rebirth beyond. A leaflet reflecting on this new memorial speaks in just such terms explicitly:

*Although* symbolising the journey towards annihilation and oblivion, facing as it does the hills of Jerusalem, the memorial *also* conveys the hope and the gift of life of the State of Israel and Jerusalem, eternal capital of the Jewish People [italics added].[27]

What is particularly striking about this reflection, is why the need was felt to use the word 'although' in almost an apologetic way. If this memorial had been constructed in Europe or America, I think the 'although' would most likely be absent. The memorial would symbolise 'the journey towards annihilation and oblivion' period. Yet this is not a memorial in Europe or America, but one 'facing ... the hills of Jerusalem'. And because it both faces the 'hills of Jerusalem' and is built into one of those hills, the word 'although' is used, and the memorial becomes one which symbolises something more than simply 'the journey towards annihilation and oblivion'. The memorial has an 'also' to it: the 'also' of the symbolism of 'the hope and the gift of life of the State of Israel and Jerusalem, eternal capital of the Jewish People'. Those words 'although ... also' can perhaps be seen as hedging around the official Israeli telling of the destruction of the 'Holocaust'.

It is there in the Warsaw Ghetto Square, where Rapoport's 'The Last March' is hedged around with the 'although ... also' of Rapoport's 'Warsaw ghetto uprising'. It is there in Naftali Bezem's Memorial Wall, which stands at the entrance to the historical exhibit. The panel 'destruction' is placed alongside the 'although ... also' of 'resistance', 'immigration to Israel' and 'rebirth'. It is there in the historical exhibit, where the sections on 'Anti-Jewish Policy in Germany 1933-1939', 'The Ghettos 1939-1941' and 'Mass Murder 1941-1945' are followed by the 'although ... also' of 'Jewish Resistance 1941-1945' and 'Liberation and Aftermath 1945 ...' In the museum, we are taken from the darkness of the 'destruction' up through a sloping, dark tunnel – 'symbolising the sewers which served as hiding places and escape routes for Jewish fighters in the Warsaw Ghetto'[28] – into the light of a display dedicated to Jewish resistance and heroism. It is there in the sacred civil space of Yad Vashem, where the Hall of Remembrance and the Children's Memorial stand alongside the 'although ... also' of 'The Pillar of Heroism' and the 'Soldiers, Partisans' and Ghetto Fighters' Monument'. It is there in the English translation of the name, where the 'martyrs' stand with the 'although ... also' of the heroes, at 'The Memorial Authority for the Martyrs and Heroes of the Holocaust'. It is there in the Hebrew name of the institution, where 'Holocaust' stands with the 'although ... also' of

'Heroism', at 'The Memorial Authority for the Holocaust and Heroism'. And it is there in the new 'Memorial to the Deportees', which speaks of 'annihilation' and 'hope'.

But it is not just there in Yad Vashem. It is there also in the ritual of State memorial days, where *Yom Hashoah Vehagevurah* – the Day of Remembrance of the Holocaust and Heroism – is followed by the 'although ... also' of *Yom Hazikkaron* – remembrance of those who died in the War of Independence – and *Yom Hatzma'ut* – Independence Day.

On the first Holocaust Day in 1951, the pro-government newspaper *Davar* led with an article that stated that 'we return and will return ... to the memory of the Holocaust and especially to the memory of the resistance fighters'.[29] That remembering the Holocaust was to 'return ... especially to the memory of the resistance fighters' was spelt out by the choice of the anniversary of the Warsaw ghetto uprising as the date to remember *Yom Hashoah Vehagevurah*, rather than the date chosen by the chief rabbinate – the fast day commemorating the Babylonian siege of Jerusalem and the destruction of the First Temple. The choice of day – anniversary of the Warsaw ghetto uprising – pointed to the remembering of the 'Holocaust' along with the 'although ... also' of 'heroism'. And yet the choice of day – a week or so before Independence Day – also pointed to the remembering of the 'Holocaust' along with the 'although ... also' of the rebirth of the State of Israel. What you see in this structuring of State memorial days is a combining then of these three elements that can be seen operating in Yad Vashem's telling of the 'Holocaust' – that is the combining of 'destruction', 'heroism' and 'rebirth'.

In some ways this mirrors the 'Judaism of Holocaust and Redemption' that Neusner has pointed to in contemporary America. That sense of being able to speak of the 'destruction' of the Holocaust in the light of the redemptive story of the 'rebirth' of Israel is clearly one which can be seen in the structuring of State memorial days, so that Independence Day follows Holocaust Day in the Israeli calendar of national holidays.

However, the linking of 'destruction and heroism' at Yad Vashem in particular, and in Israel in general, is something rather different. There is something uniquely Israeli about *Shoah Vegurah* being simultaneously about the Destruction and the 'although ... also' of Heroism. In short, telling the story of the 'Holocaust' in Israel is not about simply giving a happy ending to a horrible story, but is about telling a story which is simultaneously horrid and hopeful. The 'Holocaust' is hedged around by the 'although ... also' of 'Jewish heroism'. And this is perhaps the greatest shock that the American or European visitor to Yad Vashem gets. For a European like myself, and for my American wife, there was almost something jarring about walking through the historical exhibition, and then amongst the memorials scattered across this hill-top site. We wanted more horror, and less heroism. The 'Holocaust' we had been schooled in had gas chambers and piles of human hair cut from the victims, rather than tales of 'Jewish partisans' and illegal immigration to Palestine. This was another 'Holocaust' to the one that we knew. They shared certain things – Hitler, Nazis, Jews, Ghettos, Concentration camps – yet differed as well. We felt on safe ground at the start of the historical exhibition – 'Anti-Jewish Policy in Germany 1933-1939' followed by 'The Ghettos 1939-1941' and 'Mass Murder 1941-1945' – but not when we were being led up a sloping tunnel and into sections relating 'Jewish Resistance 1941-1945' and 'Liberation and Aftermath 1945'. We weren't used to the simultaneous – almost shamefilled – 'although ... also' which placed 'Jewish resistance' in the midst of 'Jewish suffering'. After all, in America and Europe it is the 'righteous gentiles' and the 'liberators' who are the heroes, and the Jews are simply 'victims'.

The response of Israelis to this exhibition is quite different from our response. As Young has pointed out, when confronted with the enlarged images of Germans cutting off a Jew's beard and Jewish leaders being hung, 'a group of young officer cadets required to visit the museum confess to being sickened by such photographs. But it is not the images of death or the sense of terror that offends them, they say: it is the humiliation and degradation of Jews unable to defend themselves'.[30] Their reaction, therefore, is not so much one of anger at the perpetrators, but of shame at the humiliation suffered by the diasporic Jew. In many ways a sense of shame about 'Holocaust' is perhaps the key to understanding this uniquely Israeli linking of 'destruction and heroism'. Whereas in America – and to a lesser extent in Europe – there is no shame in the 'destruction' (someone else's destruction), in Israel there is. And because of that deep sense of shame, the story of heroism has to be told, if that seemingly shameful story of destruction is also to be told. That commitment to tell both stories together and to emphasise the story of resistance, is central to the *Shoah Vegurah* tale that Yad Vashem narrates through words, images and memorials.

In Washington, DC, we were used to the placing of 'Gentile rescue' in the midst of 'Jewish suffering', but this was a museum light on Raoul Wallenberg (who rescued thousands of Jews in Budapest in 1944) and heavy on 'Jewish partisans'. And I found myself thinking, what do Jewish partisans have to do with the 'Holocaust'? While 'Jewish partisans' had very little to do with my 'Holocaust', this wasn't my 'Holocaust': this was somebody else's. It was in part the same story, and in part another story altogether. My 'Holocaust' had Raoul Wallenberg and their 'Holocaust' had Jewish partisans – with both, perhaps as much as anything, being motivated by shame. My shame used the words 'although ... also' when speaking of the European 'perpetrator' alongside the European 'rescuer'. I spoke of 'although Szálasi Ferenc oversaw the ghettoisation of the Budapest Jews, and Nyilas [the Hungarian fascist party] gangs shot hundreds of Jews into the icy waters of the Danube, it is important to also remember the work of Raoul Wallenberg in saving the lives of thousands of Budapest Jews'. Their shame used the words 'although ... also' when speaking of the Jewish 'victim' alongside the Jewish 'victor'. They spoke of commemoration involving 'recalling and mourning not only the six million Jews who perished, but also those Jewish soldiers, fighters of the Ghettos and the resistance movements who gave their lives to help smash the Nazi regime'.[31]

At Yad Vashem then, all the Jewish victims of my 'Holocaust' are resurrected in their 'Holocaust' as 'heroes' and 'martyrs'. In the historical exhibit, after being introduced to Jewish acts of resistance through the Warsaw ghetto fighters in particular, we are told that 'Jewish martyrdom ... is not only the death of a Jew who would rather give up his life than betray his religion. According to Maimonides, even a Jew killed not because he refuses to convert but simply because he is a Jew, is also a martyr'.[32] Thus Europe's Jews emerge from the Holocaust as 'martyrs and heroes', and indeed there is a sense in which all are resurrected as 'heroes'. Young points to the words of Chief Education Officer of the Army, Yitzhak Arad (the later head of Yad Vashem) at the dedication of 'The Pillar of Heroism' in 1974:

> The world wonders from where our soldiers draw their inspiration for their bravery, what are its sources? The answer is that the source of our heroism in the present lies in the heritage of the heroism of the Jewish people, a heritage that is as old as the history of the Jewish people ... In this long chain we must see the special place of Jewish heroism in the Holocaust period: the heroism of the rebels in the ghettos and the death camps, of the Jewish partisans in the forests of Eastern Europe and in the Balkan mountains, of the Jewish underground fighters all over Europe. This chain of heroism

also includes the ghetto and death camps, preserving his [sic] image as a human being, fought for his [sic] survival day after day, and thus heroically fought the battle of survival of the entire Jewish people.[33]

By including in 'this chain of heroism' those in the ghettos and camps, 'not only are past fighters united with present in Arad's address, but all victims and survivors – even those who died sanctifying the name of God – are remembered now as heroes'.[34] And they are therefore given a place in the 'chain of heroism' which provides a link between the deaths of millions of European Jews in the Holocaust and the deaths of thousands of Israelis in battle. In essence 'this chain of heroism' amounts to the 'Israelisation' of those Jews murdered in Second World War Europe. Indeed this 'Israelisation' of the victims of the Holocaust was made explicit with the passing of legislation to confer a form of posthumous Israeli citizenship upon all Holocaust 'victims'. When the memorial authority Yad Vashem was established in 1953, one of its founding tasks was 'to confer upon the members of the Jewish people who perished in the days of the Holocaust and the Resistance the commemorative citizenship of the State of Israel, as a token of their having been gathered to their people'.[35] In this unprecedented act, those who died during the 'Holocaust' are recognised as being amongst the first to die for the State of Israel, thus proving themselves worthy of the privileges of citizenship.

Given the completely unprecedented nature of conferring posthumous citizenship, the process was not without its detractors. The idea had been first put forward by Mordecai Shenhabi in 1950, who was also the central advocate of the establishing of a memorial authority. Shenhabi argued that 'the extermination of each of those millions, from the point of view of the Israeli state, was like the slaughter of a "potential citizen" ',[36] and therefore posthumous Israeli citizenship should be given to the six million victims of the Holocaust in recognition of this. However, the proposal ran into the opposition of the Israeli Foreign Ministry which pointed out the problems of conferring citizenship upon people who were already dead when the state came into being in 1948. In the event a compromise was reached whereby the citizenship to be granted to Holocaust victims was to be merely 'symbolic and abstract' 'memorial citizenship'.[37] And while this citizenship was purely symbolic, it was important symbolism none-the-less, in that it amounted to the 'Israelisation' of those European Jews killed during the Holocaust.

Yet as Segev reflects,

... there is no way of knowing which, or how many, of the Holocaust's victims considered themselves potential citizens of Israel. Many of them died precisely because they had preferred not to move to Palestine when that option was open to them. And most of the world's Jews, Holocaust survivors among them, chose not to come to Israel even after the state was founded.[38]

Not only did the majority of survivors choose to remain in the diaspora rather than emigrate to Israel but, as Segev points out, very few relatives took up Yad Vashem's offer of $12 commemorative certificates for the six million given posthumous memorial citizenship.

Despite this lack of enthusiasm on the part of surviving relatives, the granting of symbolic citizenship to the six million who died – as 'martyrs' or 'heroes' – does give the 'Holocaust' as an inheritance to Israel. Thus, Israel assumed a unique role in speaking for the dead and a virtual monopoly on the 'Holocaust'. Indeed it is ironic that Yad Vashem itself was first created largely as a result of that monopoly over the 'Holocaust' being challenged, and it seems that Yad Vashem is going to get a face-lift in 2001 in response to the challenge to its monopoly over the 'Holocaust' coming from Washington, DC. The first challenge to this monopoly came not from America, however, but from Europe and specifically from plans to establish a Holocaust memorial in Paris. These French plans were – in the words of Minister of Education Ben-Zion Dinur – evidence of 'the Diaspora instinct' and would 'give Paris the place of Jerusalem'.[39] The new government responded with top level negotiations with the man behind the Paris plan, Yitzhak Shneurson. This memorial was allowed to go ahead, but Yad Vashem was 'recognised as the central Holocaust memorial project, with the exclusive right to register the names of victims'.[40]

There is a sense perhaps in which this Israeli claim to a monopoly over 'Holocaust' memory, has become all the more important in the last two decades. The beginnings of the *Intifada* in 1987, was merely the culmination of a post-Six Day War change in perceptions whereby Israel began to be seen increasingly as the aggressor. In this context, a monopoly over the history of innocent victim-hood in the 'Holocaust' became increasingly important.

Thus Avishai Margalit claims that Yad Vashem – which she describes as 'Israel's shrine of kitsch' – in general, and the Children's' Memorial in particular have been used

... to deliver a message to the visiting foreign statesman [sic], who is rushed to Yad Vashem even before he has had time to leave off his luggage at his hotel, that all of us here in Israel are these children and that Hitler-Arafat is after us. This is the message for internal consumption as well.[41]

Thus, in the autumn of 1997, both the Czech President Václev Havel, and American Secretary of State Madeleine Albright were taken to the museum and memorial complex at Yad Vashem on their state visits to Israel. Reporting on the visit of the latter, the Yad Vashem Magazine recorded that

... at the end of her visit, leaving the Children's Memorial, Albright spoke with great emotion: 'The history remembered here at Yad Vashem is at odds with what we want to believe it was. There is an unbelievable sadness, suffering and cruelty. We must never allow ourselves to be at peace with the Holocaust. I know that I will never forget my visit'.[42]

Yad Vashem has become Israel's equivalent of the 'Tomb of the Unknown Soldier', for the stream of visiting dignitaries who come to lay wreaths and pay their respects, rather than being taken to the adjacent military cemetery or to the grave of Herzl – who can be seen in many ways as the founder of the State. There they are taken to two shrines to martyrdom: the Hall of Remembrance and the Children's' Memorial. Here, as Margalit suggests, a chain of innocent martyrdom can be developed which links the child victims of the Holocaust with present-day Israel.

Bartov points out that the lessons which Yad Vashem teaches are clear:

... the visitor should come out with the thought that had there been a Jewish state before the Holocaust, genocide would not have occurred; and since genocide did occur there must be a state. But also that just as the state can be traced back to the Holocaust, so too the Holocaust belongs to the state: the millions of victims were potential Israelis ... And more: that all Israelis are potential victims in the past, the present, and the future.[43]

Yet what is striking about such a lesson, is how times have changed. In the early days of the state, the somewhat ambivalent relationship with the Holocaust had meant that the pressure to forget as well as to remember had led to a stressing of Jewish 'heroism'. However, with the increasing perception of Israel as aggressor, the Holocaust was remembered, and remembered through the innocent victim rather than the armed resistance fighter. This is reflected upon by Margalit, who writes that

> Against the weapon of the Holocaust, the Palestinians are amateurs. True, some of them have adopted their own version of Holocaust kitsch, based on the revolting equation of the Israelis with Nazis and of themselves with Nazis' victims; but as soon as operation 'Holocaust Memory' is put into high gear by the Israeli authorities, with full-fledged sound-and-colour production, the Palestinians cannot compete.[44]

Margalit's provocative talk of 'operation "Holocaust Memory"' points to the politicisation of the 'Holocaust' within contemporary Israel. That process of politicisation has led Thomas Friedman to go as far as suggesting that 'Israel today is becoming Yad Vashem with an air force'.[45] From the 1970s onwards, the 'Holocaust' has emerged in Israeli society not simply as a cultural icon. It *is* there in movies, memorials, art-work, poetry and novels, but the 'Holocaust' in contemporary Israel is much more than simply a cultural icon. In the last thirty years in particular, a 'Holocaust discourse' has dominated political debate in Israel that has come a long way with regard to the 'Holocaust' from the ambivalent position of the early years of the State. Far from being 'forgotten', the 'Holocaust' has become central to Israeli political discourse.

Crucial in that change was the first survivor Prime Minister Menahem Begin. He was – in the words of Segev – 'the great populariser of the Holocaust' and the person who 'did more than anyone else to politicise it'.[46] During the 1950s and 1960s, Begin put himself forward as the champion of the Holocaust generation when opposing the Mapai-led government over such contentious issues as German reparations. When he became Prime Minister in 1977, the Holocaust became 'a cornerstone of the basic creed of the State of Israel and the policies of its government'.[47] In particular, Begin used the rhetoric of the 'Holocaust' to justify the government's decision to invade Lebanon in 1982: for Begin, 'the alternative is Treblinka, and we have decided that there will be no more Treblinkas'.[48] In using the rhetoric of 'Treblinka', Begin effectively determined that both support for the war, *and* opposition to the war, would be expressed by drawing lessons from the 'Holocaust'. The use of 'Holocaust' discourse in opposing Begin's stance led for example to one critic dubbing Begin's decision to invade Lebanon as 'Judeo-Nazi policy',[49] and to another choosing Yad Vashem as the site for a hunger strike in protest at both

Begin's decision to invade Lebanon and use of the 'Holocaust' to justify that decision. The hunger striker – like Begin – spoke in terms of the 'Holocaust', and yet drew very different lessons from this past:

> When I was a child of ten and was liberated from the concentration camp, I thought that we shall never suffer again. I did not dream that we would cause suffering to others. Today we are doing just that. The Germans in Buchenwald starved us to death. Today in Jerusalem, I starve myself and this hunger of mine is no less horrific. When I hear 'filthy Arabs' I remember 'filthy Jews'. I see Beirut and I remember Warsaw.[50]

The drawing of different lessons from the 'Holocaust' did not end with the Israeli withdrawal from Lebanon. Rather, the 'Holocaust' came to dominate the terms of political debate in Israel to such an extent that its lessons were used as justification for the opposing positions of the Israeli right and left throughout the remainder of the 1980s and into the 1990s. A politicised 'Holocaust' came to be used as a sort of a political football within an increasingly polarised Israel. With the breakdown of political consensus, came also a breakdown in consensus over what the 'Holocaust' meant for contemporary Israel. And in particular, what you see in this breakdown of consensus over the meaning to be drawn from the 'Holocaust', is the emerging of two radically different perspectives. Those on the right drew increasingly nationalistic lessons from the 'Holocaust', while those on the left drew universal lessons. This latter perspective can be seen in the words of the Mapam politician Yair Tsaban in a 1983 debate on 'Fifty years since the Nazi rise to power – the day and its lessons'. For Tsaban – leader of the Israeli peace movement – the 'Holocaust' warned against 'the cancerous growth of unrestrained, overpowering nationalist madness'.[51]

The drawing of universal lessons by the left in opposition to the nationalistic lessons of the right, was heightened by the rise of Kahanism in Israel during the 1980s. Former leader of the militant American Jewish Defence League, Rabbi Meir Kahane was seen as something of a joke figure on the extreme right until his election to the Knesset in 1984. Once in the Knesset, he used the 'Holocaust' to justify a number of extreme policies, none more controversial than a proposed 'Law to Prevent Assimilation between Jews and Non-Jews'. In calling for the complete separation of the Jewish and non-Jewish populations, Kahane adopted a 'Holocaust' discourse, arguing that 'as long as one gentile lives opposite one Jew, the possibility of a Holocaust remains'.[52] As had been the case with Begin's use of

'Holocaust' imagery to justify the 1982 invasion, both Kahane's supporters and opponents claimed the 'Holocaust' as the basis for their respective positions. In particular, a staple of Kahane's opponents was to draw the comparison between his anti-Arab nationalism and Hitler's antisemitism. While the Israeli right were drawing analogies between Hitler and Arafat, the Israeli left were drawing analogies between Hitler and Kahane.

This is seen perhaps nowhere as clearly as in a Knesset Rules Committee speech by Michael Eitan which was later published in the Israeli press. Eitan drew parallels between Kahane's proposed legislation before the Knesset and the legislation enacted in Nazi Germany. In essence, Kahane was portrayed as advocating a renewal of the Nuremberg Laws, with Eitan comparing, for example, Kahane's proposal with regards to extra-marital relations between Jews and non-Jews:

> It is forbidden for male and female Jews who are citizens of the state to have full or partial sexual relations of any kind with non-Jews, including outside marriage. Violation of this provision is to be punished by two years of imprisonment.
>
> A non-Jew who has sexual relations with a Jewish prostitute or a Jewish male is to be punished by fifty years in prison. A Jewish prostitute or Jewish male who has sexual relations with a non-Jewish male is to be punished by five years in prison.[53]

With the infamous Nuremberg laws which stipulated that 'extramarital relations between Jews and subjects of the state of German blood or of related blood are forbidden'.[54]

What the heated discussion in the1980s over Kahanism pointed to, was the centrality of the 'Holocaust' in Israeli political discourse. It formed the boundaries of the debate, with both left and right employing its language. As a newspaper article noted in 1984

> ... the struggle over the correct lessons to be learnt from the Nazis is by no means limited to the conflict between Kahane and his opponents; it also plays a crucial role in the more general political and cultural battle that is being fought in Israel today.[55]

And that battle over the 'correct lessons' to be drawn from the 'Holocaust' is one which takes place at all levels of Israeli society.

This contesting of meanings can be seen for example, in the decision taken by the Israeli Army in 1988 to stop visits by recruits to the Ghetto Fighters Museum at Kibbutz Lohamei Hagetaot. What emerged in the aftermath of this decision was that the tours had been stopped precisely because recruits were seen to be drawing the wrong lessons from the past. What is interesting is that those 'wrong' lessons reflected the divergent lessons being drawn by the Israeli left and right during the course of the 1980s. What worried Army chiefs was that on the one hand, 'after exposure to the museum's exhibits, some soldiers were inclined towards even greater racism and brutality when on duty in the occupied territories',[56] and that 'there were ... reports of units in which the soldiers termed themselves "Auschwitz platoons" and "Demjanjuks".'[57] On the other hand, 'other soldiers were inclined to be sympathetic to the occupying populace after seeing the museum, to the point of considering refusing to carry out orders, or even draft resistance schemes'.[58] In these divergent responses to exposure to the 'Holocaust' past the wider conflict in Israeli society between drawing nationalist and universal lessons from the 'Holocaust' is reflected.

And in some ways, one of the problems with the myth of the 'Holocaust' is that such a multitude of lessons can be drawn. The breakdown in consensus with regards to the 'Holocaust' is not simply something which reflects the increasing polarisation of the Israeli right and left. There is also a form of generational contesting of the 'Holocaust' past, seen in the current popularity of 'Holocaust' jokes amongst Israeli youth. Israeli youth are thoroughly immersed in the 'Holocaust' past. Not only do they have 'Holocaust' lessons at school – where 'since the early 1980s, questions on the Holocaust have accounted for 20 per cent of the overall score in the high school diploma examination in history'[59] – but as mentioned earlier they all visit Yad Vashem, and an increasing number visit the death camps in Europe. Nonetheless, the same Israeli teenagers who are schooled so thoroughly in the 'Holocaust', tell serial Holocaust jokes. Their telling is widespread, and yet 'their very existence continues to be a taboo of Israeli taboos, never mentioned in public, let alone to foreigners'.[60]

Segev may be in part right to interpret this phenomenon amongst Israeli teenagers as providing 'an outlet for anxiety, like the gallows humour of doctors and soldiers'.[61] However, I think there is more to Holocaust humour than that. Israel Shahak perhaps comes closer to the truth, when he concludes that they

... must probably be interpreted as manifestations of the savage scorn of their 'inventors' for their parents (regarded as 'weak' in contrast with the 'strong' young Israelis) and of delight in profaning the sacred.[62]

The widespread telling of Holocaust jokes is something unique to Israel, reflecting the unique place that the 'Holocaust' occupies in Israeli society. In contrasting 'strong young Israelis' with their 'weak parents', they mirror the ambivalent relationship that *yishuv* Israel has had with the Holocaust past of the diaspora Jewry from the earliest days of state-building. In these early years, Holocaust survivors were referred to in *yishuv* slang as 'soap', because of the widespread – but unsubstantiated – rumour that the Nazis had made soap out of the fat from Jewish bodies. Yoram Kaniuk in his novel *Man, Son of Dog*, writes: 'On the shelf in the store, wrapped in yellow paper with olive trees drawn on it, lies the Rabinowitz family'.[63] As Segev comments on this quote, 'it seems unlikely that anything could better express the contempt that native-born Israelis felt toward the survivors'.[64] One response to that sense of shame is – as I have suggested – seen in the 'although ... also' of Israeli memorial culture. Another response is the 'although ... also' of Holocaust' humour.

Yet there is more to jokes about gas and numbers tattooed on arms than dealing with a sense of shame when faced with the Holocaust. As Shahak suggests, 'Holocaust' jokes also allow for the ultimate act of youth rebellion and the breaking of the great taboo. The 'Holocaust' after all has a pseudo religious aura within contemporary Israel. It is a central plank of what Liebman and Don-Yehiya have termed Israeli 'civil religion', and thus a vital element of 'the ceremonials, myths, and creeds which legitimate the social order, unite the population, and mobilise the society's members in pursuit of its dominant political goals'.[65] Thus to joke about the 'Holocaust' in Israel, is to engage in some ways in an act of civic blasphemy. In contemporary Israel, the 'Holocaust' is simultaneously the sacred and the profane. It is both the brunt of jokes, and the object of worship.

Given the pseudo-religious aura given to the 'Holocaust' in Israeli society, Yad Vashem is nothing less than a sacred place. Walking into the Hall of Remembrance, I was given a black paper *yamuka* similar to the one I had taken from the box at the Western Wall. I was obviously walking on holy ground. Indeed as Tom Segev has noted, the very name of the Hall of Remembrance draws upon religious imagery. He points to a more apt translation of the Hebrew being 'Memorial Tabernacle',[66] rather than 'Hall of Remembrance'. This room therefore is not simply a 'hall', but a modern-day 'tabernacle'. The tabernacle established by Moses housed the Ark of the Covenant and represented the presence of God. However, this modern-day tabernacle houses the ashes of the victims and represents God's absence much more than his presence. It is perhaps the most sacred space in a new religion of the 'Holocaust'.

In a controversial article, the Israeli philosopher Adi Ophir has suggested that in Israel, the 'religious consciousness built around the Holocaust may become the central aspect of a new religion',[67] with it's own God – the Holocaust – and its own commandments to replace the ten given to Moses. Thus rather than the command 'Thou shalt have no other gods before me', Holocaust religion offers new commandments: 'Thou shalt have no other holocaust', 'Thou shalt not make unto thee any graven image or likeness', 'Thou shalt not take the name in vain', 'Remember the day of the Holocaust to keep it holy, in memory of the destruction of the Jews of Europe'.[68] As Ophir reflects, this Holocaust religion decrees that

> Absolute Evil must be remembered in exquisite detail. And already scattered throughout the land are institutions of immortalisation and documentation, like God's altars in Canaan one generation after the settlement. Already a central altar has arisen which will gradually turn into our Temple, forms of pilgrimage are taking hold, and already a thin layer of Holocaust priests, keepers of the flame, is growing and institutionalising; only, instead of rituals of sacrifices, there are rituals of memorial, remembering and repetition, since the sacrifice is completed and now all that is left is to remember'.[69]

For Ophir, this Holocaust religion turns a historical event into 'a transcendent event',[70] which he is not alone in seeing as a worrying development. The quasi-sacred status of the 'Holocaust', in contemporary Israel in general and Yad Vashem in particular, is something which Lopate also finds distasteful, reminding us that

> ... the dead of Auschwitz are not buried in Yad Vashem; believe me, I am not insulting their memories. Yad Vashem is the product of us the living, and as such it is subject to our dispassionate scrutiny and criticism. To project religious awe onto this recently built tourist attraction is idolatry, pure and simple.[71]

However, Yad Vashem is held as more than simply a 'recently built tourist attraction' within Israeli society, because the 'Holocaust' is held to be more than simply an event in history. It is an event given pseudo religious meaning, and – as I have suggested – a central element of political discourse. The implications of this politicisation are – as the well-respected historian Saul Friedlander suggests – extremely significant. He notes that

> ... significant progress toward peace between Israel and its neighbouring Arab states could possibly initiate, in the Jewish world, a recasting of the relationship between present and past. If a solution of the decades-long conflict between Zionism/Israel and its neighbours materialises, a central component of the prevailing Jewish attitudes will most likely be altered. The collective anxiety about a persistent existential threat and the ever-present collectively experienced death and mourning syndromes will recede. Jewish existence may attain a semblance of normalcy. Such an evolution will of necessity have an impact on the centrality of the *Shoah* in the narration of the Jewish past. The converse would be tragic: the possibility that the memory of catastrophes and particularly of the Holocaust will be so deeply ingrained in Jewish collective consciousness as to become an impediment to the progress toward peace.[72]

And it is not only Friedlander who has pointed to the dangers of the centrality of the 'Holocaust' being a potential 'impediment' to the peace process. As the Holocaust survivor Jehuda Elkana controversially argued in an article published in an Israeli newspaper in 1988, there is

> ... no more important political and pedagogical task for the leaders of [Israel] than to side with life, dedicate themselves to the future, and not deal constantly with the symbols, ceremonies and lessons of the Holocaust. They must eradicate the domination of this historical memory over our life.[73]

Indeed Elkana went so far as to suggest that there is

> ... no greater danger for Israel's future than a situation where the Holocaust penetrates the consciousness of the whole Israeli population – including the consciousness of most of the younger generation who have not experienced it.[74]

While 'the whole world should remember in the future',[75] Elkana's call was for Israel to 'forget' the 'Holocaust'. That sense of disquiet is not restricted to a number of writers in Israel alone, but is – as Rabbi

## 5. Yad Vashem

Wolf's words at the start of this book suggest – one increasingly expressed within sections of the American Jewish community.

# The United States Holocaust Memorial Museum, Washington, DC

If you want to view the myth of the 'Holocaust' today, the best place to find it is not in Israel, but in America. And the very best place to look is not on the periphery, but at the centre of the nation. Only a short walk from the Washington Monument which dominates the Washington, DC, skyline, the raw materials of the European Holocaust past have been used to create an Americanised 'Holocaust' present in the United States Holocaust Memorial Museum. This museum – located at the symbolic heart of America – is not simply an American 'Holocaust' museum, but *the* American 'Holocaust' museum, if not *the* 'Holocaust' museum, period.

Indeed, as mentioned earlier, with the museum's opening in April 1993, the staff at Yad Vashem expressed fears that their authoritative position in exhibiting the 'Holocaust' was seriously threatened. 'Holocaust' museums had been opening throughout the United States from the mid-1980s onwards, as the importance of the myth of the 'Holocaust' grew in the American consciousness. However, these institutions did not provide any real challenge to Yad Vashem's supremacy in the world of 'Holocaust' tourism. The first American 'Holocaust Memorial Centre' which opened in Michigan in October 1984, might have been able to claim that it was the number one tourist attraction in Detroit, but it was hardly a rival for a museum like Yad Vashem which was attracting well over one million visitors each year. In the Spring of 1993 however, not one, but two potential rivals were opened in the United States. In Los Angeles, the Simon Wiesenthal Centre's Museum of Tolerance was soon attracting over 350,000 visitors a year, and in Washington, DC, the United States Holocaust Memorial Museum brought in 20,000 visitors in the first week, 70,000 in the first month, and around two million in the first year. The volume of visitors to this mega-museum in Washington, DC, has remained more-or-less constant, with an average of around 5,000 visitors each day. Only the United States Air and Space Museum – the largest museum in the world – gets more visitors to the Mall, though visitors to the United States Holocaust Memorial Museum, spend roughly three times as long going through the museum as visitors to the Air and Space Museum. In part, the duration of the visit is determined by the nature of the museum, which presents an epic narrative of the 'Holocaust' spread over three floors alongside other changing exhibitions and a memorial complex. While the memorial complex in Washington, DC, does not rival that spread over the hillside site at Yad Vashem, the permanent exhibition is on the face of it both bigger and better. Yet this more impressive and technologically sophisticated exhibition was dismissed by the Director of the Department of Education at Yad Vashem, Shalmi Bar-Mor, as 'just a collection of gimmicks. You come out so saturated. I'm sure you come out with nothing'.[1]

Behind these apparent 'sour grapes', were fears of the 'Americanisation' of the 'Holocaust', expressed by an article in the *Jerusalem Report* which reported that with the opening of the Washington, DC, museum, 'American Jewry is implicitly declaring its independence from Israeli hegemony on Holocaust commemoration ... Now director Arad worries that American educators will stop coming to Jerusalem and look instead to Washington, undermining Israel's centrality in Holocaust studies'.[2] These words expressed fears of the cultural assimilation of the diasporic Jew, who – with the opening of the Washington, DC, museum – no longer needs to travel to Israel, because the 'Holocaust' has travelled to them. The response of Yad Vashem has been to launch a project to build something to rival the United States Holocaust Memorial Museum. The 'Holocaust' is quite literally being fought over.

America has embraced the 'Holocaust'. It is seemingly everywhere, in New York, Detroit, Los Angeles, Tampa Bay, Houston, Dallas ... One writer has noted the irony, that while 'there is no Holocaust museum in Germany', in the United States there are more than one hundred Holocaust museums and research centres, suggesting that 'the founding of Holocaust museums' is 'a particularly American phenomenon'.[3] And this surely prompts the question why the heritage industry in the United States has taken hold of what happened in Europe half-a-century ago and offered it to an American public who seem more than happy to view the 'Holocaust'? It is a question asked by Lopate, who ponders 'why both New York and Washington, DC, should have to have Holocaust memorial museums [and] ... why every major city in the United States seems to be commemorating this European tragedy in some way or another?'[4] He proceeds to recount the story of an Israeli poet proudly shown a Ohio congregation's eternal flame in memory to the six million dead:

> The poet muttered under his breath: '*Shoah* flambé'. In Israel they can joke about these matters. Holocaust monuments seem to me primarily a sign of ethnic muscle flexing, a sign that this or that Jewish community in, say, St Louis or Seattle has the financial or political clout to erect such a tribute.[5]

But there seems to be more to this proliferation of 'Holocaust' memory than simply 'ethnic muscle flexing' and a parading of wealth and power. Lopate's cynicism can be understood, but it is perhaps somewhat misplaced. Nonetheless, what is beyond dispute is that in the 1990s the 'Holocaust' is being made in America. Not only was 1993 dubbed the year of the Holocaust,[6] but the following year was described by the journalist Frank Rich as a good year for the Holocaust, 'if there's such a thing'.[7]

The fêting of the 'Holocaust' in 1990s America contrasts markedly with earlier attitudes there. Young reminds us that plans to build a memorial in Riverside Park, New York, in 1947 were never carried through, despite the initial enthusiasm of the *New York Times* which saw it to be 'fitting that a memorial to six million victims of the most tragic mass crime in history, the Nazi genocide of Jews, should rise in this land of liberty'.[8] Nothing more than a stone slab proclaiming: 'This is the site for the American Memorial to the heroes of the Warsaw Ghetto battle April–May 1943 and to the six million Jews of Europe martyred in the cause of human liberty' was laid, as proposal after proposal was rejected. The last to be considered were two memorials designed by Nathan Rapoport. These were rejected by the City Arts Commission on the grounds of being 'excessively and unnecessarily large', 'too tragic for recreational park land, too distressing for children',[9] and 'too depressing and for seeming to refer to foreign, not American, history'.[10]

The proposal to erect a memorial to 'the six million Jews of Europe' was not simply rejected by the City Arts Commission, but also by an *ad hoc* Jewish American committee which was considering the memorial plans. They concluded in 1948 that erecting such a monument in New York would be 'detrimental to the best interests of Jewry since it would stand as a perpetual reminder ... that the Jews are a helpless minority whose safety and very lives depend upon the whim of the people among whom they live or the governments who control their destinies'.[11] Therefore, one of the memorials proposed by Rapoport – Scroll of Fire – for the New York site ended up being erected in 1971 in the Martyrs' Forest outside of Jerusalem, rather than in New York. In some ways, the fate of Rapoport's memorial reflects the nature of Holocaust memory in the 1960s and early 1970s. While in the United States, the 'Holocaust' had yet to emerge in the mid 1960s, in Israel the picture was very different. In New York, only a slab marked the site of the proposed memorial. A short way from Jerusalem, however, a newly modelled Scroll of Fire was erected to remember 'the heroism and martyrdom of the *Shoah*' and celebrate 'Israel's national rebirth, leading to the reunification of Jerusalem'.[12] While in the United States in the mid 1960s the 'Holocaust' was peripheral, in Israel 'Holocaust and heroism' was becoming a central plank of national identity formation.

How things have changed. The earlier words used to dismiss Rapoport's memorial – 'too depressing and for seeming to refer to foreign, not American, history' – have been supplanted by a 'Holocaust' consciousness which sees the murder of six million European Jews as something to be remembered on American soil. Indeed the Commission established by President Carter in May 1978 to report 'on an appropriate memorial ... to the six million who were killed in the Holocaust,'[13] concluded that Americans had a 'distinct responsibility' to remember the Holocaust.[14] Rather than being peripheral to American history, the Presidential Commission saw the 'Holocaust' to be a part of American history because America had been an indifferent bystander during the 1930s and 1940s, American troops had liberated a number of concentration camps and many survivors had emigrated to the United States after the war.

For Ronald Reagan's chief arms negotiator – Max Kampelman – Americans had a special responsibility to remember this event, because of what he perceived to be a European tendency towards forgetting. He justified the building of a 'Holocaust' museum in Washington, DC, on the grounds that

> ... the Europeans probably should have built such museums in their capitals, but they haven't and most probably won't. Only Israel did, because it is a state run by Jews. But our building will demonstrate the tolerance of our culture, its ability to empathise with suffering of all its people. Our decision to build such a museum says something about our commitment to human rights and to the kind of nation we want to be.[15]

It is clear that for Kampelman this museum was to be as much about the present as it was about the past, and as much about

America as it was about the Holocaust. His words reflect the drive to 'Americanise' the 'Holocaust' which has accompanied the exporting of this European event to the United States. For Michael Berenbaum – deputy director of the Presidential Commission and later Project director of the Museum – such a process was not only inevitable, but perfectly appropriate. Yet his contention that 'it is just as appropriate to talk about the Americanisation of the Holocaust as it is to talk about the Israelisation of the Holocaust',[16] was contested by, for example, the purist Elie Wiesel for whom 'Americanisation' threatened to blur the uniqueness of this 'sacred event.

There is a sense in which bringing the 'Holocaust' to Washington, DC, inevitably meant that the Holocaust would be 'Americanised'. As Berenbaum recognised in the early 1980s – and later oversaw in the early 1990s – the museum in Washington, DC, offers a stars and stripes 'Holocaust' to visitors to the American capital. Thus it is not a direct rival to Yad Vashem. The two museums are essentially involved in quite different projects. In many ways they offer different 'Holocausts' to different audiences. Yad Vashem – as I've suggested – gives an 'although ... also ...' telling of the 'Holocaust' to Israeli schoolchildren, Israeli Defence Force recruits and foreign tourists and dignitaries. In contrast, the museum just off the Mall in Washington, DC, gives an 'Americanised' telling of the 'Holocaust' to a target audience of non– Jewish mom, dad and kids from Iowa. Yad Vashem speaks of 'martyrs' and 'heroes'. In contrast, the United States Holocaust Memorial Museum talks of 'victims'/'survivors' and 'liberators'. From Yad Vashem, we stand and look over the hills of Jerusalem. In contrast, in the United States Holocaust Memorial Museum, we catch occasional glimpses of the Washington Monument. They remember different 'Holocausts', for different people, in different places.

If Yad Vashem offers an 'Israelised' 'Holocaust' and the United States Holocaust Memorial Museum an 'Americanised' 'Holocaust', the Simon Wiesenthal Centre's Museum of Tolerance offers, 'not so much "Americanisation" of the Holocaust as "Los Angelisation".'[17] It is a self-conscious telling of the 'Holocaust' as an example of intolerance to native Los Angelians. Young reflects

> ... in keeping with its civic mandate, and now answerable to the large African-American, Hispanic, and Asian communities nearby, the Simon Wiesenthal Center's *Beit* HaShoah-Museum of Tolerance in Los Angeles examines the history of all social and ethnic prejudice and its consequences in America.[18]

Such an all-inclusive mission, is justified by the museum's curator who asks rhetorically,

> ... what is the point of having a museum which is of relevance to maybe five scholars in the whole wide world, when we live in Los Angeles, where urban violence and ethnic hatred are part of our cultural landscape. We address the issues which affect us, in this city, where we live.[19]

Sylvia Rosenblum responded to these words: ' "Poor Holocaust", I thought, but tactfully did not say!'[20]

This justification – 'we address the issues which affect us, in this city, where we live' – is not restricted to the museum in Los Angeles alone. It is the motivation of the heritage industry the world over. In Washington, DC, the museum addresses 'the issues which affect us, in this city, where we live'. In Jerusalem, Yad Vashem addresses 'the issues which affect us, in this city where we live'. In Houston, the museum addresses 'the issues which affect us, in this city, where we live'. In Oswiecim, 'Auschwitz-Land' addresses 'the issues which affect us, in this city, where we live'. Perhaps Rosenblum is right to reflect 'Poor Holocaust'. Whenever the present gets their hands on the past, the motivation is one which is as much present-centred, as it is past-centred. For all the claims to 'past' authenticity that filling museums with 'authentic' items – box-cars, suitcases, hair, bones – makes, the heritage industry does not recover an authentic past, but creates something new out of the past. Each 'Holocaust' museum uses the raw materials of the Holocaust past to create a 'Holocaust' present 'in this city where we live'.

In Washington, DC, local concerns are – in part – reflected in the conscious adoption of a focus upon the events which tie America to the Holocaust. After all, the 'Holocaust', though largely a European event, did – as the President's Commission recognised in their report – involve America. The commission acknowledged that America was a largely indifferent bystander to the Jewish emigration plans of the 1930s and the beginnings of the mass murders in the 1940s. This history of American indifference to Jewish fate features throughout the Permanent Exhibition. Panels deal with the failed Evian Conference of 1938 – when America refused to increase immigration quotas – the turning away by US coastguards of the 900 Jewish passengers aboard the *St Louis* in 1939, and the decision by the Allies not to bomb Auschwitz. These stand as an explicit judgment on past inaction, and an implicit call to America (as self-styled 'policeman of the world') not to stand idly by in the future.

Thus there is a sense in which American failures to act in the past are judged by the American present. In the Permanent Exhibition at Washington, DC, there is an acknowledging of guilt, and a recognition that not enough was done. However, this very public confession of America's failure to act during the 1930s and 1940s is overlaid by the representation of America as 'liberator' in 1945 and as refuge for the 'survivors' in the post-war period. It is these themes of 'American Holocaust history' that dominate in the museum.

Walking into the museum from the main entrance on 14th Street, we pass the flags of the 'liberating' US Army divisions, before getting into the elevators that take us up to the start of the permanent exhibition on the fourth floor or the museum. Standing, huddled together in the elevator, we are shown film footage of US troops discovering Buchenwald, Mauthausen and Ohrdruf, and hear the testimony of a US serviceman:

> The patrol leader called in by radio and said that we have come across something that we are not sure what it is. It's a big prison of some kind, and there are people running all over. Sick, dying, starved people. And you take to an American, uh, such a sight as that, you ... you can't imagine it. You, you just ... things like that don't happen.[21]

As the elevator doors open – signalling our arrival in the silent world of 'The Holocaust' – we come face-to-face with a huge black and white photograph of US troops staring at a pile of half-burnt corpses at Ohrdruf Concentration Camp. The US troops stand on the far side of the pyre, and we find ourselves – shuffling out of the elevator – standing this side of the pyre. It is as though we form a ring around this pile of half-burnt corpses. We join the 'liberators', and so become like them: 'Americans [who] encounter the camps'.[22]

We witness 1945 before we go back to 1933 (or earlier), experiencing 'liberation' before we experience 'destruction' and encountering the American liberators before we encounter the Nazi murderers. As we start out on this telling of the 'Holocaust', we have already been handed a mental map within which to operate. There is a sense of closure at the very opening of this telling of the 'Holocaust'. It is as if we go back in time to the point of liberation, before then being taken back further still to the event which demanded that liberation. It is a journey back to 1945 and a journey back to 'America' before we step into Germany.

In some ways this experiencing of closure before experiencing the 'Holocaust' is paralleled at Yad Vashem, where we are taken through the experience of rescue and rebirth, before being taken back to the destruction of 1930s and 1940s Europe. Walking down the Avenue of the Righteous Gentiles, we see rescue before we see that from which those were rescued. When we enter the museum itself, it is not to the flags of the liberators, but to a relief which talks of rebirth. We are taken back to Israel in 1948 before we are taken to Germany in 1933, or beyond. We are given an end (*the* end) to the story before we are taken to the beginning, meaning that everything we see from now on is read in the light of that ending. In Jerusalem we experience the 'Holocaust' knowing that the end of the story – the sense of closure – is the birth of the Israeli state. In Washington, DC, we experience the 'Holocaust' knowing that the end of the story – the sense of closure – is the liberation of the camps by US troops.

In giving to the past a sense of closure and an ending, these two museums offer a sense of meaning. This is particularly the case at Yad Vashem where the meaning which we are given is that of the 'Holocaust' ushering in the nation of Israel. At the United States Holocaust Memorial Museum the meaning is one of our place as 'liberator' – *not* 'perpetrator' – being strengthened as we encounter the 'Holocaust'.

Yet giving meaning to the Holocaust is to make meaningful (and more palatable) that which was and is meaningless. Rather than revealing the confusing, banal complexity of an event of ludicrous proportions, it is presented as an event which can not only be comprehended, but also as one which can be understood. And in particular understood in terms of the framework of 'rebirth' or 'liberation'. And thus in some ways the 'Holocaust' is presented as a means to an end, rather than an end in itself. Rather than the Holocaust spelling the end to six million Jewish lives, vast swathes of European Jewish culture, and perhaps also the end of Europe itself – Milan Kundera asks: 'Didn't it [Central Europe] lose its soul after Auschwitz, which swept the Jewish nation off its map?'[23] – Yad Vashem and the United States Holocaust Memorial Museum point to new beginnings through a discourse of 'rebirth' and 'liberation'. It is an event that is given redemptive closure.

The redemptive closure offered by liberation and post-war emigration from the scene of the murders, surrounds the narrative of the Permanent Exhibition at the United States Holocaust Memorial Museum. It provides the beginning of our descent into the history of destruction, and provides the end of our ascent out of that history. Our 'Holocaust' experience in Washington, DC, starts and ends with the voices of Americans ringing in our ears. The first voice is that of the US serviceman who accompanies us in the elevator that takes us to 'The Holocaust'. The last voices are those of the survivors who 'recount their experiences of loss, suffering, and anguish, as well as rescue, resistance, compassion and hope',[24] in the amphitheatre which stands at the end of the Permanent Exhibition. This theatre – whose walls are clad with stone from Jerusalem – hints at the redemption offered by Zionism, which is made more explicit in the museum's exhibition boards relating illegal emigration to Palestine and the subsequent founding of the State of Israel. As Bartov notes

> ... just like Spielberg's *Schindler's List*, the museum con-cludes with scenes of newly arrived survivors in Palestine. Zionism was, it seems, the appropriate answer to Nazism. And since Nazism is gone, and the State of Israel is alive and well, we no longer have any reason to worry.[25]

With its use of survivors the Washington, DC 'Holocaust' is given a suitably up-beat ending.

There is a similar ending at the Holocaust Museum in Houston – designed by Ralph Appelbaum who also designed the Washington, DC, Permanent Exhibition – where the survivors tell their story on film. By their very presence – albeit on celluloid – the 'survivors' speak of 'liberation'. They are the one's 'liberated' by American troops and given new life in America. Thus, it would appear that the indifference of the years 1933-1944 is atoned for by the liberation of 1945 and the emigration to the United States of the post-war years, in museums where the American history of the 'liberators' and the 'survivors' is more visible than the American history of the 'bystanders'.

While the process of 'Americanising' the 'Holocaust' does involve making this European event part and parcel of American history by stressing the role of the American 'bystander', 'liberator' and 'sur-vivor', 'Americanisation' also involves a certain distancing of 'self' from this European event. As Michael Berenbaum himself acknowl-edges, the Washington, DC, museum aims to tell the story of the Holocaust as the negation of American ideals. He writes that 'the history described here cuts against the grain of the American ethos ... While we impart no singular meaning to the events of the Holo-caust, we see in their perpetration a violation of every essential American value'.[26] The museum is therefore 'meant to serve as an ideological vaccine for the American body politic. A proper dose of Holocaust, the thinking goes, will build up the needed antibodies against totalitarianism, racism, state-sponsored mass murder',[27] and reaffirm in those who visit a commitment to American ideals.

This dynamic of making the 'Holocaust' a part of American history, and yet also representing it as alien to American values, is also achieved primarily through the use of the American 'liberators' as the eyes through which the 'Holocaust' is to be viewed. In becoming the 'American liberator' for the day, we see something which wasn't of our making. We are the liberators who chance upon that which 'they' did. And that sense of being almost accidental observers of something alien is flagged as soon as we leave the elevator that transported us to 'The Holocaust'. The words of the patrol leader – 'we have come across something that we are not sure what it is' – and the looks of disbelief and horror on the face of Eisenhower and the US troops staring at the corpses in Ohrdruf, combine to convince us of the utter 'Otherness' of what we are witnessing. This is not America the photographs say, as the GI in the elevator had reminded us that 'you take to an American, uh, such a sight as that, you ... you can't imagine it. You, you just ... things like that don't happen'. As we embark on 'The Holocaust', we are being told that 'things like that don't happen here'. We have become fellow American 'liberators' encountering camps in a foreign land and therefore witnessing what 'they' did. Already a framework is established that teaches us to see the 'Holocaust' as an un-American crime. We – like the US troops – have encountered someone else's crime, and stare – hands-on hips – with a mixture of disgust and fascination.

The brutality of the 'Other' is a thing that both horrifies and comforts. It is horrific to see what the 'Other' has done, but it merely serves to confirm our knowledge of their 'Otherness', and thus to strengthen our own identity as 'liberators' vis-à-vis 'they' who are the 'perpetrators'. Perhaps we are voyeurs, but at least we are voyeurs who stand on moral highground: ground high enough to allow us to peep over walls which shroud TV monitors showing the forbidden fruit of what 'they' – Mengele, the Nazis ... – did.

It becomes possible to show what 'they' did to all those Jews in all its horror. And those who visit the museum stand – peering over the low wall – transfixed by the horror show on offer. As the journalist Philip Gourevitch noted on his visit to the museum, these tend to be places in the exhibition where 'the crowd – which was impossibly dense throughout the gallery – was even thicker than usual'.[28] It was the same on the day that I visited the museum, and when Liliane Weissberg visited and found 'the largest crowds in front of the video terminals that show medical experimentation or the burying of the dead'.[29] Like her, I found the experience of staring over the wall disturbing. As she recounts, 'small walls built around the video stations let me view the images from a skewed angle only' with the result that 'while hoping to protect children from these images, the architecture produces the effect of peep shows'.[30]

Transfixed by the film footage of the *Einsatzgruppen* murdering Europe's Jews being shown on the museum's video monitors, Gourevitch starts to take notes:

> Peepshow format. Snuff films. Naked women led to execution. People are being shot. Into the ditch, shot, spasms, collapse, dirt thrown in over. Crowds of naked people. Naked people standing about to be killed, naked people lying down dead. Close-up of a woman's face and throat as a knife is plunged into her breast – blood all over. Someone holds a severed head in his hand. Mass graves of thousands. Naked. Naked corpses. Naked corpses. Street beatings. The gun, the smoke, a figure crumbles. Naked corpses. Naked women dragged to death. Shooting. Screaming. Blackout. The film begins again.[31]

And this peepshow Holocaust, is the one which is offered elsewhere in America. It is offered in a less sophisticated way by the cabinet of horrors at the Dallas Memorial Centre. It is given to us in Spielberg's filmic 'Holocaust' with its scenes of the clearing of the ghetto and the naked women from amongst Schindler's Jews being herded into what turns out to be a shower room at Auschwitz. It is also offered in Goldhagen's best-selling popular history of the Holocaust which does not hold back on graphic descriptions of mass murder.

In part, I think that Gourevitch is right to suggest that this peepshow telling of the Holocaust fits with cultural norms. He claims that 'violence and the grotesque are central to the American aesthetic, and the Holocaust museum provides both amply' in an exhibition which has the 'potential for excitement, for titillation, and even for seduction by the overwhelmingly powerful imagery'.[32] Yet I think this peepshow version of the Holocaust is about more than simply a desire for 'titillation' in an America schooled in Hollywood's celebration of technicolour violence. I think it is more about a sense of the 'Holocaust' being the 'Other', and thus being portrayed as the great antithesis to all-American values.

This is where Washington, DC, differs so markedly from Yad Vashem. At Washington, DC, the 'Holocaust' is being portrayed as 'their' story. At Yad Vashem the Holocaust is being portrayed as 'our' story. And therefore at Washington, DC, there is a rejection of the twinning of 'Holocaust and Heroism' so central to the Israeli telling of the 'Holocaust' at Yad Vashem. It is the American troops and the righteous gentiles who are the 'heroes' and not the Jews. The Jews are 'victims' not 'heroes', and their story of victimisation is revealed on the TV-monitors which we crane our necks to view. As Berenbaum himself states resolutely, 'the Holocaust offers no happy ending, no transcendent meaning, no easy moralism. And even if we pause occasionally to learn of courage and valour, of heroism and decency, the overriding theme of the Holocaust is evil perpetrated by individuals, organisations, and governments'.[33]

There is no place for 'Holocaust and [Jewish] heroism' in Washington, DC, but only Jewish victimisation, and the telling of the story of the 'Holocaust' in all its gory horror. This story is 'not [one of] regeneration and rebirth, goodness or resistance, liberation or justice, but death and destruction, dehumanisation and devastation, and, above all, loss'.[34] Here on the Mall – in this sacred civil space of American memorials, monuments and museums – it is safe to tell the 'Holocaust' as a story of death, destruction, dehumanisation, devastation and loss. This is a telling on American soil, and not on the hills of Jerusalem or in a field in Southern Poland. Indeed, there is a strong sense in which telling the story in *all* its horror just a few hundred yards from the Washington Monument is a powerful tool in this museum about the most un-American of crimes.

Something of this emerges in a money-raising letter written by Chairman of the Museum Council, Miles Lerman. In it, he described the experience of walking around the museum and then emerging into the landscape of the Mall. This familiar landscape would – he suggested – be seen afresh, because 'having witnessed the nightmare of evil, the great American monuments to democracy that surround each departing visitor will take on new meaning as will the ideals for which they stand'.[35] As Alvin Rosenfeld notes – commenting on these words -

> ... these national monuments have the effect of re-establishing museum visitors in the familiar and consoling realities of American space, and in so doing they can also have the effect of telling them that the exhibits they just saw, for all of their horror, signify an essentially European event.[36]

Part of the attraction of the 'Holocaust' to contemporary America is the very foreignness of the 'Holocaust'. It is a European event which can be included in American national history, but within the parameters that Americans were the 'liberators' and 'Nazis' the 'perpetrators' and therefore that it can be observed from the outside.

Rather than creating a museum of American pluralism, tolerance, democracy and human rights on the Mall, an anti-museum has been created of Nazi racism, intolerance, dictatorship and persecution. In a similar manner, rather than building a 'Museum of Tolerance' in Los Angeles, a museum has been created which details an act of intolerance. At this anti-museum we are self-consciously told what it means to be 'American' by being given a taste of what it means to not be 'American'. Entering the museum from Raoul Wallenberg place, we are confronted by two inscriptions well known to all Americans. The first is taken from the Declaration of Independence with its assurance of the right of all citizens to 'life, liberty, and the pursuit of happiness'. The other is taken from the words of George Washington, who stated that 'the government of the United States ... gives to bigotry no sanction, to persecution no assistance'. And these words echo in our heads as we encounter an exhibition which details a history of 'bigotry' and 'persecution' and of a regime which took 'life, liberty, and the pursuit of happiness' away from millions of European Jews.

There is a sense in which the United States Holocaust Memorial Museum is essentially established as an un-American museum, telling the story of an un-American crime to Americans. As we walk through this anti-museum, we reaffirm who we are in opposition to the historical 'them'. It is so much easier to look at someone else's racism, intolerance, dictatorship and persecution in the past, than to confront the racism, intolerance, dictatorship and persecution in either our own past or our own present. Rather than learning from the past, we can leave comforting ourselves in the present that we are not like that. It carries the danger of inducing in us a feeling of self-righteousness. This is something which the American journalist Alison Owings signals when reflecting on her own experience of writing a book which involved interviewing German women – 'perpetrators', 'victims' and 'bystanders' – who had lived through the Third Reich. She writes of 'an admonition that whipped the early wind out of my sails' given to her by survivor Reinhard Bendix, who had said to her: 'I do hope your book won't make Americans feel smug'.[37]

In many ways, at Washington, DC, we walk through a museum where horror and smugness meet. It is a bizarre mix. As one visitor confessed,

> ... to have walked through this exhibition alongside fellow Americans ... all in their bright summer tourist garb, left me feeling strangely comforted and surprisingly proud. Comfort and pride are no part of what one feels upon leaving the remains of the Nazi camps in Germany or Poland or upon

concluding a visit to Yad Vashem in Israel. Why, therefore, are such feelings evoked at the United States Holocaust Memorial Museum? The answer probably lies less in what is shown in the one place and not in the others than in the site itself and the democratic ideals that America's capital exemplifies.[38]

Here – just off the Mall – the relics from the death camps are uprooted from their original context and given new meaning in a new site. In Washington, DC, the relics from 'Auschwitz' are given a specifically 'American' twist in a museum which aims at the defence of 'the core American – indeed the core human – values of individual dignity, social justice, and civil rights'.[39] The 'Holocaust' becomes a lesson in the dangers of discrimination, and the piles of shoes evidence of what happens when the values espoused by American society are neglected. They become on the one hand relics of warning, and on the other hand a confirmation of the essential rightness of American values.

But the use of thousands of relics in the Permanent Exhibition in Washington, DC, serves another purpose. They are imbued with meaning in a museum that 'Americanises' the 'Holocaust', but as in Auschwitz they are also presented as authentic evidence of the historicity of the 'Holocaust'. That this is in part the aim of the museum, becomes clear as we are introduced to 'The Holocaust' up on the fourth floor of the building. Alongside the large photograph of American troops staring at half burnt corpses, a smaller photograph of General Dwight D. Eisenhower at Ohrdruf is accompanied by his words:

The things I saw beggar description ... The visual evidence and the verbal testimony of starvation, cruelty and bestiality were ... overpowering ... I made the visit deliberately in order to be in a position to give firsthand evidence of these things in ever, in the future, there develops a tendency to charge these allegations merely to 'propaganda'.[40]

These words are described as a 'prophetic quotation' which 'museum visitors encounter ... at the beginning of the Permanent Exhibition'.[41] They form another part of the mental map with which to negotiate 'The Holocaust'. Eisenhower's words – and those of the GI whose testimony we heard in the elevator – come to us to authenticate what we are about to embark on. In the context of the claims of 'Holocaust deniers', we are being told that what we will see and hear is not merely 'propaganda' but 'firsthand evidence'. The oral testimony of the soldier in the elevator is given weight by the written testimony of someone of the stature of Eisenhower – the all-American hero – and this authenticity is transferred to the remainder of the exhibit. We have been initiated into the role of witnesses of a horrific reality, rather than simply museum-goers.

Throughout the museum, there is an obvious concern on the part of the exhibition designers with authenticity. This is not simply a place to introduce us to an American telling of the 'Holocaust', or to reaffirm our belief in American values. It is also a place which – through the presentation of material evidence – aims to convince us of the reality of the murder of six million European Jews in the face of the claims of Holocaust deniers. Such a concern is foreign to Yad Vashem, located as it is within a society where Holocaust denial is unheard of. However, in an American setting, the dissemination and acceptance of 'revisionist' claims is no small fear on the part of survivors especially. And thus the United States Holocaust Memorial Museum is – in part – designed to stand against such claims and disprove them through an impressive marshalling of material evidence. The hope is that, after their visit to Washington, DC, the 'Iowa farm family' won't believe the internet claims of the so-called 'revisionist' Institute for Historical Review.

Thus the material artefacts on display in the museum are more than simply things to look at. They are self-consciously also building blocks of evidence. Over the course of a number of years, an impressive array of relics was collected from East-Central Europe and the former Soviet Union. In particular, a large number of relics were imported from Poland, including artefacts from Auschwitz. On 20 June 1989, a delegation from the United States Holocaust Memorial Museum had met with officials from the museum at Auschwitz and negotiated the loan of exhibits from the Museum for display in Washington. In November, crates of relics from Auschwitz arrived in Washington DC. In addition to a wooden barracks building from Auschwitz-II, the museum received rubble from the crematoria, empty Zyklon B containers, and piles of shoes and suitcases.

These artefacts provide the building blocks of the 3D 'Holocaust' experience which takes the visitor through a virtual ghetto constructed of relics: a casting of the largest remaining segment of the Warsaw ghetto wall, a sewer cover from the Warsaw ghetto, the Lodz ghetto hospital door and a handcart from Theresienstadt. And then the pace quickens and the visitor is taken on a virtual 'Holocaust' deportation journey through 'a 15 ton "Karlsruhe" freight car, one of several types that were used to deport Jews',[42] which sits on rails from Treblinka, past discarded cases and the contents of those cases, underneath a casting of the *Arbeit macht frei* gateway from Auschwitz-I and into part of a wooden barracks complete with wooden bunks from Auschwitz-Birkeneau. Arriving at 'The Concentration Camp Universe', the visitor becomes an observer of the gas chambers at Auschwitz. As Weissberg reflects, 'with the help of the US government and the Holocaust Memorial Council, Auschwitz has come to you'.[43]

For the exhibition planners who created the permanent exhibition, the self conscious aim was that we the visitors would experience the same journey as the victims. As exhibition designer Ralph Appelbaum himself put it:

> ... we realised that if we followed those people under all that pressure as they moved from their normal lives into ghettos, out of ghettos onto trains, from trains to camps, within the pathways of the camps, until finally to the end ... if visitors could take that same journey, they would understand the story because they will have experienced the story'.[44]

And thus we are taken through a freight car and under the Auschwitz-I gateway, so that in some sense we experience the myth of the 'Holocaust'.

Yet this is not the real thing. We know that we are in a 'Holocaust' museum looking at 'Holocaust' artefacts. As we walk through the freight car in Washington, DC, or pause in the shortened freight car which forms the entrance to the museum in Dallas, we aren't taking the same 'journey' that Holocaust victims took, but the 'journey' of tens of thousands of tourists. As Bartov comments, while the use of authentic artefacts

> ... is meant to bring the visitors closer to the 'reality' of the event and simultaneously to repudiate the challenge of the deniers of the Holocaust ... the result is rather to create a false sense of 'reality' while trivialising the genocide.[45]

That aim of bringing us closer to the 'reality' of the 'Holocaust', clearly underlies the decision of the museum planners to issue visitors with the identity card of a 'Holocaust' victim when they embark on their tour of the Permanent Exhibition. The use of identity cards is a conscious attempt by the museum designers to 'personalise the concept of victims',[46] and ensure that 'at the United States Holocaust Memorial Museum, visitors do not learn at a distance; rather, they are brought inside the story' through the gaining of an 'exhibition "twin" ',[47] or 'companion'.[48]

Initially cards were created to match the visitor's age and gender, which were then updated during the exhibition by inserting the card into machines. These proved, however, to be unreliable. Completed identity cards were issued, therefore, with the visitor turning the next page at the end of each floor of the exhibition. These completed cards cover a total of 558 individuals: 260 of whom are murdered during, and 298 of whom survive, the 'Holocaust'. The chances of your 'exhibition "twin" ' making it out of the museum alive are thus slightly greater than fifty-fifty. You are therefore much more likely to make it out of the museum's 'Holocaust' alive than any East European Jew was in the 1940s. In this 'Holocaust' the majority survives – as in the one offered by *Schindler's List*, there are more winners than losers. I was relieved to discover that I was a winner, not a loser. My 'exhibition "twin" ' survived. I had chosen to become 'Mendel Rozenblit' a Jew from Llukow, for the day. Born in 1907, Mendel was married with an eight-year-old son and four-year-old daughter when the Nazis invaded Poland. Taken to the Warsaw Ghetto and then on to Auschwitz, Mendel survived the war but the rest of his family were murdered. The card ends by informing me that 'in 1947 Mendel emigrated to the United States where he began a new family'.[49]

In taking the card of an East European Jew, I had adopted an identity which most of my fellow visitors had also adopted. The majority of the 558 Washington, DC, 'Holocaust' victims are Jewish, with 364 being Eastern European Jews and 115 Western European Jews. Nonetheless, in this 'Americanised Holocaust', non-Jewish victims are remembered alongside the Jews. Identity cards also feature Polish prisoners (47), Jehovah's Witnesses (20), Homosexuals (9), Gypsies (3) and those killed during the Euthanasia programme (2). Victimhood is after all a powerful community identity at the end of the twentieth century, and the 'status' of 'Holocaust victim' is one which has been fought over.

But choosing to become 'Mendel Rozenblit' – a 'victim' of Nazism – for just one day, felt artificial. After all what do I – a British non-Jew from Preston – know about being a 'victim' of Nazism? And wouldn't I be a fool to choose victimhood anyway? I wasn't a victim of Nazism, so why should I choose to be one now? I tried but I couldn't do it very well. I felt like an outsider rather than an insider. I *am* an outsider not an insider after all, and when it comes to the Holocaust incredibly thankful not to have been an insider. If this elevator is a time machine taking us back in time to 1930s and 1940s Europe then I think I'd prefer to be someone other than Mendel Rozenblit, a Polish Jew from Llukow. I'd prefer to be living in Preston rather than Llukow, and to be a British non-Jew rather than a Polish Jew. How authentic do they want this identifying with the victims to be? Do I end up dead somewhere on the second floor after being taken into the ghetto and Auschwitz? I couldn't summon up the energy to 'adopt' the *persona* of this 'ghostly companion'.

I felt confused – as Gourevitch confessed to being – about which identity was being demanded of me. I'd been herded into the elevator by a museum guide who had told me to choose a 'victim's' identity, from the tray of victim's identities on the table up against the wall. But then, once in the elevator I was being asked to relate to the US serviceman whose voice accompanied the scenes on the video monitor. Being transported up to the world of the 'Holocaust', I'm trying to do two things at once. I'm trying to read the first page of my I.D. Card, and I'm trying to watch the TV monitor fixed to the roof of the elevator. I'm trying to become the 'victim Mendel', but I'm also trying to be the US serviceman who liberates the camp in the film footage being shown on the monitor. For all I know, Mendel might be in this film footage (alive or dead). I can't assume both the identity of 'victim' and 'perpetrator' in the twenty or so seconds that it takes for the elevator to take me up to the 4th floor where the 'Holocaust' is waiting. As Gourevitch comments, it's 'an odd spin, this: clutching their I.D. cards, museumgoers are asked to identify simultaneously with the victims and their saviours'.[50] 'The museum', Weissberg notes, 'does not want me solely to assume the role of victim. It asks me to be victim and victor at once'.[51]

Yet I couldn't manage to do both things at once. The elevator doors opened and I stood, holding my I.D. Card, staring at the photograph of American soldiers looking at a pile of corpses. Perhaps Mendel was one of those half burnt corpses, but I forgot about him as this photograph gave me the cue that my 'Holocaust' would be seen through the eyes of the 'liberator' not the 'victim'. My dilemma of struggling with a dual identity was solved as I stood in silence and looked at US servicemen looking at the 'Holocaust'. I was relieved really. I didn't want to be Mendel and experience the 'Holocaust' as 'victim'. I didn't even want to be a 'liberator' and smell the corpses. I would be an outside looking at soldiers looking at corpses. I would see the 'Holocaust' through their eyes. I would be a non-Jew from Preston who had been born a safe twenty-five years after the Holocaust. I would be myself.

And why is it so much easier to build a museum which offers the opportunity to be a 'liberator' or a 'victim', rather than a 'perpetrator' for the day? There isn't a museum in Washington, DC, which gives you the identity card of a 'perpetrator', but one which gives you the identity card of a 'European victim' killed by a 'European perpetrator' ... or in the case of Mendel a 'European victim' who found salvation in the United States. Why don't they give out the cards of perpetrators and bystanders as well as victims, so that somewhere towards the end of the second floor I come to the shocking understanding that I'm a member of a German battalion which is involved in killing Jews in 1942, or a Hungarian municipal official involved in drawing up plans for the local ghetto in 1944? Or failing all that, why not simply let me be a museum visitor and release me from the pressure to empathise with that which is impossible to empathise with, and the pressure to experience that which no survivor would wish upon anyone.

Yet the museum designers aim at giving to visitors an authentic experience. As Donald Horne suggests, 'authenticity is the special magic of museums',[52] and Holocaust museums are no exception. He goes on to comment how

> ... in a technological museum, it is not that this is the kind of steam engine that Watt constructed that makes it interesting, but that it is the very steam engine Watt constructed. In an art museum, it is not that this painting is beautiful, but that it is an authenticated Rembrandt. In a history museum, it is not that this is the kind of hat that Napoleon wore, but that this is the very hat Napoleon wore.[53]

His words hold true for Washington, DC, where it is not that this is the kind of barracks that inmates at Auschwitz lived in, but that this is one of the barracks that Auschwitz inmates lived in. The aim was 'to create patches of Holocaust space within a building that has removed people from American space and has placed them in the artificial world of exhibition space'.[54] Within this artificial space, an authentic 'Holocaust' experience would be created through the use of authentic artefacts.

While the barracks are described as ones which 'housed Jews deported from the Theresienstadt ghetto in Czechoslovakia',[55] the exhibition designers do not make such claims of authenticity of the railroad truck which is one of the central objects in the museum. Despite the box-car being given to the museum by the Polish Government 'with written attestation that the car had been used to transport Jews from the Warsaw ghetto to their death in the gas chambers of Treblinka',[56] this claim could not be confirmed. Therefore

– with a clear eye to the potential accusations of Holocaust deniers – 'the historian who was responsible for writing labels and captions insisted that the label for the car be worded accordingly, explaining that "the walkway goes through a 15-ton freight car, one of several types that were used to deport Jews," rather than "this car was used to deport ...".'[57]

At Dallas however, they are bolder in their speculation over the wartime past of their 'shortened Belgian railroad car [which] may once have stood at the railroad siding at Auschwitz-Birkeneau [Auschwitz-II], the notorious ramp where Jews were selected on arrival, or carried the property of those who were murdered'.[58] On the label attached to the railroad car they simply speculate that it 'may' have transported Jews, but they go further on the back of a postcard where the car is described as one 'that *was* used for transporting people to the concentration camps' (italics added),[59] in the centre's information brochure which includes a photograph of 'Holocaust survivor Mike Jacobs lead[ing] visitors through a Belgian boxcar used to transport Jews'[60] and in the filmic telling which claims that 'this boxcar was actually used to carry Jews and other prisoners for days at a time'.[61] It is the largest and most impressive relic on display and the one through which all visitors enter the centre – the sign reads 'Please enter through the boxcar' – and where school parties are instructed to pause for an 'authentic' (shortened) experience of deportation (in a shortened railroad car). However, some survivors have no wish to pause for such an 'authentic' (second) experience of deportation. They have been 'given their own, hidden entrance, a secret door for survivors'.[62]

Box-cars are a popular – and sought-after – 'authentic' object. Alongside the ones in Washington, DC, and Dallas, the only other one in an American Holocaust museum is housed at the Tampa Bay Holocaust Museum. There is one at Yad Vashem – perched precariously on severed track in the Memorial to the Deportees – and one is being sought by the Imperial War Museum in London for their new Holocaust display. But it is not simply box-cars that are being chased for Holocaust museums across the globe. The *Beit Hashoah* – Museum of Tolerance in Los Angeles has 'actual bunks from the Majdanek death camp, suitcases with the names of the victims on them',[63] and the small Holocaust museum at The Dallas Memorial Center for Holocaust Studies has a number of glass cases filled with authentic artefacts and 'memorabilia of the Holocaust'.[64] Each artefact is labelled, and its authenticity attested.

Thus a shaving brush and soap becomes transformed into a 'shaving brush and soap used in the Warsaw Ghetto'. A whip becomes a 'whip used by concentration camp guards'. Barbed wire is 'barbed wire from Birkeneau found near the crematoria at Auschwitz-Birkeneau'. Bricks and rocks are 'bricks from the crematorium at Auschwitz-Birkeneau' and 'rocks from the crematorium at Auschwitz-Birkeneau'. Rusty spoons are 'spoons from Auschwitz-Birkeneau'. An old shoe is 'from the more than 800,000 shoes stored at Majdanek'. A bolt was 'taken from the railway track near the crematorium at Auschwitz-Birkeneau'. Another bar of soap was 'soap used in the camps'. A toothbrush and razor are 'from Majdanek'. A water cup was 'used by prisoners at Majdanek'. A 'shower head from Majdanek'. A blanket was 'used by prisoners at Birkeneau'. A pair of trousers were 'worn by prisoners in Majdanek Concentration Camp'. In Donald Horne's words on museums in general, 'such an emphasis on authenticity provides a radiance of value and scarcity that hallows the object in itself, so that often the museum provides not an account of social processes but a collection of isolated objects, sacred in themselves'.[65]

But perhaps the most sacred artefacts in American Holocaust Museums, are the phials of ashes and fragments of bone brought from Europe's killing fields. At Dallas, alongside the 'toothbrush and razor from Majdanek' and 'personal and household items of victims of Nazi Genocide at Auschwitz', lie small piles of 'women's hair from Majdanek' and Auschwitz-Birkeneau, 'Charred bones from Treblinka' and 'Human bones from Majdanek'. In the 'Memorial Room', there are further fragments of human remains. A 'Star of David Shaped Urn' contains 'human bones and ashes' and a small glass scent bottle – with a silver stopper – holds 'ashes from Majdanek'.

These, like the other artefacts on display, have been donated by individuals who collected them in situ. The majority have been brought back from Europe by the Jacobs family, who provided the impetus behind setting up the museum and memorial centre. The 'women's hair' was 'brought by Mike Jacobs from Auschwitz-Birkeneau', the 'Human Bones from Majdanek' were 'donated by Mike and Ginger Jacobs, September 1990' and the human bones and ashes in the 'Star of David Shaped Urn' were 'brought back from the crematoriums of Birkeneau-Auschwitz by Mike Jacobs and were laid to rest on January 29, 1984'. The small bottle of ashes from Majdanek was 'donated by the Hon. D. John McClellan Marshall who collected them at the site in Poland in 1993', in a small scent bottle with a silver stopper engraved with the letter 'M' for 'McClellan Marshall' (and 'Majdanek'?).

This freelance collecting of human remains by survivors is something noted by Dorothy Rabinowitz in a fascinating description of the return of one Holocaust survivor to Majdanek. Here she crawls into the crematoria oven to collect some ashes, which she takes back to America in 'the vinyl envelope that had held her pocket rain bonnet'.[66] Rabinowitz recounts how

> ... once home, just as she expected, everyone she knew wanted some of the ashes. Other people might not understand why you would want something like those ashes from the oven at Majdanek, but to her and her friends it was natural enough: they had no graves to visit; the ashes were all they had for a memorial. Perhaps the survivors' group she belonged to might even one day build a monument to their dead, as had been done in other American cities, and the ashes could be kept there. For now, she kept what she had, little gravelly bits of uneven size, in a white envelope.[67]

That desire on the part of survivors to have some sort of memorial is surely a major motivation behind the building of so many museums-cum-memorials in the United States during the course of the last two decades. Museums such as those in Washington, DC, and Houston are more than simply museums. Like Dallas, they house fragments of human remains and thus in some way become symbolic mass graves. In the memorial room in Houston, a small case on one wall contains earth from Auschwitz, Buchenwald, Dachau, Majdanek, Mauthausen and Treblinka. At Washington, DC, the official groundbreaking ceremony in October 1985 saw the co-mingling of 'the nation's most sacred soil' with ' "holy soils" from European concentration and death camps and venerated cemeteries: Auschwitz, Bergen-Belsen, Dachau, Theresienstadt, Treblinka, and the Warsaw Jewish Cemetery'.[68] Once the building was completed, a similar co-mingling of 'sacred' American and European soil took place with the burying of soil from 39 Holocaust sites and soil from Arlington National Cemetery underneath the eternal flame in the Hall of Remembrance. This represented the coming together – in death – of the victims and the liberators.

With the reburial of human remains in the memorial rooms of museums such as those in Washington, DC, Dallas and Houston, there is a sense in which these institutions themselves are transformed into sites of sacred space. In a similar manner to the spread of medieval religious relics, the relics of the Holocaust have spread to new sacred sites. Coleman and Elsner's reflections on pilgrimage provide a parallel:

... sometimes (rather as relics spread the influence of a person or site) the charisma of a place is even diffused by the 'replication' of that place far from its original location. Benares, for instance, has many smaller counterparts in the Indian subcontinent; Walsingham provides an Anglo-Saxon equivalent of Nazareth; a 'second Mecca' is said by some Muslims to exist in Ajmer.[69]

With the reburial of sacred 'soil' and ashes from Europe's concentration camps the Holocaust museums to Washington, DC, Dallas or Houston have become to Auschwitz what Ajmer is to Mecca. While the pilgrimage to Auschwitz remains the ultimate destination of Holocaust pilgrimage, the emergence of sacred sites throughout the United States offers the next best thing for the would be Holocaust pilgrim. The need to go to the killing fields is lessened when the killing fields have symbolically come to you.

Like Auschwitz, these museums-cum-memorials have become sites of both Holocaust tourism and Holocaust pilgrimage. In many ways those dual roles are accommodated through the demarcation of space into clearly defined 'museum' space and 'memorial' space. Through this separation of space in the museum, the roles of learning and remembering are clearly divided. We are taken through the museum to learn of the Holocaust, and then we are taken into the memorial to remember the victims of the Holocaust whose ashes have symbolically been laid to rest. Thus at Washington, DC, and Houston the permanent exhibition is separated from the 'memorial' space of the Hall of Remembrance and the Memorial Room. This 'memorial' space is designed – at Houston – as 'a place to contemplate what was seen in the permanent exhibition and also to remember those who perished in the Holocaust',[70] and in Washington – as 'America's national memorial to the victims of the Holocaust' where 'visitors are encouraged to light a candle in their memory'.[71]

At Dallas, this division between museum space and memorial space is there in name at least, through the designating of distinct 'Memorial Room' and 'Museum' room. However, fragments of human remains are present in both the memorial and museum space. The presence of 'charred bones from Treblinka' and 'Human Bones from Majdanek' in the display cases in the museum room effectively make this space as sacred as that of the Memorial Room with its 'Star of David Shaped Urn' containing 'human bones and ashes ... from the crematoriums of Birkeneau-Auschwitz' and glass bottle containing 'ashes from Majdanek'. Both the museum and the memorial are repositories for human remains, although in the former the bones and hair are exhibits in glass display cases, while in the latter they are symbolically buried in an urn.

The question of whether it was acceptable to display human remains as a museum exhibit was one raised by the arrival of nine kilograms of human hair from Auschwitz at Washington, DC. Some on the museum's Content Committee saw this material as powerful evidence that the Holocaust had taken place, and thus argued that it should be displayed in the permanent exhibition. Indeed, for Hilberg it was vital that it be displayed as testimony to the 'ultimate rationality of the destruction process'.[72] Others, however, objected to the display of this 'sacred material'. Museum consultant Alice Greenwald and Director of Temporary Exhibits Susan Morgenstein wrote that they could not 'endorse the use of a wall of human hair, or ashes and bones' as 'these relics of once vital individuals, which do not belong in a museum setting but rather in a memorial setting. You run the very real risk of creating a cabinet of horrible curiosities by choosing to use them'.[73] In the end the decision was made to exhibit a large photograph of the piles of hair on display at Auschwitz, and to keep the hair itself in storage.

The phrase 'cabinet of horrible curiosities' is something which comes to mind as you walk around the museum room in Dallas, with its glass display cases with their carefully labelled small piles of human hair and bones. Perhaps these artefacts are better placed in an urn or beneath an eternal flame in memorial space. But by choosing not to display the hair itself in its fragile physicality, Director of the Exhibition Department Martin Smith argued that the museum in Washington, DC, pulled back from telling the whole truth about the Holocaust. It reflected – he claimed – the fact that

> ... there are people so concerned about not upsetting people that they actually are willing to hold back on telling the truth of the Holocaust, because I think what the hair does is to actually bring you to a different layer of truth. But it's not going to be there, and this is part and parcel of the whole problem of a museum about this subject, being in Washington, DC, and being on the Mall. In the end, you mustn't upset too much. And I don't think one can ever upset people too much about this.[74]

Linenthal – in his book on the museum in Washington, DC – argues that

> ... the decision not to display human hair illustrates the clash between the different voices which shaped the museum, the

commemorative and the educational. In this particular case, the commemorative voice, the privileged voice of the survivor, won out. For, as Raul Hilberg once remarked, one of the problematic 'rules' of Holocaust speech is that any survivor, no matter how inarticulate, is superior to the greatest Holocaust historian who did not share in the experience.[75]

For Elie Wiesel, a survivor, there is a sense in which the attempt at understanding that which will never be understood, is bound to trivialise. His preference was thus more for commemoration than education, and he therefore offered – in 1983 – a very different vision of the visitor's encounter with the 'Holocaust' at Washington, DC, than the one displayed. Wiesel's vision was of

... a kind of hall and we enter that hall and it seems endless. And I would like that hall to be covered with photos ... of Treblinka ... From all the far corners of exile and memory people have come there, to die there ... And then I would like maybe a voice or a guide to speak softly, to whisper ... 'look at the faces, look at them well. You don't understand, don't try. Just remember.' ... This is the way I would begin ... I want those people who go there to come out 2,000 years old.[76]

As Linenthal reflects, Wiesel's vision was of a museum which existed

... not to provide proof to counter Holocaust deniers, or as an agent of civic revitalisation, or as institutional prescription for the pathology of modern culture, but as an initiatory centre ... [where] the sacred mystery that was the Holocaust would stamp itself on individual psyches, and visitors would, ideally, emerge with a renewed appreciation of its mystery.[77]

The museum would be, for Wiesel, 'a place where the impossibility of knowing existed alongside the traditional ways of "knowing" in a museum'.[78] And that in many ways captures the essential dilemma provided by these museums-cum-memorials. It is the dilemma of making the 'Holocaust' known and yet also conveying something of the 'unknowability' of an event which has been imbued with a near sacred status by survivors such as Wiesel.

Holocaust museums are difficult to design. Rather than amassing a collection of beautiful items, they seek to provide a narrative of a horrific historical event, and to engage in an act of memory. And both

Houston and Washington, DC, do an effective job in communicating how the Holocaust unfolds. They are powerful museums. Perhaps – as others have commented – the most powerful element of the museum in Washington, DC, is the tower of photographs taken between 1890 and 1941 of the Jews of Eishishok, Lithuania. Murdered over the course of two days in 1941, these Jews are not remembered in their absence through shoes, suitcases, toothbrushes and mounds of hair. They are not even remembered as corpses. Rather they are remembered alive. They are remembered as people who lived vibrant and varied lives.

Walking through this tower of photographs as you make your way down through the permanent exhibition, is to be reminded again of the sheer stupidity of murdering all of these people, of destroying this lively community, of ending 900 years of Jewish life and culture in two days. And again – as in Auschwitz – I am left with the desire to turn the clock back to the days in 1941 before the SS entered Eishishok and let these people live again. But the thing that is frustrating about history is the utter feeling of helplessness when you realise that clocks can't be turned back and Eishishok can't be brought back to life. That is history.

And it is then that I feel a certain sympathy for Wiesel's mystical plans for the museum at Washington, DC. Rather than pretending that we understand how and why all this happened, perhaps it would be better to have simply this tower of photographs and a voice which says, quietly: 'look at the faces, look at them well. You don't understand, don't try. Just remember.' Because thinking that we understand may just be about the most dangerous thing of all.

# Epilogue

> I believe it more and more. History: a lucky dip of meanings.
> Events elude meaning, but we look for meanings. Another
> definition of Man [sic]: the animal who craves meaning – but
> knows ...[1]

The words of history teacher Tom Crick, in Graham Swift's novel
*Waterland*, seem an appropriate ending to a book on the emergence
of the myth of the 'Holocaust' over the course of the last three to four
decades. After all, the myth of the 'Holocaust' involves, above everything else, an attempt to extract meaning from this troubling past.
Due to the nature of this past, the craving for meaning – after the
initial silence – verges on the obsessive. And yet, *despite* the nature
of this past, the tendency has been to opt for meanings that discern
some sort of redemption in the Holocaust.

The myth of the 'Holocaust' has chosen to adopt what Langer calls,
'a discourse of consolation' rather than 'a discourse of ruin'.[2] This
consoling discourse offers us 'a persisting myth about the triumph of
the spirit that colours the disaster with a rosy tinge and helps us to
manage the unimaginable without having to look at its naked and
ugly face'.[3] From 'Anne Frank' onwards, there has been a tendency for
the myth of the 'Holocaust' to temper representations of this ugly
past with stories of redemption. At Yad Vashem it is the 'although ...
also' telling of the past in terms of 'Holocaust and heroism' and
'Holocaust and rebirth', and at the United States Holocaust Memorial
Museum it is the closure offered by 'liberation', which provides the
rose coloured spectacles through which the 'Holocaust' is seen. In
both cases, there is a sense in which 'a discourse of consolation' has
been adopted to deal with this disturbing past.

Yet while a shared seeking for redemption characterises the
tellings of this past to the present, at the end of the twentieth
century, a multitude of meanings have been drawn from the murder

of six million Jews. Holocaust history is to some extent at least, 'a lucky dip of meanings'. It can be used – as Liebman and Don-Yehiya acknowledge – to

> ... point to the possibility of evil or the reality of evil. It can suggest that we must guard against the aberration of Nazism, or that in a crisis the world will not rescue Jews in mortal peril. It can point to the world's indifference to the murder of Jews, or to the courage of a few, who stood up to Nazi terror on behalf of Jews. It can mean Nazi against Jew, or German against Jew, or Christian against Jew, or *goy* against Jew – or evil against good, strong against weak. It can suggest how monstrous a few can become, or how readily all of us can, by our silence or inaction, become complicit in monstrous crimes. It can point to the weakness of Eastern European Jews who allowed themselves to be murdered, or to the heroism and inner resources required to face death with dignity and faith, or to the courage of Jews who resisted and rebelled. Or the Holocaust can be understood as a demonstration of Jewish helplessness in the Diaspora and the consequent importance of 'Jewish power', which the State of Israel represents.[4]

While 'the facts do not necessarily lend equal support to each of these meanings', Liebman and Don-Yehiya suggest that 'a sufficient factual basis can be found to reinforce any one to which primary sentiments and world views might predispose a person'.[5] And this, I think, is the attraction of the myth of the 'Holocaust' to the contemporary world. The 'Holocaust' past is one to which a multitude of meanings can be attributed, and one from which a multitude of lessons can be drawn.

As the three people and the three places which have formed the focus for this reflection on the nature of the myth of the 'Holocaust' reveal, quite different lessons have been drawn from this past in Europe, the United States and Israel during the last three to four decades. Reflecting on what has happened to Anne Frank, Adolf Eichmann, Oskar Schindler, Auschwitz, Yad Vashem and the United States Holocaust Memorial Museum, is in many ways to experience a similar journey to the one made by the journalist Judith Miller who notes, 'as I travelled in Europe and America, I heard different people describe different Holocausts'.[6] At the end of the twentieth century, there is not one homogenous 'Holocaust' out there. Andreas Huyssen reminds us that,

... the same facts have generated significantly different accounts and memory. In Germany, the Holocaust signifies an absence of Jews and a traumatic burden on national identity, in which genuine attempts at mourning are hopelessly entangled with narcissistic injury, ritual breast-beating, and repression. Thus in Germany, until recently, there has been little public knowledge of, or interest in, what was actually lost through the destruction. In Israel, the Holocaust became central to the foundation of the state, both as the end point of a disavowed history of Jews as victims, and as a starting point of a new history of nation, self-assertion, and resistance. In the Israeli imagination, the Warsaw ghetto uprising has thus been invested with the force of a mythic memory of resistance and heroism unfathomable in Germany. The American focus of the Holocaust concentrates on America as liberator of the camps and haven for refugees and immigrants, and American Holocaust memorials are structured accordingly. In the Soviet account, the genocide of the Jews lost its ethnic specificity and simply became part of the story of the Nazi suppression of international communism in general to an extent which now requires a rewriting of the narratives of East European and Soviet memorial sites.[7]

This summary of the diversity of meanings given to the 'Holocaust' within different national contexts, resonates with the sense of different 'Holocausts' which I have been talking about in this book. There can be little doubt that the representation of the 'Holocaust' has differed – often-times quite radically – over space. That sense of difference is quite striking when walking through the national representations of the 'Holocaust' on show at Yad Vashem and the United States Holocaust Memorial Museum. Both are exhibiting the same historical event, but there are radical differences in what is – and is not – seen to be significant. As Huyssen is right to point out, the Israeli telling at Yad Vashem stresses resistance in general and the Warsaw ghetto uprising in particular. In contrast, these themes are given far less weight at the United States Holocaust Memorial Museum, which reflects an American concern with liberation and the post-war immigration of the survivors. While Israel tells the narrative with 'heroes and martyrs' as the central characters, America tells the narrative with rescuers and survivors as the central characters.

Not only do Israel and America tell different versions of the same story, but they tend to draw different lessons from that story. Thus in Israel, the 'Holocaust' was seen – in the 1950s and 1960s in particular

– to provide examples of – as Liebman and Don-Yehiya phrase it – 'the heroism and inner resources required to face death with dignity and faith' and 'the courage of Jews who resisted and rebelled'. As I have suggested, these layers of meaning have – more recently – been overlaid with lessons of victimhood and the 'world's indifference to the murder of Jews'. Underlying these have been the constant assumption that 'the Holocaust can be understood as a demonstration of Jewish helplessness in the Diaspora and the consequent importance of "Jewish power", which the State of Israel represents'.

By contrast, in the United States, rather different lessons are drawn. In Spielberg's 'Holocaust' movie, 'the courage of a few, who stood up to Nazi terror on behalf of Jews' is the lesson drawn from the telling of the 'Holocaust', through the person of Oskar Schindler. Something of this same lesson is seen at the United States Holocaust Memorial Museum, with its focus upon both rescuers and liberators. However, in Washington, DC, the stress is perhaps more upon the 'Holocaust' as both the reality and 'possibility of evil', which becomes the 'Other' against which the American self can be constructed.

In general terms, it appears possible to distinguish – as Omer Bartov suggests – between two broad strands of meanings which have been given to the 'Holocaust'. Bartov is no doubt reflecting upon his experience of visiting both Yad Vashem and the United States Holocaust Memorial Museum when he writes that

> ... Holocaust museums seem to offer two narrative options: one that presents Zionism as the ultimate answer to Jewish persecution by host gentile nations; another that argues in favour of toleration and understanding for cultural and ethnic minorities. The first is a nationalist narrative, the second a humanist one. These are not mutually contradictory messages, but they do reflect the social and intellectual environment in which they tend to be disseminated.[8]

In some ways, the former – dubbed by Bartov 'a nationalist narrative', although it can also be described as a Zionist narrative – can be seen to be most influential in Israel, while the latter – dubbed by Bartov 'a humanist' narrative, although it can also be described as a universal narrative – can be seen to be most influential in the United States. As Liebman and Don-Yehiya note with regard to meanings given to the 'Holocaust' in Israel, 'among those close to the religious tradition there is greater propensity to view the Holocaust in terms of Israel against the Nations, than there is among nonreligious Jews, just as more Israelis than American Jews view the Holocaust this way'.[9]

However, within both Israel and the United States, it is possible to discern both narratives. Thus, there has been a tendency to draw universal lessons from the Holocaust in the United States but, as *Schindler's List* reveals, these universal lessons can stand side-by-side with a Zionist narrative. More significantly perhaps – as I have suggested – there has been a breakdown of consensus within Israeli society as to what lessons should be drawn from the 'Holocaust'. This breakdown in consensus is less about the 'Holocaust' past than it is about the Israeli present and future. In particular, the Israeli left has reacted to the claims of the nationalist right that the 'Holocaust' teaches Israel of the need to stand alone versus the nations. In direct contrast, more universal lessons have been drawn by the left, who have pointed to the 'Holocaust' teaching, 'how readily all of us can ... [Israelis included] become complicit in monstrous crimes.'

Thus while different national tellings of the 'Holocaust' can be broadly discerned, it would be wrong to paint a picture of monolithic national versions of this 'myth'. The representation of the 'Holocaust' after all does not simply vary over space, *but* also – as I have tried to explore in this book – over time. In short, history matters. For example, the shifting representation of 'Anne Frank', and the changing meanings given to the 'Holocaust' at 'Auschwitz' and Yad Vashem, all point to the importance of chronology in understanding the changing shape of the myth of the 'Holocaust' in the last fifty years.

With 'Anne Frank', there is a sense in which the division that Bartov draws between 'universal' and 'nationalist' meanings can be taken chronologically rather than geographically. As I have suggested, 'Anne Frank' assumes a universal meaning in the immediate post-war context, which comes to be overlaid with a more specifically Jewish set of meanings once the myth of the 'Holocaust' has emerged. The result of this, is that the contemporary 'Anne Frank' is very much a product of history. In order to understand the different meanings given to the 'Holocaust', we need to think both about different national *and* historical experiences. And the reality at the end of the twentieth century, is that the myth of the 'Holocaust' is a complex mixture of historically and geographically situated narratives and meanings which have accumulated over the course of the last five decades in Europe, Israel and the United States.

In many ways, the myth of the 'Holocaust' seems flexible enough to cope with those competing narratives and conflicting meanings. It does seem to be a bottomless 'lucky dip' which can mean all things to all people. However, there are times when that flexibility appears to be stretched to breaking point, as revealed by the battle over brand-name 'Auschwitz'. Auschwitz is a site which has accumulated layers of meaning from the time of its liberation by the Red Army. In the period before the emergence of the myth of the 'Holocaust' it came to represent Fascist aggression within a Soviet bloc narrative of the war. With the emergence of the myth of the 'Holocaust' however, the site's Jewishness was reasserted, as this place came above all other places to represent the Nazi murder of Jews, and thus to become a synonym for the 'Holocaust'. Parallel to this however, a process of 'Catholicising' Auschwitz can be seen as taking place. And then with the rise of the myth of the 'Holocaust' – and the fall of the Berlin Wall – this site became a place of both pilgrimage and 'Holocaust tourism' for Western-European, American and Israeli tour groups. The result is that the place and symbol called 'Auschwitz' has been increasingly contested. The Carmelite Convent controversy was the highpoint of that contestation, but by no means the end point.

At the end of the twentieth century, it is not simply 'Auschwitz' that has been contested, but the 'Holocaust' itself. The 'Holocaust' – like 'Auschwitz' – is a desirable icon and a contested brandname. One aspect of that contestation, can be seen in the last decade, as the centre of gravity of the 'Holocaust' has shifted westwards. This has resulted – in Israel in particular – in increasing disquiet at the perceived 'Americanisation of the Holocaust'. Israel had her 'year of the Holocaust' back in 1961 – at the time of the Eichmann Trial – but the United States has had her 'year of the Holocaust' much more recently – in 1993. The result is – as I have suggested – that if you want the 'Holocaust' in the 1990s, then America is a better place to go looking for it than either Europe or Israel.

The major products of the American 'year of the Holocaust' – the 'Holocaust' museums in Los Angeles and Washington, DC, and Spielberg's filmic 'Holocaust' – were heavily criticised in Israel. Loshitzky points to Israeli journalist Tom Segev's 'vicious' criticism of *Schindler's List*, which she sees as expressing 'latent hostility toward the American Jew who "stole our *Shoah*" '.[10] And I think this gets right to the heart of the matter. Underlying the Israeli critiques of American tellings of the 'Holocaust', is a sense that Israel – rather than America – should have a monopoly over this past. However, as 1993 proves, that monopoly has not simply been challenged but effectively overturned.

Yet Israel is fighting back, and in particular Yad Vashem is seeking to claim back the '*Shoah*' from Washington, DC. With the launching of the Yad Vashem 2001 project, there is a self-conscious attempt to establish *the* definitive 'Holocaust' museum on the hills on the outskirts of Jerusalem, rather than on the Mall in Washington, DC. This is to be a bigger and better 'Holocaust' museum which 'will provide for the needs and requirements of the 2 million visitors expected annually'.[11] It is perhaps not entirely coincidental that the expected number of visitors equals the number of 'Holocaust tourists' already visiting the United States Holocaust Memorial Museum each year. To cater for these increased tourist numbers, the museum space is to be more than doubled and totally restructured.

There has long been a perceived need for restructuring at Yad Vashem. Given the age of the museum and a shortage of state funding, its permanent exhibition is rather dated. You don't get the slick presentation or the mass of 'authentic' objects of the United States Holocaust Memorial Museum, but 'a poor man's exhibit' which 'contains some photographs, a slide show, a film, a few "authentic" requisites, mainly partisans' weapons'.[12] However, all of that is set to change, with the creation of a new museum which will 'relate to the visitors of the 21st century in the language they speak'.[13] This means amongst other things, 'providing direct access to the state-of-the-art databases',[14] and presenting 'many more artefacts, diaries, documents and modes of transmitting the information including the use of multimedia equipment and computer stations'.[15] It will amount to nothing less than 'vast museological changes'.[16]

However, while there is clearly an attempt to copy the United States Holocaust Memorial Museum's success in using multimedia displays and artefacts to communicate the 'Holocaust' to a late 20th century audience, Yad Vashem 2001 is not going to be simply a United States Holocaust Memorial Museum in Jerusalem. Rather, it will quite self-consciously continue to tell an Israeli – not an American – version of the 'Holocaust'. Chairman of the Yad Vashem Directorate Avner Shalev writes that in the new museum, 'the displays, presented from a Jewish perspective, will emphasise the Jewish reality during the Holocaust, providing a detailed picture of the terror of daily life under German Nazis and their collaborators, and the varying responses by the local Jewish populations'.[17] It is to be a museum which will address the question of

> ... Jewish life between the two world wars, the complexities of existence and survival under Nazi occupation for the Jews and their leadership, focusing on the ways of coping and forms of resistance, among many other issues. The new museum will emphasise Jews as subjects rather than as objects in the hands of the Nazis as has been presented until recently.[18]

Thus it is clear that there will be a continued emphasis upon the 'although ... also' of Jewish resistance which has characterised the Israeli myth of the 'Holocaust'.

Yet while there is to be much in the way of continuity with existing elements of the Yad Vashem myth of the 'Holocaust', it seems likely that there will also be changes. As the promotional material acknowledges, 'the masses of data based on archival material, research and testimonies that have been gathered over the past few decades' means that 'there is an urgent need to expand, alter and add additional emphases to the existing historic exhibition'.[19] Thus, 'the Museum's conceptual foundations have been readdressed. The exhibits of the story of the Holocaust will be a blend of chronology and themes and will include subjects that to this date have not been explored in depth'.[20]

Such changes will no doubt be in part influenced by new research findings on the Holocaust past, but they will also be influenced by shifting present concerns. And one of those increasingly important present concerns – rescue – is something which will feature in a museum where

> ... the deeds of the murderers, accomplices, and those 'bystanders' who chose to remain silent will be accurately depicted, while in stark contrast, special attention will be drawn to the acts of the Righteous Among the Nations who proved that courage can vanquish the greater evil, and that their behaviour was in fact, very human.[21]

The language 'courage can vanquish the greater evil' sounds somewhat reminiscent of the 'Holocaust' lessons offered by Spielberg's *Schindler's List*. and I can't help wondering if Yad Vashem isn't going to be – in some ways at least – 'Schindlerised'.

As I have reflected, Yad Vashem has changed over the course of the last thirty or so years. However, these changes have largely been accumulative. Thus they have involved the steady addition of memorials, which has created a site which is effectively a number of layers of memory. Yet Yad Vashem 2001 is to see – to some extent at least – the destruction of what has gone before, and its replacing with what is seen to be a better, more up-to-date, and more 'powerful' telling of the 'Holocaust'. And faced with that, part of me sees this to be vandalism of sorts. Reading the Yad Vashem 2001 – Masterplan material, I have a feeling of affection for the old Yad Vashem with its cafeteria, 'poor man's exhibit' and pillar of heroism. Much of this is to be swept away and replaced with a 'Holocaust' for the 21st century.

Leaving the original Yad Vashem alongside the Yad Vashem 2001 would prove strangely effective. In essence what such a decision would do, is to open the eyes of the visitor to the reality that what is on display here is the representation of the 'Holocaust', and that that representation changes shape over time as well as space. Thus, we could visit a 1950s-60s Israeli 'Holocaust' and a 2001 Israeli 'Holocaust', and through that gain an insight into how this event has been – and is being – remembered by Israel.

One option for the heritage industry is to lay the very process of 'heritagisation' bare, and to invite visitors to think about how and why the past is remembered the way it is. Setting the new improved Yad Vashem alongside the old Yad Vashem, would allow for just that sort of reflective encounter. It would enable visitors to reflect on the changing shape of 'Holocaust' memory which may actually – as James Young argues – be one of the best ways of remembering this horrific event. Young has suggested that

> ... the best memorial to the fascist era and its victims in Germany today may not be a single memorial at all – but only the never-to-be-resolved debate over which kind of memory to preserve, how to do it, in whose name, and to what end. Imagine, for example, a series of annual competitions, whereby the proposed designs and jury's debate are exhibited in lieu of an installed winner. Visitors to such a memorial installation would be invited to submit their own evaluations of designs, which would in turn be added to the overall memorial text. Instead of a fixed figure for memory, the debate itself – perpetually unresolved amid ever-changing conditions – would be enshrined.[22]

Yad Vashem, could potentially offer something similar. Rather than bulldozing the old permanent exhibition and entry way, and building a new, 'improved' 'fixed figure for memory', the old and new could stand side by side and thereby point to the impact of 'ever-changing conditions' in the present, upon memory of the past. Rather than giving the visitor what is perceived as a bigger, better and more technically accomplished experience of the 'Holocaust', this memorial site could give to visitors two 'Holocaust' museums (one old, one new) which would force visitors to ask themselves how and why the two are different.

That idea of leaving the old representation when inserting the new, is something being discussed at present with regard to Bergen-Belsen. Driving back from Bergen-Belsen to Hannover, the site's director – Thomas Rahe – told me of recent calls for a memorial text which would remember the full diversity of victims of this concentration camp. At present the text on the main memorial is that agreed upon by the British, who had control of the camp in the immediate post-war years. Their decision was to invite all nations whose citizens had been incarcerated at the camp to submit a phrase to be included on the memorial wall. Thus there are texts in, for example, Hungarian, despite those who were taken to Bergen-Belsen being taken there not as 'Hungarians' but as Jews. While there are texts in Hebrew and Yiddish, the memorial tends to downplay the Jewishness of the majority of the victims, by representing them primarily in terms of nationality rather than ethnicity. But rather than tearing down the old, and putting up a new memorial in its place – as happened when the old texts were removed from the memorial at Auschwitz-II – the proposal is for a second memorial to be built alongside the memorial wall erected in 1947. This second memorial would be dated, and contain texts relating the 'ethnicity' and 'identity' – rather than nationality – of victims. It would thus remember hitherto unrepresented groups of victims such as homosexuals.

Visitors would discover two memorials side-by-side, which reflect a changing history of remembering the 'Holocaust'. If this new memorial were to be built, it would become the sixth major memorial on the site of this former concentration camp. A short distance from the memorial wall and the proposed site for the new memorial, stands a stone memorial unveiled in 1946 by those Jews who survived the war and remained in Bergen-Belsen when it was transformed into a Displaced Persons Camp. Next to this, is a stone dedicated by Israeli President Chaim Herzog in 1987. A ten minute walk away, are a Soviet memorial in the cemetery for Soviet Prisoners of War which was also erected in 1946, and a German memorial from 1968. Thus, if the proposed memorial gets the go-ahead, visitors to Bergen-Belsen will encounter six layers of memorials in one site, and be forced to ask themselves who erected these, when they were erected, and – perhaps most importantly – why they were erected. In the process, visitors would be forced to ask the perhaps rather disquieting question as to what has been forgotten – or suppressed – at particular times in recent history, as much as what has been remembered.

By keeping the old Yad Vashem alongside the new, and creating a multi-layered site of 'Holocaust' memory, visitors would be forced to ask the same sort of questions at this hilltop site on the outskirts of Jerusalem. Rather than entering the new entrance plaza and heading onto the new museum, the visitor would be forced to decide whether to go to the old 'Yad Vashem' or the new 'Yad Vashem' first.

More importantly, the visitor would be led to ask the bigger question of why it was decided – in 2001 – that there needed to be a bigger 'Holocaust' museum, and to reflect upon what the differences between the two permanent exhibitions were. This would focus upon the visitor a sense of self-reflectiveness, which is precisely what the proposed erecting of a new memorial alongside the old at Bergen-Belsen aims at doing.

In part, perhaps, the idea of having effectively two 'Yad Vashems' on the same hill is a reflection of postmodern sensibilities. I could perhaps be described – in John Urry's words – as one of the growing number of 'post-tourists' who,

> ... finds pleasure in the multitude of games that can be played and knows that there is no authentic tourist experience. They know that the apparently authentic fishing village could not exist without the income from tourism or that the glossy brochure is a piece of pop culture. For the post-tourist there is no particular problem about the inauthentic. It is merely another game to be played at, another pastiched surface feature of post-modern experience.[23]

For this particular 'post-"Holocaust" tourist', there is no authentic 'Holocaust tourist' experience. Rather there are many 'mythical' tellings of this historical event. And yet the problem is that far from the 'Holocaust' heritage industry acknowledging that its products are only a museum or a movie which gives a partial – and ideologically laden – telling of this event called the 'Holocaust', the tendency has been for 'Holocaust' heritage to make far grander claims. Thus the museum in Washington, DC, aims through the use of 'authentic' artefacts to take us on the journey that the Holocaust victims took, and Steven Spielberg claims to have acted as a 'witness' in making what is a Holocaust 'document'. But walking through a 'Holocaust' museum or watching a 'Holocaust' movie – however 'realistic' they attempt to be – is not to experience the Holocaust. The United States Holocaust Memorial Museum and *Schindler's List* are not the Holocaust, but simply representations of the 'Holocaust'.

And because they are representations, these museums and movies – as Frank Rich acknowledges – have a 'limited shelf life'. Rich suggests that 'the occasional Disneyland touches in the Washington Holocaust Museum – the you-are-there "passport" assigning each visitor an individual camp prisoner, for instance – may not survive the theme-park-crazed America that spawned them'.[24] And the result is that in coming decades, the United States Holocaust Memorial Museum will look as dated as Yad Vashem presently does. No doubt the response will then be to undertake the same kind of refit that Yad Vashem is presently planning, so as to produce a more up-to-date, bigger and better 'Holocaust'. However, as I have suggested with Yad Vashem, the most positive thing to do may be to keep those 'out-dated' representations of this event as a document which reflects the meanings given to the 'Holocaust' in 1990s America – 'Disneyland touches' and all.

After all, doing this would be to acknowledge that representations by definition are historically situated, and therefore partial. The implications of acknowledging representations to be historically situated is to accept that Yad Vashem's historical museum tells us as much about how 1970s Israel remembers the 'Holocaust' as it does about the 'Holocaust' itself, and that the United States Holocaust Memorial Museum's permanent exhibition tells us as much about how 1990s America remembers the 'Holocaust' as it does about the 'Holocaust'. Thus rather than going to Yad Vashem to learn lessons from the Holocaust, we should perhaps go to learn about 1970s Israel by seeing how the 'Holocaust' has been represented. And rather than go to the United States Holocaust Memorial Museum to learn about America in the 1990s by seeing how this particular national museum has chosen to represent this troubling past. There is a sense in which we learn more from critically examining the lessons we are being offered than in simply passively taking them in, because the lessons being offered tell us as much about the society and the generation doing the remembering, as they do the historical reality itself. This can be seen, I think, from Omer Bartov's reflections after visiting the Museum of Tolerance in Los Angeles. He notes down the lessons which he had been bombarded at this site of 'Holocaust tourism':

What is needed to avoid another Holocaust (or LA riot) argues the museum is tolerance. All we need to do is tolerate, nay, love each other, and then we can return to our respective slums or villas wholly transformed, accepting of our fate and fortune. Prejudice, we are told, was at the root of genocide, hence we must eliminate prejudice (not its causes) and all will be well. Not a change of material realities, but a change of heart, not a transformation of the conditions that perpetuate frustration and violence, but a transformation of our perception of these conditions.[25]

These are surely lessons which tell us as much about 1990s Los Angeles as they do about the 'Holocaust'. But saying that is not to invalidate them. After all, learning about 1990s Los Angeles may not be a bad thing to do.

But the problem comes when 'Holocaust' museums – and 'Holocaust' movies – aren't up front about the fact that the lessons being offered are the products of that particular time and place, more than they are lessons drawn directly from this event which is called the 'Holocaust'. History is after all a complex reality and thus notoriously difficult to draw any simple lessons from. However, at the end of the twentieth century, 'Shoah business' is quick to draw lessons from this past. And yet the lessons drawn are in reality lessons inspired much more by present needs than understanding of the past.

There is a misplaced optimism at present, in the redemptive potential of engaging with this event we call the 'Holocaust' and learning lessons from this past. Bus-loads of schoolchildren are taken on guided tours of 'Holocaust' museums and American presidents and chat show hosts urge us to watch 'Holocaust' movies, because the assumption is that engaging with this past will make us better citizens. Shalev even goes so far as to promise us that 'Yad Vashem paves the way for a better future'.[26] And yet such optimism, seems to me to be woefully misplaced. As Langer suggests, we do well to remember that the idea of learning from history cuts two ways. He recalls

> I can hardly remember a Holocaust conference I've attended during the past decade where someone hasn't echoed George Santayana's solemn platitude that those who ignore the past are doomed to repeat it. The so-called ethnic cleansing in Yugoslavia is only one of a dozen episodes in recent years to prove that Santayana's maxim is nothing more than a piece of rhetorical excess ... Indeed, it could be argued about the violence in Bosnia that the contending forces not only have not ignored the past of the Holocaust, but have paid careful attention to it in order to learn more about how to dehumanise their enemy in the name of some purifying ideology.[27]

And yet despite the inherent dangers that Langer points out, there continues to be an optimistic assumption that knowledge about the 'Holocaust' is a guarantee that racially motivated mass murder will not happen again. That assumption lies behind the badges emblazoned with the logo 'Never Again', which Gourevitch found on sale at the United States Holocaust Memorial Museum bookshop for $1. The implicit subtitle to these badges is – I think – 'Never again, because this museum guarantees that this thing will never happen again'.

While our faith in the power of *'Shoah* business' to prevent the Holocaust happening again may be a comfort of sorts, it is surely false comfort. To pin our hopes on the myth of the 'Holocaust' having the potential to prevent the Holocaust happening again is to fail to recognise that engaging with the 'myth' is rather different from engaging with the reality. A degree of confusion exists between the myth of the 'Holocaust' and the historical event itself. The critical distinction between the two tends to be neither stressed by the heritage industry nor picked up on by the increasing numbers of 'Holocaust tourists'.

I was reminded of this when visiting the Anne Frank House, where we stood in line in the giftshop to add our names to a visitors' book which is filled with the sort of statements – 'never again', 'this has changed my life' – which seem to be chanted every time that the 'Holocaust' is represented. And I have to admit that I feel a little cynicism every time I hear and read those familiar phrases.

I couldn't help but wonder what all these well-meaning people had meant when they lined up to write those phrases in this visitors' book. What was it – after walking through the Anne Frank House – that they were remembering anyway? The exhibition is very minimal in this unfurnished house which relies on its aura as the 'real thing' where history happened. We learn next to nothing about the historical event called the 'Holocaust', and relatively little about the Frank family. So what is it that is being commemorated and what must never happen again? And how can this experience of shuffling around a small unfurnished house in the centre of Amsterdam change anyone's life? I felt that these lofty sentiments were induced more by guilt than by understanding.

There is a strong sense in which, half a century after the event, there is far more guilt about the 'Holocaust' than there is understanding. Yara Dekking's words with specific reference to the Netherlands in the 1980s would appear to have a wider significance.

> Yes, people are interested now ... But the screaming and demands often are a way of coping with shame. The uproar, I think, is a way of masking our inability to examine and analyse these shameful events in our past. Even Jews who yell "never again" are engaging in a form of self-defence. They are not really confronting the fact that it did happen, and that it happened here, and that it could happen again. Perhaps not in the same way or perhaps not to them, but to others.[28]

Dekking's words surely cause us to reflect on what good all this contemporary obsession with the 'Holocaust' actually does.

Despite – or perhaps even because of – all the noise about the 'Holocaust' there is little comprehension of what this thing really was. Rosenfeld notes that an American Jewish Congress poll found that '38% of American adults and 53% of high school students either do not know or offer incorrect answers to the question "What does the term 'the Holocaust' refer to?" ', leading them to conclude that a 'serious knowledge gap exists for both adults and youth in the US with regard to basic information about the Holocaust'.[29] There is – Rosenfeld suggests – a 'seeming paradox' in that 'while the Americans know the least about the Holocaust, they seem to care the most, with large percentages of those polls replying that they deem it "essential" or "important" that Americans "know about and understand the Holocaust".'[30]

It is almost as if we have this sense that this thing is important, but don't quite know what it really is. We are, therefore, perhaps not really that much closer to making sense of the Holocaust. Myth has replaced reality, and indeed myth has become more important than reality. And in one sense there is nothing wrong with that. Perhaps myth is always more powerful than reality. But when we engage with that 'myth' let's not kid ourselves that we are engaging with the reality of this thing that has become known as the 'Holocaust'. *Schindler's List* is after all just a movie, and the United States Holocaust Memorial Museum is just a museum, despite all claims to the contrary.

Something of that sense of the 'Holocaust' museum in Washington, DC, being just a museum emerges in Gourevitch's account of how his visit to the United States Holocaust Memorial Museum ended:

> After I left the museum, I bought a soda and strolled along the Mall. When I finished my drink, I found a trash can and was about to toss in my bottle when I noticed a familiar-looking grey card sitting atop the garbage already there. I reached in and pulled it out: Holocaust museum identity card No. 1221, Maria Sava Moise, Gypsy, had survived the war, only to wind up as a part of the litter of a Washington tourist's afternoon.[31]

Gourevitch's words raise the question of whether visiting the Washington, DC, museum is nothing more than one more stop on the crowded itinerary of a busy tourist to Washington, DC. And the answer is – I would suggest – that of course it is. And I see nothing terribly wrong with that. Why not go to this museum as you would any other. But one should avoid giving this museum or any museum some special sacred status because of the event that it refers to. In the case of the Washington, DC, museum, it is a museum which tells us as much about contemporary America as it does the Holocaust, because it is a museum which gives us an Americanised myth of the 'Holocaust'.

The myth of the 'Holocaust' is much more interested in meaning than memory, and thus ultimately much more interested in the present than the past. One aspect of that present is – in the case of the United States in particular – the reality of Holocaust denial. Museums such as the United States Holocaust Memorial Museum and movies such as *Schindler's List* have as a self-conscious goal not simply teaching the public lessons from this past, but also the aim of disproving the claims of those who deny the Holocaust. These claims – which are fairly widespread in the United States – have done much to encourage the expansion of '*Shoah* business' in the United States in particular. For survivors, the claims of 'Holocaust deniers' are not simply galling, but also downright offensive. The response of financing museums to tell the 'truth' about the Holocaust is perfectly understandable. And that is the response that has been seen over the course of the last couple of decades. As Alvin Rosenfeld notes, the 'more than 100 Holocaust institutions throughout the United States and Canada ... which are dedicated to educating the public about the Holocaust ... exist largely because Holocaust survivors in North America have seen to it that they exist'.[32] For many survivors, there is a strong sense that there needs to be concrete reminders of the Holocaust to prove the reality of this past when there are no more living witnesses to counter the claims of Holocaust deniers. A building programme which seeks to fix the 'Holocaust' in both the American landscape and consciousness is not so much fuelled simply by a fear that the Holocaust will simply be forgotten, but by a fear that the Holocaust will be erased from memory.

Nonetheless, building museums and making movies may not be the best strategy for dealing with 'Holocaust deniers'. After all, it amounts to attempting to counter the questioning of the reality of the Holocaust, by offering in its place a representation of the 'Holocaust'. Indeed, building museums and making movies may be the worst possible strategy. As I have suggested, there is a danger that 'Holocaust' museums and movies play into the hands of deniers, because they tend to blur the critical distinction between reality and representation. Cole's critique of Auschwitz-I is surely an object lesson here.

More critically however, the assumption that '*Shoah* business' can defeat Holocaust denial is fundamentally misplaced because ironically 'Shoah business' may actually produce denial. In many ways, 'Holocaust denial' has emerged only within the context of the emergence of the myth of the 'Holocaust'. It was not until the 'Holocaust' emerged as an iconic event that it was perceived to be an event which was deemed to be worth denying. There is after all a lot of history out there which someone could choose to deny ever happened if they felt so inspired. That the 'Holocaust' has been signalled out for denial is because of its present iconic status rather than anything else. It is not that surprising that Anne Frank's diary and the gas chambers at Auschwitz have been chosen by deniers as central elements of their own myth-making.

In essence, 'Holocaust denial' is much more an attack on the myth of the 'Holocaust' than it is an attack on the historical event itself, because denying the Holocaust is primarily a product of present concerns, rather than an engagement with the past. At the end of the twentieth century one by-product of the myth of the 'Holocaust' is the 'denial of the Holocaust'. There is – I think – an unintended symbiotic relationship of sorts between the two. The result is that building more 'Holocaust' museums is – if anything – likely to feed yet more 'Holocaust denial' claims, which is – if anything – likely to result in the building of yet more 'Holocaust' museums. It is perhaps only when the 'Holocaust' is not perceived as the iconic event of the twentieth century and when 'Shoah business' is no longer big business, that the focus of the attacks of 'Holocaust' deniers will shift elsewhere. If this is the case, our contemporary obsession with the 'Holocaust' may not simply be doing us less good than we often claim. It may actually be doing us harm.

# Notes

## Prologue

1. Wolf, A.J., 'The Centrality of the Holocaust is a Mistake' in M. Berenbaum, *After Tragedy and Triumph. Essays in Modern Jewish Thought and the American Experience* (New York, 1990) pp. 44-5.

2. Glazer, N., *American Judaism* (Chicago, 1972) pp. 114-15.

3. Jick, L.A., 'The Holocaust: Its Use and Abuse within the American Public', *Yad Vashem Studies* 14 (1981) p. 307.

4. Linenthal, E.T., *Preserving Memory. The Struggle to Create America's Holocaust Museum* (New York, 1997) p. 7.

5. Marrus, M.R., *The Holocaust in History* (Harmondsworth, 1993) p. 200.

6. Jick, op. cit., (1981) p. 309.

7. Lopate, P., 'Resistance to the Holocaust', *Tikkun* 4, No. 3(1989) p. 65.

8. ibid., p. 62.

9. Rabinowitz, D., *New Lives. Survivors of the Holocaust Living in America* (New York, 1977) p. 196.

10. Liebman, C.S. and Don-Yehiya, E., *Civil Religion in Israel. Traditional Judaism and Political Culture in the Jewish State* (Berkeley, 1983) p. 7.

11. Langer, L.L., *Admitting the Holocaust* (Oxford, 1995) p. 33.

12. Lopate, op. cit., (1989) p. 56.

13. Mosse, G.L., *Fallen Soldiers. Reshaping the Memory of the World Wars* (New York, 1990) p. 7.

14. Winter, J., *Sites of Memory, Sites of Mourning* (Cambridge, 1995) pp. 17-18.

15. Mosse, op. cit., (1990) p. 7.

16. Linenthal, op. cit., (1997) p. 1. (Emphasis mine)

17. Huyssen, A., 'Monument and Memory in a Postmodern Age' in J.E. Young (ed.) *The Art of Memory. Holocaust Memorials in History* (New York, 1994) p. 9.

18. Eliach, Y., 'President's Commission on the Holocaust: Reflections' cited in Linenthal, op. cit., (1997) p. 13.

19. Hilberg, R., 'Developments in the Historiography of the Holocaust' in A. Cohen, J. Gelber and C. Wardi (eds) *Comprehending the Holocaust* (Frankfurt am Main, 1988) p. 21.

20. *Oxford English Dictionary*. Second Edition (Oxford, 1989)

21. Rosenfeld, A.H., 'The Americanisation of the Holocaust' in A.H. Rosenfeld (ed.), *Thinking About the Holocaust: After Half a Century* (Bloomington, 1997) p. 121

22. *Oxford English Dictionary*. Second Edition (Oxford, 1989)

23. Jick, op. cit., (1981) p. 309.

24. ibid., p. 310.

25. Smith, T.W., 'The Polls – A Review. The Holocaust Denial Controversy', *Public Opinion Quarterly* 59, No. 2 (1995) p. 272.

26. Young, J.E., *The Texture of Memory. Holocaust Memorials and Meaning* (New Haven, 1993) p. 211.

27. ibid., p. 211.

28. Young, J.E., *Writing and Rewriting the Holocaust. Narrative and the Consequences of Interpretation* (Bloomington, 1990) p. 118.

29. Ibid., p. 132.

30. De Mildt, D., *In the Name of the People: Perpetrators of Genocide in the Reflection of their Post-War Prosecution in West Germany* (The Hague, 1996) p. 12.

31. ibid., footnote 79, p. 333 referring to R.L. Braham, *The Eichmann Case: A Source Book* (New York, 1969)

32. Rabinowitz, op. cit., (1977) p. 193.

33. Amitai Etzioni cited in Bauman, Z., *Modernity and the Holocaust* (Cambridge 1991) p. 167.

34. Neusner, J., *Death and Birth of Judaism. The Impact of Christianity, Secularism, and the Holocaust on Jewish Faith* (New York, 1987) p. 275.

35. ibid., p. 279.

36. Lipstadt, D.E., 'The Holocaust: Symbol and "Myth" in American Jewish Life', *Forum* on the Jewish People, Zionism and Israel 40 (1980-1)p. 78.

37. Finkelstein, N., 'Daniel Jonah Goldhagen's "Crazy" Thesis: A Critique of Hitler's Willing Executioners', *New Left Review* 224 (July/August, 1997) pp. 84-5.

38. ibid., p. 84.

39. Miller, J., *One, By One, By One. Facing the Holocaust* (New York, 1990) pp. 224-5. (Emphasis mine)

40. Berenbaum, op. cit., (1990) p. 4.

41. Neusner, op. cit., (1987) p. 282.

42. Loshitzky, Y., 'Introduction' in Y. Loshitzky (ed.), *Spielberg's Holocaust. Critical Perspectives on Schindler's List* (Bloomington, 1997) p. 7.

43. Cited in Shandler, J., 'Schindler's Discourse. America Discusses the Holocaust and its Mediation, from NBC's Mini-Series to Spielberg's Film' in Y. Loshitzky (ed.), op. cit., (1997) p. 154.

44. Loshitzky, op. cit., (1997) p. 7.

45. Abrams, E., *Faith or Fear. How Jews Can Survive in a Christian America* (New York, 1997) p. 128.

46. Shandler, op. cit., (1997) footnote 9, p. 165.

47. Cited in ibid., p. 154.

48. Avisar, I., *Screening the Holocaust: Cinema's Image of the Unimaginable* (Bloomington, 1988) p. 129.

49. Miller, op. cit., (1990) p. 43.

50. Avisar, I., 'Holocaust Movies and the Politics of Collective Memory' in A.H. Rosenfeld (ed.), op. cit., (1997) p. 44.

51. Vidal-Naquet, P., *Assassins of Memory: Essays on the Denial of the Holocaust* (New York, 1993) p. xii and p. xviii.

52. Hilberg cited in Linenthal, op. cit., (1997) p. 11.

53. Berenbaum, op. cit., (1990) pp. 40-1.

54. ibid., p. xviii.

55. Shandler, op. cit., (1997) p. 164.

56. Hansen, M.B., *'Schindler's List* is not *Shoah*. Second Commandment, Popular Modernism and Public Memory' in Loshitzky (ed.), op. cit., (1997) p. 98.

57. ibid., pp. 98-9.

58. Miller, op. cit., (1990) p. 232.

59. Cited in ibid., p. 232.

60. Finkelstein, op. cit., (1997) footnote 76, p. 83.

61. Mosse, op. cit., (1990) p. 8.

62. ibid., p. 126.

63. Cited in Wollaston, I., *A War Against Memory? The Future of Holocaust Remembrance* (London, 1996) p. 24.

64. Tran, M., 'Superman Lands in Holocaust Row', The *Guardian* (27 June 1998) p. 17.

65. Margalit, A., 'The Kitsch of Israel', The *New York Review of Books* 35, No. 18 (24 November 1988) p. 24.

66. Bauer, Y., 'The Significance of the Final Solution' in D. Cesarani (ed.) *The Final Solution: Origins and Implementation* (London, 1994) p. 306.

## Chapter 1. Anne Frank

1. Miller, *op. cit.*, (1990) p. 10.

2. Rosenfeld, A.H., 'Popularisation and Memory: The Case of Anne Frank' in P. Hayes (ed.), *Lessons and Legacies. The Meaning of the Holocaust in a Changing World* (Evanston, 1991) p. 244.

3. van Galen Last, D. and Wolfswinkel, R., *Dutch Holocaust Literature in Historical perspective* (Amsterdam, 1996) p. 13.

4. Cited in Doneson, J.E., 'The American History of Anne Frank's diary', *Holocaust and Genocide Studies* 2, No. 1 (1987) p. 152.

5. Tory, A., *Surviving the Holocaust. The Kovno Ghetto Diary* (London, 1991)

6. Barnouw, D. and Van Der Stroom, G., (eds), *The Diary of Anne Frank. The Critical Edition* [Hereafter *Critical Edition*] (London, 1989) p. 576 (diary entry for 28 March 1944).

7. *Critical Edition*, p. 582 (diary entry for 31 March 1944).

8. Rosenfeld, A.H., *A Double Dying: Reflections on Holocaust Literature* (London, 1986) p. 17.

9. ibid., p. 51.

10. Rosenfeld, op. cit., (1991) p. 245.

11. Cited in Van Der Stroom, G., 'The Diaries, *Het Achterhuis* and the Translations', in *Critical Edition*, p. 67.

192

12. The article is translated and reproduced in ibid., pp. 67-8.

13. van Galen Last and Wolfswinkel, op. cit., (1996) p. 141.

14. Rosenfeld, op. cit., (1991) p. 258.

15. Van Der Stroom, 'The Diaries ...' in *Critical Edition*, p. 74.

16. *Critical Edition* p. 189 (diary entry for 16 June 1942), & Paape, H., '... Originally from Frankfurt-am-Main', in *Critical Edition*, p. 7.

17. *Critical Edition*, p. 274 (diary entry for 9 October 1942).

18. ibid., pp. 313-14 (diary entry for 17 November 1942).

19. ibid., p.600 (diary entry for 11 April 1944).

20. ibid., p. 643 (diary entry for 11 May 1944).

21. ibid., p. 601 (diary entry for 11 April 1944).

22. ibid., p. 657 (diary entry for 22 May 1944).

23. Van Der Stroom, 'The Diaries ...' in *Critical Edition*, pp. 72-3.

24. ibid., p. 72.

25. Cited in ibid., p. 72.

26. *Der Spiegel* (1 April 1959) Cited in ibid., p. 73.

27. *Critical Edition*, p. 545 (diary entry for 18 March 1944).

28. ibid., p. 567 (diary entry for 24 March 1944).

29. *Critical Edition* and Frank, O.H., and Pressler, M., *Anne Frank. The Diary of a Young Girl. The Definitive Edition* (Harmondsworth, 1997)

30. Rayner, J., 'Anne Frank's Father Censored Her Diaries to Protect the Family', The *Observer* Review (23 August 1998) p. 5.

31. Kushner, T., 'I want to go on living after my death: The memory of Anne Frank', in M. Evans and K. Lunn (eds.) *War and Memory in the Twentieth Century* (Oxford, 1997) p. 7.

32. Review in the *National Jewish Post* (30 June 1952) cited in Barnouw, D., 'The Play', in *Critical Edition*, p. 78.

33. Bordman, G., *The Oxford Companion to American Theatre* (Oxford, 1984) p. 199.

34. 'Acting version of the play' cited in Doneson, op. cit., (1987) p. 153.

35. Cited in Graver, L., *An Obsession with Anne Frank. Meyer Levin and the Diary* (Berkeley, 1995) p. 89.

36. Letter from the Hacketts to Otto Frank (3 July 1956) cited in Doneson, op. cit., p. 154.

37. Letter from Otto Frank to the Hacketts (9 November 1955) cited in ibid., p. 154.

38. Flinker, M., *Young Moshe's Diary: The Spiritual Torment of a Young Boy in Nazi Europe* (Jerusalem, 1979).

39. Young, J.E., op. cit., (1990) p. 27.

40. Allan, E. (ed.) *A Guide to World Cinema* (London, 1985) p. 137.

41. Letter from John Stone to George Stevens (23 December, 1957) cited in Doneson, op. cit., (1987) pp. 154-5.

42. ibid., p. 155.

43. ibid., p. 158.

44. *Critical Edition*, p. 273 (diary entry for 9 October 1942).

45. Cited in Rosenfeld, op. cit., (1991) p. 258.

46. ibid., p. 258.

47. Ozick, C., 'Who Owns Anne Frank?', The *New Yorker* (6 October 1997) p. 86.

48. Rosenfeld, op. cit., (1991) p. 276.

49. 'How "Cheerful" is "Anne Frank"?', *Variety* (1 April 1959) p. 2. (I'm assuming that this is not an April Fool's joke!)

50. Langer, L.L., 'The Americanisation of the Holocaust on Stage and Screen', in S.B. Cohen (ed.) *From Hester Street to Hollywood. The Jewish-American Stage and Screen* (Bloomington, 1983) p. 214.

51. ibid., p. 216.

52. *Critical Edition*, p. 694 (diary entry for 15 July 1944).

53. Bettelheim, B., 'The Ignored Lesson of Anne Frank', in B. Bettelheim, *Surviving the Holocaust* (London, 1986) p. 125. (Essay originally published in *Harpers* Magazine, November 1960).

54. Beller, S., ' "Your Mark is our Disgrace": Liberalism and the Holocaust', *Contemporary European History* 4, No. 2 (July 1995) p. 212.

55. Ozick, op. cit., (1997) p. 78.

56. Rosenfeld, op. cit., (1991) p. 254.

57. ibid., p. 254.

58. Levin's review in the *New York Times Book Review* (15 June, 1952) cited in ibid., p. 250 cf. His review in Congress Weekly (16 June, 1952) cited in ibid., p. 273.

59. ibid., p. 251.

60. Roosevelt, E., 'Introduction' to *Anne Frank: The Diary of a Young Girl* (New York, 1952) cited in ibid., p. 249. Graver, op. cit., p. 24 notes that the introduction was 'actually written by Barbara Zimmerman [an editor at Doubleday] and signed by Mrs. Roosevelt'

61. Birstein, A., & Kazin, A., (eds.), 'Introduction' to *The Works of Anne Frank* (New York, 1959) cited in ibid., p. 251.

62. ibid., p. 251.

63. *Trouw* (12 October 1956) cited in Barnouw, D., 'The Play', in *Critical Edition*, p. 80.

64. ibid., p. 80.

65. Muhlen, N., 'The Return of Anne Frank', *The ADL Bulletin* (June 1957) cited in Rosenfeld, op. cit., (1991) p. 266.

66. *Theater der Zeit* (June 1957) cited in ibid., p. 266.

67. ibid., p. 271.

68. Young, J.E., 'The Anne Frank House. Holland's Memorial "Shrine of the Book" ', in Young (ed.) op. cit., (1994) p. 131.

69. Young, op. cit., (1990) pp. 109-10.

70. Roth, P., *The Ghost Writer* (New York, 1979) pp. 157-8.

71. Weinberg, J., and Elieli, R., The Holocaust Museum in Washington (New York, 1995) p. 105.

72. Anne Frank Stichting, *Anne Frank: A History for Today* (Amsterdam, 1996) p. 5.

73. Anne Frank Stichting, *Anne Frank in the World 1929-45* (Amsterdam, 1994) p. 5.

74. Anne Frank Educational Trust, 'Anne Frank: A History for Today Exhibition' (n.d. leaflet)

194

75. *Anne Frank: A History for Today* p. 91.

76. Abner Katzman cited in Miller, op. cit., (1990) p. 96.

77. Paape, H., 'The Betrayal' in *Critical Edition* pp. 28-30.

78. Interim report of the Political Investigation Branch of the Amsterdam Police (1 April 1948) cited in ibid., p. 34.

79. Wiesenthal, S., *The Murderers Amongst Us* (New York, 1967) cited in Pick, H., *Simon Wiesenthal. A Life in Search of Justice* (London, 1996) pp. 173-4.

80. Wiesenthal, S., *Justice Not Vengeance* (London, 1989) p. 335.

81. Harwood, R., *Did Six Million Really Die? The Truth at Last* (Richmond, 1974) cited in Barnouw, D., 'Attacks on the Authenticity of the Diary' in *Critical Edition*, p. 91.

82. Butz, A.R., *The Hoax of the Twentieth Century* (Richmond, 1975) cited in ibid., p. 92.

83. Irving, D., *Hitler und seine Feldherren* (Frankfurt-am-Main, 1975) cited in ibid., p. 91.

84. Bauer, op. cit., (London, 1994) p. 307.

## Chapter 2. Adolf Eichmann

1. Cited in Levy, A., *The Wiesenthal File* (London, 1993) p. 135.

2. Aharoni, Z. and Dietl, W., *Operation Eichmann. The Truth about the Pursuit, Capture and Trial* (London, 1996) p. 140.

3. de Mildt, op. cit., (1996) p. 12.

4. Roger Veilland cited in Gouri, H., 'Facing the Glass Booth', in G.H. Hartman (ed.), *Holocaust Remembrance. The Shapes of Memory* (Oxford, 1994) p. 157.

5. Cited in Pearlman, M., *The Capture and Trial of Adolf Eichmann* (London, 1963) p. 148.

6. ibid., p. 9.

7. Cited in ibid., p. 12.

8. Cited in Ben-Gurion, B., *Israel. A Personal History* (New York, 1971) p. 573.

9. Cited in ibid., p. 581.

10. Wiesenthal, op. cit., (1989) p. 78.

11. Pick, op. cit., (1997) p. 146.

12. ibid., p. 136.

13. Aharoni and Dietl, op. cit., (1996) p. 83.

14. ibid., p. 181.

15. Wiesenthal, op. cit., (1989) p. 77.

16. Amit, M., 'Foreword' in Aharoni and Dietl, op. cit., (1996) p. 7.

17. Wiesenthal, op. cit., (1989) p. 76.

18. ibid., p. 70.

19. Cited in Levy, op. cit., (1993) p. 122.

20. Pick, op. cit., (1997) p. 138.

21. Cited in Segev, T., *The Seventh Million. The Israelis and the Holocaust* (New York, 1994) p. 334.

22. ibid., p. 325.

23. Diary entry for 6 December 1959 cited in ibid., p. 325.

24. Aharoni and Dietl, op. cit., (1993) p. 84.

25. Liebman and Don-Yehiya, op. cit., (1983) p. 98.

26. Cited in Segev, op. cit., (1994) p. 437.

27. Liebman and Don-Yehiya, op. cit., (1983) p. 106.

28. *The Times* (28 May 1960) p. 5.

29. *New York Times* Magazine (18 December 1960) p. 62.

30. Segev, op. cit., (1994) p. 155.

31. Cited in ibid., p. 183.

32. Cited in Ben-Gurion, op. cit. (1971) p. 575.

33. Cited in Arendt, H., *Eichmann in Jerusalem. A Report on the Banality of Evil* (London, 1963) p. 16.

34. Bettelheim, op. cit., (1986) p. 139.

35. Cited in Pearlman, op. cit., (1963) pp. 562-3.

36. Arendt, H., op. cit., (1963) pp. 204-5.

37. ibid., p. 108.

38. ibid., p. 106.

39. ibid., p. 111.

40. Cited in Pearlman, op. cit., (1963) p. 358.

41. Weitz, Y., 'The Holocaust on Trial: The Impact of the Kasztner and Eichmann Trials on Israeli Society', *Israel Studies* 1, No. 2 (Fall 1996) p. 12.

42. Hausner, G., *Justice in Jerusalem* (London, 1967) p. 292.

43. ibid., p. 291.

44. Cited in Segev, op. cit., (1994) p. 332.

45. ibid., pp. 332-3.

46. Hausner, op. cit., (1967) p. 291.

47. Cited in Segev, op. cit., (1994) p. 351.

48. Cited in Pearlman, op. cit., (1963) p. 304.

49. ibid., p. 304.

50. Herman, S.N., Peres, Y. and Yuchtman, E., 'Reactions to the Eichmann Trial in Israel: A Study in High Involvement', *Scripta Hierosolymitana* 14 (1965) pp. 99-100.

51. Gouri, op. cit., (1994) p. 157.

52. Hausner, op. cit., (1967) p. 296.

53. Gouri, op. cit., (1994) p. 154.

54. ibid., p. 155.

55. Arendt, op. cit., (1963) p. 6.

56. Liebman and Don-Yehiya, op. cit., (1983) p. 107.

57. Gouri, op. cit., (1994) p. 155.

58. ibid., pp. 156-7.

59. *New York Times* Magazine (18 December 1960) p. 7.

60. Cited in Ben-Gurion, op. cit., (1971) p. 575.

61. Cited in Pearlman, op. cit., (1963) p. 146.

62. Cited in Segev, op. cit., (1994) pp. 329-30.

63. Cited in Wighton, C., *Eichmann. His Career and Crimes* (London, 1961) p. 20.

64. Gouri, op. cit., (1994) p. 155.

65. Hartman, G., *The Longest Shadow. In the Aftermath of the Holocaust* (Bloomington, 1996) p. 143.

66. Ezrahi, S., 'Revisioning the Past', *Salmagundi* 68-9 (Fall 1985) pp. 260-61.

67. Cited in Papadatos, P., *The Eichmann Trial* (London, 1964) p. 29.

68. Arendt, op. cit., (1963) p. 49.

69. Cited in Pearlman, op.cit., (1963) p. 611.

70. Arendt, op. cit., (1963) p. 22.

71. Cited in Papadatos, op. cit., (1964) footnote 31, p. 28.

72. Bettelheim, op. cit., (1986) p. 134.

73. Cited in Ben-Gurion, op. cit., (1971) p. 588.

74. Hausner, op. cit., (1967) pp. 342-3.

75. ibid., p. 344

76. Pearlman, op. cit., (1963) p. 89.

77. Hilberg, R., 'Significance of the Holocaust' in H. Friedlander and S. Milton (eds), *The Holocaust: Ideology, Bureaucracy and Genocide* (New York, 1980) p. 101.

## Chapter 3. Oskar Schindler

1. Keneally, T., 'Foreword' in E.J. Brecher, *Schindler's Legacy. True Stories of the List Survivors* (London, 1994) p. xvi.

2. Cited in Horowitz, S.R., 'But is it Good for the Jews? Spielberg's Schindler and the Aesthetics of Atrocity' in Y. Loshitzky (ed.) *Spielberg's Holocaust. Critical Perspectives on Schindler's List* (Bloomington, 1997) p. 119.

3. Cited in Hoberman, J., '*Schindler's List*. Myth, Movie and Memory', *Village Voice* (29 March 1994) p. 24.

4. Cited in Shandler, op. cit., (1997) p. 158.

5. Manchel, F., 'A Reel Witness: Steven Spielberg's Representation of the Holocaust in *Schindler's* List', *The Journal of Modern History* 67 (March 1995) p. 84.

6. Bernstein, M.A., 'The *Schindler's List* Effect', *The American Scholar* 63 (1994) p. 429.

7. ibid., p. 430.

8. ibid., p. 432.

9. Avisar, I., op. cit., (1997) p. 49 and Zelizer, B., 'Every Once in a While. *Schindler's List* and the Shaping of History' in Loshitzky (ed.), op. cit., (1997) p. 23.

10. Bresheeth, H., 'The Great Taboo Broken. Reflections on the Israeli Reception of *Schindler's* List' in Loshitzky (ed.), op. cit., (1997) p. 206.

11. Karpf, A., 'The Last Jews of Kraków Cringe', The *Guardian* (28 October 1995) p. 27. and Ronson, J., 'Hotel Auschwitz', BBC Radio 4 (9 October 1997)

12. Hansen, M.B., '*Schindler's List* is Not *Shoah*. Second Commandment, Popular Modernism and Public Memory' in Loshitzky (ed.), op. cit., (1997) p. 83.

13. Manchel, op. cit., (1995) p. 84.

14. Avisar, op. cit., (1997) p. 50.

15. Manchel, op. cit., (1995) pp. 87-8.

16. Langer, op. cit., (1983) p. 214.

17. Urs Jenny cited in Loshitzky, op. cit., (1997) pp. 14-5.

18. Hoberman, op. cit., (1994) p. 31.

19. ibid., p. 31.

20. Cited in Manchel, op. cit., (1995) p. 96.

21. Text on the video jacket of *Schindler's List* distributed by Universal Pictures.

22. Bartov, O., *Murder in Our Midst. The Holocaust, Industrial Killing, and Representation* (Oxford, 1996) p. 167.

23. Bershen, W., Round-table interview in Hoberman, op. cit., (1994) p. 27.

24. Manchel, op. cit., (1995) p. 92.

25. Bartov, op. cit., (1996) p. 169.

26. Loshitzky, op. cit., (1997) p. 3.

27. Loshitzky, 'Holocaust Others. Spielberg's *Schindler's List* Versus Lanzmann's *Shoah*' in Loshitzky (ed.) op. cit., (1997) p. 107.

28. Uri Schin cited in Bresheeth, op. cit., (1997) p. 201.

29. Brecher, op. cit., (1994) p. xix.

30. Bernstein, op. cit., (1994) p. 430.

31. Spiegelman, A., Round-table interview in Hoberman, op. cit., (1994) p. 30.

32. Cited in Loshitzky, op. cit., (1997) p. 114.

33. Cited in Schemo, D.J., 'Good Germans. Honouring the Heroes. And Hiding the Holocaust', The *New York Times* (12 June 1994) Section 4 p. 6.

34. Rosenfeld, op. cit., (1997) p. 141.

35. Bartov, op. cit., (1996) pp. 169-70.

36. Loshitzky, op. cit., (1997) p. 107.

37. Avisar, op. cit., (1997) p. 54.

38. Manchel, op. cit., (1995) p. 89.

39. ibid., p. 97.

40. Rosenfeld, op. cit., (1997) pp. 142-3.

41. Horowitz, op. cit., (1997) p. 138.

42. Browning, C.R., *Ordinary Men. Reserve Police Battalion 101 and the Final Solution in Poland* (New York, 1993) pp. 188-9.

43. Cited in Bernstein, op. cit., (1994) p. 431.

44. Bauer, op. cit., (1994) p. 308.

45. Lanzmann, C., *Shoah. An Oral History of the Holocaust. The Complete Text of the Film* (New York, 1985) p. 200.

46. Bartov, O., 'Spielberg's Oskar. Hollywood Tries Evil' in Loshitzky (ed.) op. cit., (1997) p. 45.

47. ibid., footnote 5, p. 59.

48. Rosenfeld, op. cit., (1997) p. 137.

49. ibid., p. 140

50. ibid., p. 139.

51. Brecher, op. cit., (1994) p. xx.

198

52. Koch, G., Round-table interview in Hoberman, op. cit., (1994) p. 29.

53. ibid., p. 29.

54. Keneally, op. cit., (1994) pp. xiv-v.

55. Rosenfeld, op. cit., (1997) p. 137.

56. Bartov, op. cit., (1996) p. 169.

57. Rosenfeld, op. cit., (1997) p. 144.

58. ibid., p. 144.

59. Fogelman, E., *Conscience and Courage. Rescuers of Jews During the Holocaust* (New York, 1994) p. 301.

60. ibid., p. 301.

61. Charlesworth, A., 'Towards a Geography of the *Shoah*', *Journal of Historical Geography* 18, No. 4 (1992) p. 469.

62. Cited in Rosenfeld, op. cit., (1997) p. 146.

63. Brecher, op. cit., (1994) p. xix.

64. ibid., p. xix.

65. Bartov, op. cit., (1996) p. 170.

66. Koch, op. cit., (1994) p. 29.

67. Loshitzky, op. cit., (1997) p. 3.

68. ibid., p. 4.

69. Hoberman cited in Hansen, op. cit., (1997) p. 80.

70. Loshitzky, op. cit., (1997) p. 112.

71. Cited in Shandler, op. cit., (1997) p. 161.

72. Wieseltier, L., 'Washington Diarist. Close Encounters of the Nazi Kind', The *New Republic* (24 January 1994) p. 42.

## Chapter 4. Auschwitz

1. Kushner, T., 'The Memory of Belsen' in J. Reilly, D. Cesarani, T. Kushner and C. Richmond (eds.), *Belsen in History and Memory* (London, 1997b) p. 188.

2. Smolen, K., *Auschwitz 1940-1945. Guidebook through the Museum* (Óswiecim, 1974) p. 114.

3. Charlesworth, A., 'Contesting Places of Memory: The Case of Auschwitz', *Environment and Planning D: Society and Space* 12 (1994) p. 583.

4. Smolen, op. cit., (1974) pp. 114-15.

5. Kushner, op. cit., (1997b) p. 188.

6. Adorno, T.W., 'Cultural Criticism and Society', *Prisms* (1955).

7. Kushner, op. cit., (1994) p. 195.

8. Charlesworth, op. cit., (1994) p. 585.

9. Cited in Wollaston, I., 'Sharing Sacred Space? The Carmelite Controversy and the Politics of Commemoration', *Patterns of Prejudice* 28, No. 3-4 (1994) p. 25.

10. Montague IJA Research Report (October 1987) cited in ibid., pp. 25-6.

11. ibid., p. 21.

12. Cited in Bartoszewski, W.T., *The Convent at Auschwitz* (London, 1990) p. 7.

13. Cited in ibid., p. 45.

14. Cited in ibid., p. 45.

15. Cited in ibid., p. 121.

16. Wollaston, op. cit., (1994) p. 22.

17. Young, op. cit., (1993) p. 142.

18. Cited in Bartoszewski, op. cit., (1990) p. 103.

19. Cited in Wollaston, op. cit., (1994) p. 27.

20. ibid., p. 27.

21. Van Pelt, R.J. and Dwork, D., *Auschwitz 1270 to the Present* (New Haven, 1996) p. 374.

22. ibid., p. 374.

23. Ryback, T.W., 'Evidence of Evil', The *New Yorker* (15 November 1993) p. 78.

24. Van Pelt and Dwork, op. cit., (1996) p. 364.

25. ibid., p. 362.

26. Utley, A., 'The Auschwitz Horror Show', *THES* (21 August 1992) p. 32.

27. Sellars, R.W., 'Why Take a Trip to Bountiful – Won't Anaheim Do? Perception and Manipulation of the Historic Past', *Landscape* 30, No. 3 (1990) p. 18.

28. Horne, D., *The Great Museum. The Re-Presentation of History* (London, 1984) p. 10.

29. Levine, P.A., 'To Choose to Go to Birkeneau. Reflections on Visiting a Death Camp, August 1996', *Multiethnica* 18/19 (November 1996) p. 8.

30. Young, op. cit., (1993) pp. 127-32.

31. Smolen, K., *Auschwitz-Birkeneau. Guide Book* (Oswiecim, 1993) map facing p. 1.

32. Young, op. cit., (1993) p. 128.

33. ibid., p. 127.

34. Ryback, op. cit., (1993) p. 70.

35. Rojek, C., *Ways of Escape. Modern Transformations in Leisure and Travel* (Houndmills, 1993) p. 136.

36. Charny, I.W., *How Can We Commit the Unthinkable? Genocide: The Human Cancer* (Epping, 1982) p. 28.

37. Webber, J., 'Personal Reflections on Auschwitz Today', in T. Swiebocka (ed.) *Auschwitz. A History in Photographs* (Warsaw, 1993) p. 282.

38. Walter, T., 'War Grave Pilgrimage', in I. Reader and T. Walter (eds.) *Pilgrimage in Popular Culture* (London, 1993) p. 69.

39. Rodman, G.B., *Elvis After Elvis. The Posthumous Career of a Living Legend* (London, 1996) p. 107.

40. Ronson, op. cit., (1997).

41. Young, op. cit., (1993) pp. 152-3.

42. Levine, op. cit., (1996) p. 8.

43. Cited in Bunting, M., 'Queen Hit by Row over Auschwitz', The *Guardian* (23 March 1996).

44. Cited in ibid.,

45. Cited in ibid.,

46. Karpf, op. cit., (1995) p. 27.

47. Kugelmass, J., 'Missions to the Past. Poland in Contemporary Jewish Thought and Deed' in P. Antze and M. Lambek (eds), *Tense Past. Cultural Essays in Trauma and Memory* (London, 1996) p. 201.

48. Horn, D., 'On Filling Shoes', *Hadassah Magazine* (November 1992) p. 21 cited in Kugelmass, J., 'Why We Go to Poland. Holocaust Tourism as Secular Ritual' in Young, op. cit., (1994) p. 183.

49. ibid., p 175.

50. Lopate, op. cit., (1989) p. 64.

51. Ryback, op. cit., (1993) p. 78.

52. A. Scharir, 'Consequences of Auschwitz', *Yedioth Ahronoth* (22 April 1988) cited in Zuckermann, M., 'The Curse of Forgetting: Israel and the Holocaust', *Telos* 78 (Winter 1988-9) p. 51.

53. ibid., p. 52.

## Chapter 5. Yad Vashem

1.  Young, op. cit., (1993) pp. 250-1.

2.  Segev, op. cit., (1994) p. 423.

3.  Bennett, T., *The Birth of the Museum. History, Theory, Politics* (London, 1995) p. 6.

4.  'Martyrs' and Heroes' Remembrance (Yad Vashem) Law, 5713-1953' cited in Dafni, R., (ed.) *Yad Vashem. The Holocaust Martyrs' and Heroes' Remembrance Authority, Jerusalem* (Jerusalem,1990: Fifth Edition) p. 4.

5.  Segev, op. cit., (1994) pp. 184-5.

6.  Reinharz J., and Friesel, E., 'The Zionist Leadership Between the Holocaust and the Creation of the State of Israel', in Rosenfeld, op. cit., (1997) p. 110.

7.  Shapira, A., 'The Holocaust and World War II as Elements of the *Yishuv* Psyche Until 1948', in Rosenfeld, op. cit., (1997) p. 75.

8.  Dan Horowitz cited in ibid., p. 70.

9.  Liebman and Don-Yehiya, op. cit., (1983) p. 8.

10. Segev, op. cit., (1994) p. 185.

11. Ezrahi, op. cit., (1985) p. 257.

12. Dafni, op. cit., (1990) p. 25.

13. Segev, op. cit., (1994) p. 510.

14. Young, op. cit., (1993) p. 257.

15. Dafni, op. cit., (1990) p. 18.

16. ibid, p. 18.

17. Segev, op. cit., (1994) pp. 179-80.

18. Elon, A., *The Israelis. Founders and Sons* (Harmondsworth, 1983) p. 286.

19. ibid., p. 286.

20. Young, op. cit., (1993) p. 258.

21. Cited in Segev, op. cit., (1994) p. 472.

22. Cited in ibid., pp. 394-5.

23. Liebman and Don-Yehiya, op. cit., (1983) p. 152.

24. Segev, op. cit., (1994) p. 444.

25. ibid., p. 495

26. Young, J.E., 'Israel's Memorial Landscape: Sho'ah, Heroism, and National Redemption' in Hayes (ed.), op. cit., (1991) p. 303.

27. Yad Vashem, 'The Memorial to the Deportations' (n.d. pamphlet)

28. Dafni, op. cit., (1990) p. 8.

29. Cited in Liebman and Don-Yehiya, op. cit., (1983) p. 103.

30. Young, op. cit., (1993) p. 252.

31. Dafni, op.cit., (1990) p. 18.

32. Segev, op cit., (1994) p. 424.

33. Cited in Young, op. cit., (1993) p. 256.

34. ibid., p. 257.

35. 'Martyrs' and Heroes' Remembrance (Yad Vashem) Law, 5713-1953' cited in Dafni, op. cit., (1990) p. 5.

36. Cited in Segev, op. cit., (1994) p. 432.

37. ibid., p. 433.

38. ibid., p. 432.

39. ibid., p. 431.

40. ibid., p. 431.

41. Margalit, op. cit., (1988) p. 23.

42. *Yad Vashem Magazine* 7 (Fall 1997) p. 18.

43. Bartov, op. cit., (1996) p. 178.

44. Margalit, op. cit., (1988) p. 24.

45. Cited in Young, op. cit., (1991) footnote 1, p. 371.

46. Segev, op. cit., (1994) pp. 397-8.

47. ibid., p. 399.

48. Cited in ibid., p. 399.

49. Yeshayahu Leibowitz cited in ibid., p. 401.

50. Shlomo Schmelzman cited in Cromer, G., 'Negotiating the Meaning of the Holocaust: An Observation on the Debate about Kahanism in Israeli Society', *Holocaust and Genocide Studies* 2, No. 2 (1987) p. 290.

51. Cited in Segev, op. cit., (1994) p. 403.

52. Cited in Cromer, op. cit., (1987) p. 290.

53. Article in *Hadashot* (16 November 1984) cited in ibid., p. 293.

54. ibid., p. 293.

55. ibid., p. 295.

56. Shahak, I., 'History Remembered, History Distorted, History Denied', *Race and Class* 30, No. 4 (April-June 1989) p. 80.

57. Segev, op. cit., (1994) p. 408.

58. Shahak, op. cit., (1989) p. 80.

59. Segev, op. cit., (1994) p. 482.

60. Shahak, op. cit., (1989) p. 81.

61. Segev, op. cit., (1994) p. 487.

62. Shahak, op. cit., (1989) p. 81.

63. Cited in Segev, op. cit., (1994) p. 183.

64. ibid., p. 183.

65. Liebman and Don-Yehiya, op. cit., (1983) p. ix.

66. Segev, op. cit., (1994) p. 426.

67. Ophir, A., 'On Sanctifying the Holocaust: An Anti-Theological Treatise', *Tikkun* 2, No.1 (1987) p. 61.

68. ibid., p. 62.

69. ibid., pp. 62-3.

70. ibid., p. 63.

71. Lopate, op. cit., (1989) p. 60.

72. Friedlander, S., *Memory, History and the Extermination of the Jews of Europe* (Bloomington, 1993) pp. xi-xii.

73. Jehuda Elkan, 'A Plea for Forgetting', *Ha'aretz* (2 March 1988) cited in Zuckermann, op. cit., (1988-9) p. 43.

74. ibid., p. 44.

75. ibid., p. 44.

## Chapter 6. The United States Holocaust Memorial Museum, Washington, DC

1.  Cited in *Internet on the Holocaust and Genocide* 43 (April 1993) p. 2.

2.  Cited in ibid., p. 2.

3.  Weissberg, L., 'Memory Confined', *Documents* 4 (Spring 1994) p. 84.

4.  Lopate, op. cit., (1989) pp. 59-60.

5.  ibid., p. 60.

6.  Shandler, op. cit., (1997) p. 164.

7.  Rich, F., 'Journal: The Holocaust Boom. Memory as an Art Form', The *New York Times* (7 April 1994) Section A, p.27

8.  Young, op. cit., (1993) p. 289.

9.  ibid., p. 291.

10. Young, op. cit., (1994) p. 34.

11. Arad, G.N., 'Rereading an Unsettled Past. American Jews During the Nazi Era' in Rosenfeld (ed.), op. cit., (1997) p. 199.

12. Young, op. cit., (1993) p. 221.

13. Cited in Linenthal, op. cit., (1997) p. 20.

14. Cited in ibid., p. 37.

15. Cited in Miller, op. cit., (1990) p. 234.

16. Cited in Linenthal, op. cit., (1997) p. 44.

17. Rosenblum, S., 'Are Museums the Best Places for the Memorialisation of the Holocaust?', *International Network on Holocaust and Genocide* 11, No. 4 (1996) p. 17.

18. Young, op. cit., (1994) pp. 34-5.

19. Rosenblum, op. cit., (1996) p. 17.

20. ibid., p. 17.

21. Cited in Linenthal, op. cit., (1997) p. 167.

22. Exhibition text (Washington, DC).

23. Kundera, M., 'The Tragedy of Central Europe', The *New York Review of Books* 31, No. 7 (26 April 1984) p. 37.

24. Weinberg and Elieli, op. cit., (1995) p. 148.

25. Bartov, op. cit., (1996) pp. 180-1.

26. Berenbaum, M., *The World Must Know. The History of the Holocaust*

*as Told in the United States Holocaust Memorial Museum* (Boston, 1993) p. 2.

27. Gourevitch, P., 'Behold Now Behemoth. The Holocaust Memorial Museum: One More American Theme Park', *Harper's Magazine* (July 1993) p. 56.

28. ibid., p. 60.

29. Weissberg, op. cit., (1994) p. 90.

30. ibid., p. 90.

31. Gourevitch, op. cit., (1993) p. 60.

32. ibid., p. 61.

33. Berenbaum, op. cit., (1993) p. 2.

34. ibid., p. 220.

35. Cited in Rosenfeld, op. cit., (1997) p. 127.

36. ibid., p. 127.

37. Owings, A., *Frauen. German Women Recall the Third Reich* (Harmondsworth, 1995) p. xxxvi.

38. Estelle Gilson cited in Rosenfeld, op., cit., (1997) p. 129.

39. Berenbaum, op. cit., (1993) p. 235.

40. Exhibition text (Washington, DC).

41. Weinberg and Elieli, op. cit., (1995) p. 76.

42. Exhibition text (Washington, DC).

43. Weissberg, op. cit., (1994) p. 88.

44. Cited in Linenthal, op. cit., (1997) p. 170.

45. Bartov, op. cit., (1996) p. 182.

46. Weinberg and Elieli, op. cit., (1995) p.72.

47. Berenbaum, op. cit., (1993) p. 235.

48. Weinberg and Elieli, op. cit., (1995) p. 72.

49. I.D. Card number 5934.

50. Gourevitch, op. cit., (1993) p. 58.

51. Weissberg, op. cit., (1994) p. 89.

52. Horne, op. cit., (1984) p. 16.

53. ibid., pp. 16-7.

54. Linenthal, op. cit., (1997) p. 163.

55. Weinberg and Elieli, op. cit., (1995) p. 124.

56. ibid., p. 153.

57. ibid., p. 153.

58. Exhibition text (Dallas).

59. Museum postcard (Dallas).

60. 'The Dallas Memorial Center for Holocaust Studies' (n.d. brochure).

61. Introductory Film Commentary (Dallas).

62. Young, op. cit., (1993) p. 298.

63. The Simon Wiesenthal Center, *'Beit Hashoah* – Museum of Tolerance' (n.d. brochure)

64. 'The Dallas Memorial Center for Holocaust Studies' (n.d. brochure).

65. Horne, op.cit., (1984) p. 17.

66. Rabinowitz, op. cit., (1977) p. 162.

67. ibid., p. 164.

68. Linenthal, op. cit., (1997) p. 57.

69. Coleman, S., and Elsner, J., 'Epilogue – Landscapes Reviewed' in *Pilgrimage. Past and Present. Sacred Travel and Sacred Space in the World Religions* (London, 1995) p. 208.

70. 'Holocaust Museum Houston. Education Center and Memorial' (n.d. brochure)

71. 'United States Holocaust Memorial Museum Visitors Guide' (n.d. brochure)

72. Cited in Linenthal, op. cit., (1993) p. 214.

73. Cited in ibid., p. 212.

74. Cited in ibid., p. 215.

75. ibid., pp. 215-6.

76. Cited in ibid., p. 122.

77. ibid., p. 122.

78. ibid., p. 122.

## Epilogue

1.  Swift, G., *Waterland* (London, 1992) p. 140.

2.  Langer, op. cit., (1995) p. 7.

3.  ibid., p. 3.

4.  Liebman and Don-Yehiya, op. cit., (1983) p. 142.

5.  ibid., p. 142.

6.  Miller, op. cit., (1990) p. 11.

7.  Huyssen, op. cit., (1994) p. 15.

8.  Bartov, op. cit., (1996) p. 183.

9.  Liebman and Don-Yehiya, op. cit., (1983) p. 142.

10. Loshitzky, op. cit., (1997) p. 8.

11. 'Yad Vashem 2001 – Masterplan. The New Museum Complex and the Visitors' Centre' (n.d. promotional brochure) p. 21.

12. Bartov, op. cit., (1996) p. 176.

13. 'Yad Vashem 2001 – Masterplan', p. 5.

14. ibid., p. 8.

15. ibid., p. 21.

16. ibid., p. 22.

17. ibid., p. 5.

18. ibid., p. 21.

19. ibid., p. 21.

20. ibid., p. 21.

21. ibid., p. 5.

22. Young, op. cit., (1993) p. 81.

23. Urry, J., 'The "Consumption" of Tourism', *Sociology* 24, No. 1 (1990) p. 34.

24. Rich, op.cit., (1994) p. 27.

25. Bartov, op. cit., (1996) pp. 183-4.

26. 'Yad Vashem 2001 – Masterplan', p. 6.

27. Langer, op. cit., (1995) p. 179.

28. Cited in Miller, op. cit., (1990) pp. 109-10.
29. Rosenfeld, op. cit., (1997) p. 120.
30. ibid., p. 120.
31. Gourevitch, op. cit., (1993) p. 62.
32. Rosenfeld, op. cit., (1997) pp. 137-8.

# Select Bibliography

Abrams, E., *Faith or Fear. How Jews Can Survive in a Christian America* (New York, 1997)

Aharoni, Z. and Dietl, W., *Operation Eichmann. The Truth about the Pursuit, Capture and Trial* (London, 1996)

Arendt, H., *Eichmann in Jerusalem. A Report on the Banality of Evil* (London, 1963)

Avisar, I., *Screening the Holocaust: Cinema's Image of the Unimaginable* (Bloomington, 1988)

Barnouw, D., and Van Der Stroom, G. (eds), *The Diary of Anne Frank. The Critical Edition* (London, 1989)

Bartoszewski, W.T., *The Convent at Auschwitz* (London, 1990)

Bartov, O., *Murder in our Midst. The Holocaust, Industrial Killing, and Representation* (Oxford, 1996)

Bauman, Z., *Modernity and the Holocaust* (Cambridge, 1991)

Beller, S., ' "Your Mark is our Disgrace": Liberalism and the Holocaust', *Contemporary European History* 4, No. 2 (July 1995)

Ben-Gurion, D., *Israel. A Personal History* (New York, 1971)

Berenbaum, M., *After Tragedy and Triumph. Essays in Modern Jewish Thought and the American Experience* (New York, 1990)

Berenbaum, M., *The World Must Know. The History of the Holocaust as Told in the United States Holocaust Memorial Museum* (Boston, 1993)

Bernstein, M.A., 'The *Schindler's List* Effect', *The American Scholar* 63 (1994)

Bettelheim, B., *Surviving the Holocaust* (London, 1986)

Brecher, E.J., *Schindler's Legacy. True Stories of the List Survivors* (London, 1994)

Browning, C.R., *Ordinary Men. Reserve Police Battalion 101 and the Final Solution in Poland* (New York, 1993)

Charlesworth, A., 'Contesting Places of Memory: The Case of Auschwitz', *Environment and Planning D: Society and Space* 12 (1994)

Cohen, A., Gelber, J. and Wardi, C., *Comprehending the Holocaust* (Frankfurt am Main, 1988)

Cromer, G., 'Negotiating the Meaning of the Holocaust: An Observation on the Debate about Kahanism in Israeli Society', *Holocaust and Genocide Studies* 2, No. 2 (1987)

Doneson, J.E., 'The American History of Anne Frank's diary', *Holocaust and Genocide Studies* 2, No. 1 (1987)

Elon, A., *The Israelis. Founders and Sons* (Harmondsworth, 1983)

Epstein, J., 'A Dissent on *Schindler's* List', The *New York Review of Books* 41, No. 8 (21 April 1994)

Ezrahi, S.D., 'Revisioning the Past:The Changing Legacy of the Holocaust in Hebrew Literature', *Salmagundi* 68-9 (Fall 1985)

Finkelstein, N., 'Daniel Jonah Goldhagen's "Crazy" Thesis: A Critique of Hitler's Willing Executioners', *New Left Review* 224 (July/August 1997)

Fogelman, E., *Conscience and Courage. Rescuers of Jews During the Holocaust* (New York, 1994)

Friedlander, H. and Milton, S. (eds), *The Holocaust: Ideology, Bureaucracy and Genocide* (New York, 1980)

Friedlander, S., *Memory, History and the Extermination of the Jews of Europe* (Bloomington, 1993)

van Galen Last, D and Wolfswinkel, R., *Dutch Holocaust Literature in Historical Perspective* (Amsterdam, 1996)

Goldhagen, D.J., *Hitler's Willing Executioners. Ordinary Germans and the Holocaust* (London, 1997)

Gourevitch, P., 'Behold Now Behemoth. The Holocaust Memorial Museum: One More American Theme Park', *Harper's Magazine* (July 1993)

Graver, L., *An Obsession with Anne Frank. Meyer Levin and the Diary* (Berkeley, 1995)

Hartman, G.H. (ed.), *Holocaust Remembrance. The Shapes of Memory* (Oxford, 1994)

Hartman, G.H., *The Longest Shadow. In the Aftermath of the Holocaust* (Bloomington, 1996)

Hausner, G., *Justice in Jerusalem* (London, 1967)

Hayes, P. (ed.), *Lessons and Legacies. The Meaning of the Holocaust in a Changing World* (Evanston, 1991)

Herman, S.N., Peres Y. and Yuchtman, E., 'Reactions to the Eichmann Trial in Israel: A Study in High Involvement', *Scripta Hierosolymitana* 14 (1965)

Hilberg, R., *The Destruction of the European Jews* (London, 1961)

Hoberman, J., '*Schindler's List*. Myth, Movie and Memory', *Village Voice* (29 March 1994)

Jick, L.A., 'The Holocaust: Its Use and Abuse within the American Public', *Yad Vashem Studies* 14 (1981)

Kugelmass, J., 'Missions to the Past. Poland in Contemporary Jewish Thought and Deed' in P. Antze and M. Lambek (eds), *Tense Past. Cultural Essays in Trauma and Memory* (London, 1996)

Kushner, T., 'I Want to Go On Living After My Death: The Memory of Anne Frank' in M. Evans and K. Lunn (eds), *War and Memory in the Twentieth Century* (Oxford, 1997)

Kushner, T., 'The Memory of Belsen' in J. Reilly, D. Cesarani, T. Kusner and C. Richmond (eds), *Belsen in History and Memory* (London, 1997)

Langer, L.L., 'The Americanisation of the Holocaust on Stage and Screen' in S.B. Cohen (ed.), *From Hester Street to Hollywood. The Jewish-American*

*Stage and Screen* (Bloomington, 1983)

Langer, L.L., *Admitting the Holocaust* (Oxford, 1995)

Levine, P.A., 'To Choose to Go to Birkeneau. Reflections on Visiting a Death Camp, August 1996', *Multiethnica* 18/19 (November 1996)

Levy, A., *The Wiesenthal File* (London, 1993)

Liebman, C.S. and Don-Yehiya, E., *Civil Religion in Israel. Traditional Judaism and Political Culture in the Jewish State* (Berkeley, 1983)

Linenthal, E.T., *Preserving Memory. The Struggle to Create America's Holocaust Museum* (New York, 1997)

Lipstadt, D.E., 'The Holocaust: Symbol and "Myth" in American Jewish Life', *Forum* on the Jewish People, Zionism and Israel 40 (1980-1)

Lopate, P., 'Resistance to the Holocaust', *Tikkun* 4, No. 3 (1989)

Loshitzky, Y., *Spielberg's Holocaust. Critical Perspectives on Schindler's List* (Bloomington, 1997)

Manchel, F., 'A Reel Witness: Steven Spielberg's Representation of the Holocaust in *Schindler's* List', The *Journal of Modern History* 67 (March 1995)

Margalit, A., 'The Kitsch of Israel', The *New York Review of Books* 35, No. 18 (24 November 1988)

Marrus, M., *The Holocaust in History* (Harmondsworth, 1993)

Miller, J., *One, By One, By One. Facing the Holocaust* (New York, 1990)

Neusner, J., *Death and Birth of Judaism. The Impact of Christianity, Secularism, and the Holocaust on Jewish Faith* (New York, 1987)

Ophir, A., 'On Sanctifying the Holocaust: An Anti-Theological Treatise', *Tikkun* 2, No. 1 (1987)

Ozick, C., 'Who Owns Anne Frank?', The *New Yorker* (6 October 1997)

Papadatos, P., *The Eichmann Trial* (London, 1964)

Pearlman, M., *The Capture and Trial of Adolf Eichmann* (London, 1963)

Pick, H., *Simon Wiesenthal. A Life in Search of Justice* (London, 1996)

Rabinowitz, D., *New Lives. Survivors of the Holocaust Living in America* (New York, 1977)

Rich, F., 'Journal: The Holocaust Boom. Memory as an Art Form', The *New York Times* (7 April 1994)

Rosenblum, S., 'Are Museums the Best Places for the Memorialisation of the Holocaust?', *International Network on Holocaust and Genocide* 11, No. 4 (1996)

Rosenfeld, A.H., *A Double Dying: Reflections on Holocaust Literature* (London, 1986)

Rosenfeld, A.H., *Thinking About the Holocaust: After Half a Century* (Bloomington, 1997)

Ryback, T.W., 'Evidence of Evil', The *New Yorker* (15 November 1993)

Schemo, D.J., 'Good Germans. Honouring the Heroes. And Hiding the Holocaust', The *New York Times* (12 June 1994)

Segev, T., *The Seventh Million. The Israelis and the Holocaust* (New York, 1994)

Shahak, I., 'History Remembered, History Distorted, History Denied', *Race and Class* 30, No. 4 (April-June 1989)

Swiebocka, T. (ed.), *Auschwitz. A History in Photographs* (Warsaw, 1993)

Utley, A., 'The Auschwitz Horror Show', *THES* (21 August 1992)

Van Pelt, R.J. and Dwork, D., *Auschwitz 1270 to the Present* (New Haven, 1996)

Webber, J., *The Future of Auschwitz. Some Personal Reflections* (Oxford, 1992)

Weinberg, J. and Elieli, R., *The Holocaust Museum in Washington* (New York, 1995)

Weissbeg, L., 'Memory Confined', *Documents* 4 (Spring 1994)

Weitz, Y., 'The Holocaust on Trial: The Impact of the Kasztner and Eichmann Trials on Israeli Society', *Israel Studies* 1, No. 2 (Fall 1996)

Wieseltier, L., 'Washington Diarist. Close Encounters of the Nazi Kind', The *New Republic* (24 January 1994)

Wiesenthal, S., *Justice Not Vengeance* (London, 1989)

Wollaston, I., 'Sharing Sacred Space? The Carmelite Controversy and the Politics of Commemoration', *Patterns of Prejudice* 28, No. 3-4 (1994)

Wollaston, I., *A War Against Memory? The Future of Holocaust Remembrance* (London, 1996)

Young, J.E., *Writing and Rewriting the Holocaust. Narrative and the Consequences of Interpretation* (Bloomington, 1990)

Young, J.E., *The Texture of Memory. Holocaust Memorials and Meaning* (New Haven, 1993)

Young, J.E. (ed.), *The Art of Memory. Holocaust Memorials in History* (New York, 1994)

Zuckermann, M., 'The Curse of Forgetting: Israel and the Holocaust', *Telos* 78 (Winter 1988-9)

# Index